D1756560

Standard Arabic
An advanced course
Teacher's handbook

This course is designed for students who have completed a first-level course in Arabic and wish to pursue the subject to degree level. It aims to develop thoroughly the four basic language skills of reading, writing, speaking and listening, making extensive use of authentic Arabic materials. Each of the twenty chapters is based around a particular topic relating to the culture, history, politics, geography or society of the Arab Middle East, to give students an insight into important aspects of the region. This topic-based approach allows students to tackle vocabulary and structures in a coherent and concentrated manner.

Each chapter contains materials for translation into and from Arabic, aural texts, précis passages, suggested oral discussion topics, and a variety of exercises including comprehension in English and Arabic.

James Dickins has held lectureships in Arabic at Heriot-Watt University in Edinburgh and the University of Durham, and has also taught Arabic at the universities of Cambridge and St Andrews. His research work has concentrated on functional linguistics, and Sudanese Arabic grammar and lexicography, and his book *Extended Axiomatic Linguistics* appeared in 1998.

Janet Watson has held lectureships in Arabic at the universities of Edinburgh, Durham and Salford, and has also taught at Manchester University. She travels regularly to the Middle East and has spent extended periods in Yemen and Egypt. A specialist in Yemeni Arabic, her book publications include *A Syntax of San'ani Arabic and Ṣbaḥtū! A Course in San'ani Arabic*.

Standard Arabic
An advanced course

Teacher's handbook

JAMES DICKINS
University of Durham

JANET C. E. WATSON
University of Durham

PUBLISHED BY THE PRESS SYNDICATE OF THE UNIVERSITY OF CAMBRIDGE
The Pitt Building, Trumpington Street, Cambridge CB2 1RP, United Kingdom.

CAMBRIDGE UNIVERSITY PRESS
The Edinburgh Building, Cambridge, CB2 2RU, United Kingdom e.mail http:/www/cup.cam.ac.uk
40 West 20th Street, New York, NY 10011–4211, USA e.mail http:/www/cup.org
10 Stamford Road, Oakleigh, Melbourne 3166, Australia

First published 1998

Printed in the United Kingdom at the University Press, Cambridge

Typeset in Times 10/12.5

A catalogue record for this book is available from the British Library

ISBN 0 521 63161 0 hardback

Contents

Introduction to the teacher's handbook

There are a large number of exercises in *Standard Arabic: an advanced course*. Many of these exercises such as paraphrase in Arabic, comprehension in Arabic, vocabulary identification and synonym exercises are designed to encourage students to talk and to think in Arabic. Potential answers to these exercises are not given in this teacher's handbook. The handbook provides suggested translations into English and into Arabic, answers to comprehension questions in English, suggested structure translations into Arabic, complete transcriptions of aural texts, and, for the précis section, guidance questions around which one might structure a précis in Arabic of the text concerned. The key vocabulary section with suggestions as to how it should be approached is mentioned only in the material to chapters 1–4. This section in remaining chapters should be dealt with in a similar way. In structure translation exercises we have provided the relevant portion of the original text in curly brackets in the first five chapters, but not in subsequent chapters. At various points additional exercises are included in the teacher's handbook. Typically, these involve English translations and relate to features of Arabic which are most effectively brought into relief by considering English translation equivalents of aspects of the Arabic text in question.

It is not our intention to dictate the way in which exercises or the book as a whole should be used, and none of the translations are intended to be taken as an ideal version. Teachers should feel free to select texts and even chapters as they think fit and use or adapt exercises suggested for the texts. In teaching a media Arabic course teachers may wish to add current newspaper or broadcast material, particularly in chapters of political interest such as *The Arab–Israeli conflict*, *Islamic fundamentalism*, or *Democracy*.

1
Geography of the Middle East

3. Key vocabulary

The key vocabulary section should be used as a means of expanding students' vocabulary within specific fields. The idea behind this section is to encourage students to seek out and learn new vocabulary from the texts in each chapter. One way of approaching the key vocabulary section in class is to get students to work in pairs collecting certain terms or types of terms from one or a number of texts within the chapter. A time limit of say five or ten minutes should be set. Students then write up ten of the terms they have collected and the teacher can encourage discussion around these terms in Arabic. Discussion can begin by considering the meaning of a particular term and its wider semantic connotations. If students come up with the word واد 'valley', for instance, the teacher can then ask مـا هـي أهم الـوديـان فـيَّ الـعـالم الـعـربي؟, looking at the use of a term in specific instances. The key vocabulary section can be used as a support section for essay writing classes or oral classes.

4. Written Arabic texts 1

(a) Suggested translation of الـعـالم الـعـربي.

> In the Arab world there are seas, gulfs, rivers, valleys, deserts, islands and mountains. The Persian Gulf lies in the East of the Arabian Peninsula, while the Gulf of Aqaba lies to the South of Jordan. The Mediterranean divides North Africa from Europe, and the Red Sea divides Egypt from Saudi Arabia. The Suez Canal is in Egypt and links the Mediterranean with the Red Sea. The Arabian Sea lies to the South-East of the Arabian Peninsula and the Straits of Hormuz and the Gulf of Oman are found between the Arabian Sea and the Persian Gulf.
>
> The most important rivers in the Arab world include the Nile in Egypt and Sudan, the Euphrates in Syria and Iraq and the river Jordan in Jordan. The most important valleys in the Arab world are in Egypt and they are the Nile valley and the Valley of the Kings.
>
> The Arab world has a large number of deserts including the Sinai

desert in Egypt, the Nafud desert in the Kingdom of Saudi Arabia and the Sahara in North Africa. The Arab world is well-known for its many deserts. Some of the islands in the Arab world include the island of Bahrain in the Persian Gulf, the island of Masira in the Arabian Sea and the island of Socotra in the Gulf of Aden.

There are many mountains in most of the Arab countries such as Mount Hermon in Lebanon, Mount Arafat in the Kingdom of Saudi Arabia, and the Atlas mountains in North Africa. The Rock of Gibralter, known in Arabic as Jabal Tariq, lies between the Atlantic Ocean and the Meditteranean.

(b) **i** Answers to comprehension questions relating to المملكة العربية السعودية.

1. The Kingdom of Saudi Arabia is in the Arabian Peninsula.
2. Five of the countries which border Saudi Arabia are Iraq, Kuwait, Bahrain, the United Arab Emirates and Yemen (also Oman and Jordan).
3. Most Saudis in the past were nomads who travelled from place to place in the desert in search of fodder for their animals.
4. Today most people in Saudi Arabia live in towns and cities.
5. The four Saudi cities mentioned in the text are Jeddah, Riyadh, Mekka (Mecca) and Medina.
6. The area of Saudi Arabia is a third of the area of Europe.
7. The dunes in the desert are said to be 600 metres high or more and to be several kilometres in length.
8. The Empty Quarter is the same size as France.
9. The Nafud is located to the North of the Empty Quarter.
10. Large lava fields are said to be a legacy of volcanic activity in the past.

iii Additional exercise: further questions to المملكة العربية السعودية.
This text is very simple, as are the questions relating to it. It can be used in conjunction with the other texts in this section to provide a quick picture of Sudan in relation to the other countries mentioned. Additional questions could be added in class comparing Sudan with, say, Iraq and Saudi Arabia. Questions could relate to geographical features, ways of life of the inhabitants and could also include subjective questions such as:

- هل زرت السودان/العراق/المملكة العربية السعودية؟

- ما رأيك في البلاد؟

- هل ترغب في زيارة دولة عربية {أخرى}؟

5. Written Arabic texts 2

(a) **i** Answers to comprehension questions relating to جغرافية عمان.

1. The countries which border Oman include the Kingdom of Saudi Arabia, the

United Arab Emirates and the Republic of Yemen.

2. The seas and stretches of water which border Oman include the Gulf of Oman, the Arabian Sea and the Straits of Hormuz.
3. Oman's link with the sea has enabled it to dominate the Straits of Hormuz from the South.
4. The approximate area of Oman is 312,000 square kilometres.
5. Oman's territories can be divided into the coastal plains in the far South-East and the inner territories.
6. The inner territories are characterised by a chain of mountains called the Hijr.
7. The height of the highest mountain in Oman is approximately 3075 metres (above sea level).

ii Suggested translation of جغرافية عمان.

As is well-known,[1] Oman is situated in the far South-East of the Arabian peninsula. It is bordered to the East by the Gulf of Oman and the Arabian Sea, to the West by the Kingdom of Saudi Arabia and the United Arab Emirates, to the North by the Straits[2] of Hormuz, and to the South by the Republic of Yemen. Because of its geographical position,[3] Oman has developed[4] its own special geographical character. Its link with the sea is[5] one of its most obvious features, and has enabled it to dominate the southern entrance to the straits of Hormuz[6] – those straits which were once[7] the starting point of the trade route from the east to the Mediterranean basin and and to Europe, and which are now the main global oil lane, providing[8] the world with more than 60% of its oil needs.

Thus, Oman's geographical position is as important today as it was in the past.[9] Oman is[10,11] the second largest[12] country[13] in the Arabian peninsula,[14] covering[15] approximately 312,000 square kilometres. The physical geography of the country[16] differs considerably[17] from one region to another, and, from the point of view of surface features (elevations), the country can be divided into a number of sub-regions. Firstly,[18] there are the coastal plains which cover more than 1,700 kilometres from the far south east on the Arabian Sea to the Gulf of Ra's Masandam in the North. The most important of these are the fertile Batina plain[19] north-west of Musqat, which covers 270 kilometres, and the southern coastal plain,[20] which stretches from Raysut in the West to Taqah in the East, where it ends in[21] the lush[22] green plain of Salalah.

Bordering[23] the coastal plain are the inland regions which are dominated by[24] a mountain chain known as al-Hajar. This chain runs parallel to the coast from Brimi in the North to a point[25] near Sur in the South. There are also mountainous areas near[26] the coast of Dhofar in the south. The highest mountain in Oman is[27] around 3,075 metres, and is known as al-Jabal al-Axdhar (the Green Mountain).

Notes

1. Lit: 'It is well known that ...'
2. Singular in Arabic.
3. Lit: 'This position has led to Oman ...'
4. Lit: 'Has become to Oman [its special geographical characteristics]'.
5. Lit: 'has become'.
6. Lit: 'the Straits of Hormuz from the southern end'. Word order changed in order (i) to produce a more idiomatic sounding English phrase, (ii) to get 'Straits of Hormuz' to the end of the phrase, so that it can be naturally picked up again by the following 'those Straits'.
7. 'Once' added to provide contrast with subsequent 'now'.
8. Metaphor in Arabic الشريان 'artery', translated here as 'global oil lane' ('global' added here for naturalness). التي تمد translated as 'providing' instead of 'which provides' in accordance with sense required in English.
9. Lit: 'has been of utmost importance in old and modern [times]'.
10. أما ... فـ (cf. ch. 2, 7aii; ch. 17, 7a).
11. تُعتبَر (cf. ch. 1, 7d).
12. 'Largest' added to compensate for the removal of equivalent to مساحة earlier in the sentence.
13. 'Arab' not included in translation, since 'Arab country' might suggest that there are some non-Arab countries in the Arabian peninsula (which is not the case).
14. Lit: 'the region of the Arabian peninsula'.
15. Lit: 'its land(s) area reaches'.
16. Lit: 'these lands differ'.
17. Absolute accusative in Arabic تتباين ... تبايناً كبيراً (cf. ch. 18, 7aii).
18. Lit: 'There are ...'. 'Firstly' added to make explicit in English that this is the first element in a list.
19. الباطنة is given as the name of the coastal plane of eastern Oman (Wehr).
20. Lit: 'The coastal plain in the southern region'.
21. حيثُ. Lit: 'where, such that' (cf. ch. 12, 7f).
22. يانع Lit: 'mellow', 'ripe' (cf. Wehr).
23. يلي منطقةَ السهول السحلية، المناطقُ الداخلية lit: 'Borders the region of the coast plains [object], the inner regions [subject]'.
24. Lit: 'which are characterised by the presence of'.
25. 'A point' added in English to avoid the slightly inelegant 'to near'.
26. Lit: 'which overlook'.
27. Lit: 'The height of the highest mountain summit in Oman reaches'.

iii Additional exercise: comparison of translations of جغرافية عمان.
This passage presents a number of problems from a translation point of view, some of which are dealt with in the notes. Students could be asked to compare their versions with the suggested translation given above.

(b) Suggested translation of مضيق هرمز.

> The Straits of Hormuz are an extremely wide waterway whose width is no less than forty-five miles from the Omani coast to the Iranian coast, but this width is [effectively] somewhat narrower when we take into consideration a number of islands in the region: the distance between the Omani island of Ans and the Iranian island of Lark is approximately twenty-five miles. Thus the Straits are a lot wider than people imagine them to be.
>
> These days eight million barrels of oil a day pass through the Straits of Hormuz. This amount is a lot lower than that which used to pass through the Gulf a few years ago. Then it was estimated to be around twenty million barrels a day. As a result of this reduction the importance of the Straits is less than it was at the time of the Iranian Revolution in 1979.

6. Written Arabic texts 3 (classical)

(a) **ii**

• The places mentioned in this text include: Mekka, the Qibla, Abadan, Bahrain, Oman, Mahra, Hadramawt, Yemen, Jedda, Madyan, Eilat, al-Qulzum, Ba'lbak, Damascus, Palestine, Palmyra, Kufa, Hira, Basra, Homs (ancient Emesa), Hawran, the plain of Balka, Taran, Jubaylan, al-Bathaniya.
• The rivers mentioned in this text include: the Euphrates and the Tigris.
• The seas mentioned in this text include: the Persian Sea, the Red Sea, the Dead Sea.

(c) Suggested translation of أقمت في ضيافة سلطان اليمن.

> I spent a few days as a guest of the Sultan of Yemen. He treated me well and gave me a mount, and I went on to the city of Sana'a. It is the main city in Yemen; it is a large town with beautiful buildings built of baked brick and plaster; it has many trees, fruits and crops, a moderate climate, and good water. An odd fact about India, Yemen and Ethiopia is that the rain falls only in high summer; during this period it mainly falls in the afternoon each day. Travellers hurry up around noon in order to avoid the rain. The people of the town take refuge in their houses because the rain is extremely heavy.
>
> The city of Sana'a is paved throughout, and when the rain comes, it washes and cleans all the alleys. The Great Mosque of Sana'a is one of

the most beautiful mosques [in the world]. Inside is a tomb of one of the prophets, may peace be upon them.

I then travelled from Sana'a to the town of Aden, the port of Yemen on the coast of the Indian Ocean. Aden is surrounded by mountains and you can only enter from one side. It is a large town without agriculture, trees or water. It has a large cistern where the water collects during the rainy season. The water is some distance away from the town. The bedouins have often blocked it off and made it inaccessible to the town's inhabitants in order to get them to give them money and clothes. Aden is extremely hot; it is [used as] a port by the people of India, and great boats come there from Kanabayt, Tanah, Kulum, Calcutta, Fandarayna, Sindpur and other places. Indian merchants live there, as well as Egyptian merchants.

8. Aural Arabic texts 1

i   Complete transcription of حصاد الشهر, no. 6, side 1, item 1, مضيق باب المندب ١.

يبلغ طول البحر الأحمر نفسه حوالى الفي كيلومتر ويبلغ أقصى عرضه ثلاث مائة وستين كيلومتراً ولكن باب المندب وهو ذلك الممر المائي الضيق الذي يفضي للبحر الأحمر من طرفه الجنوبي لا يزيد عرضه عن حوالى عشرين كيلومتراً. ولا بد بالطبع لجميع السفن المتجهة إلى قناة السويس من المحيط الهندي والسفن المتجهة إلى ميناء إيلات الإسرائيلي وميناء العقبة الأردني أن تمر عبره. ويحد البحر الأحمر من الجانب الإفريقي غربا إثيوبيا والسودان ومصر وتمتد قناة السويس بعدئذ من خليج السويس شمالا إلى البحر الأبيض المتوسط وهي من أعظم الممرات المائية المصطنعة في العالم. وإلى الشرق من شبه جزيرة سيناء يقع خليج العقبة ويقع على رأسه ميناء العقبة الأردني وميناء إيلات الإسرائيلي وعلى الجانب الآخر من البحر الأحمر وهو الجانب الشرقي توجد سواحل للمملكة العربية السعودية والجمهورية العربية اليمنية وإلى الجنوب قليلا من باب المندب حيث ينفرج الخط الساحلي ويفضي إلى المحيط الهندي تقع جمهورية اليمن الديموقراطية الشعبية إلى الشرق والمستعمرة الفرنسية السابقة جيبوتي إلى الغرب على الساحل الإفريقي.

ii Answers to comprehension questions relating to مضيق باب المندب ١.

1. The length of the Red Sea is approximately 2,000 kilometres.

2. The greatest width of the Red Sea is 360 kilometres.
3. The Mandib Straits lead to the Red Sea in the South.
4. The width of the Mandib Straits does not exceed twenty kilometres.
5. Ships heading for the Suez Canal and the ports of Eilat and Aqaba require passage through the Mandib Straits.
6. The African countries which border the Red Sea to the West are Ethiopia and Sudan.
7. The Suez Canal runs from the Gulf of Suez to the Meditteranean Ocean.
8. The Gulf of Aqaba lies to the East of the Sinai peninsula.
9. The ports of Aqaba and Eilat lie at the head of this Gulf.
10. The countries situated to the East of the Red Sea are Saudi Arabia and the Yemen Arab Republic [today the Republic of Yemen].
11. The People's Democratic Republic of Yemen is situated to the South-East of the Mandib Straits.
12. The former French colony of Djibouti is situated to the South-West of the Mandib Straits.

9. Aural Arabic texts 2

i   Complete transcription of حصاد الشهر, no. 26, side 2, item 3, مضيق باب المندب ٢

مضيق باب المندب عظيم الأهمية لأنه منفذ يربط بين البحر الأحمر
وبين المحيط الهندي . ومعلوم أن البحر الأحمر يؤدي شمالاً إلى قناة
السويس والبحر الأبيض المتوسط . واتساع مضيق باب المندب لا يزيد
على خمسة وعشرين كيلومترا عند أضيق نقطة . فالسفن المارة
يستطيع ملاحوها أن يشاهدوا كلاً من آسيا وأفريقيا . والمضيق قريب
من السواحل العربية لا يفصله عنها سوى قناة ضيّقة وقليلة العمق لا
يسهل على السفن أن تجتازها . وعندها جزيرة «مايم» التي لا تزيد
رقعتها على ثمانية كيلومترات مربعة ولا يقيم فيها سوى بضعة مائات
من السكان لأنها تفتقر إلى الماء وإلى الزراعة . وهي بالرغم من ذلك
عظيمة الأهمية من الناحية الاستراتيجية . وقد أدرك البريطانيون
أهميتها عام ألف وسبع مائة وتسعة وتسعين فاحتلّوها يوم كان الجيش
الفرنسي في مصر بقيادة نابليون بونابرت فأراد البريطانيون منعه
من التوغل في جنوب البحر الأحمر خشيةً أن يكتسح الهند . وعندما
زال خطر نابليون جلا البريطانيون عن جزيرة «مايم» . لكنهم في عام
ألف وثماني مائة وسبعة وخمسين احتلوها مرة أخرى كيلا يحتلها
الفرنسيون .

ii Answers to comprehension questions relating to ٢ مضيق باب المندب.

1. The Mandib Straits are extremely important because they link the Red Sea with the Indian Ocean.
2. The Red Sea leads North to the Suez Canal and the Mediterranean Sea.
3. The Mandib Straits are twenty-five kilometres wide at their narrowest point.
4. Sailors in passing ships can see both Asia and Africa.
5. The Straits are separated from the Arabian coast by a narrow and shallow channel which ships cannot easily negotiate.
6. The island of Mayum is less than eight kilometres square.
7. A fcw hundred people live there.
8. The number of inhabitants is so few because there is very little water and agriculture.
9. The British occupied it in 1799.
10. They hoped to prevent the French army from advancing into the southern Red Sea by occupying Mayum.
11. They reoccupied Mayum in 1857.
12. They reoccupied Mayum in order to prevent the French from doing so.

iii Structure translations based on ٢ مضيق باب المندب.

١ – هذا الأمر عظيم الأهمية.

٢ – تربط قناة السويس بين البحر الأبيض المتوسط وبين البحر الأحمر.

٣ – لا يسهل على الحكومة أن تحلّ هذه المشكلة.

٤ – تفتقر الحكومة الحالية إلى العلم الضروري.

٥ – ماذا عملت يوم غزا العراق الكويت؟

٦ – لم أفعل شيئاً خشيةً أن تزعل.

10. Written English texts
(a) Suggested translation of 'Republic of Yemen: geography'.

جغرافية الجمهورية اليمنية

اندمجت الجمهوريةُ العربيةُ اليمنيةُ وجمهوريةُ اليمن الديموقراطيةُ الشعبيةُ يومَ اثنينِ وعشرينَ مايو عامَ ألفٍ وتسعمئةٍ وتسعينَ لتُشكّلا الجمهوريةَ اليمنيةَ . وكانت الجمهوريتانِ اليمنيتانِ السابقتانِ قد احتوتا على الزاوية

الجنوبية الغربية للجزيرة العربية – وتشمل هذه الزاوية المرتفعات الواقعة داخل البلاد والشريط الساحلي المقابل للبحر الأحمر والمستعمرة البريطانية السابقة عدن البالغة مساحتها مائة وخمسة وتسعين كيلومتراً مربعاً ومحمية الجزيرة العربية الجنوبية البالغة مساحتها حوالي ثلاث مئات وثلاثة وثلاثين ألف كيلومتر مربع بالإضافة إلى جزيرة بارم البالغة مساحتها ثلاثة عشر كيلومتراً مربعاً وجزيرة كمران البالغة مساحتها سبعة وخمسين كيلومتراً مربعاً، وتقع الجمهورية اليمنية في الطرف الجنوبي للجزيرة العربية وتحدّها المملكة العربية السعودية من الشمال وسلطنة عمان من الشرق. أما عاصمة اليمن فمدينة صنعاء الواقعة على هضبة الجهال.

(b) Suggested translation of 'Egypt: the centre of gravity'.

مصر .. مركز الثقَل

يبلغ عدد سكان مصر تسعةً وثلاثين مليونَ نسمة ويُعتبر هذا العدد أكبر بكثير من عدد سكان أي دولة عربية أخرى ، حيث يُوجد ثلثُ سكان الأمة العربية في مصرَ ، وتزيد الكثافةُ السكانيةُ في مناطق مصرَ الآهلة [/المأهولة] على تلك في أي دولة أخرى في العالم العربي، لأنّ مصرَ – وبرغم تساوي مساحتها مع مساحة كلتى فرنسا وإسبانيا – لا يقطنها ناس إلا في وادي النيل ودلتاه ، باستثناء بضعة آلاف ساكنين في واحات الصحراء الغربية، ولا تزيد مساحةُ هذه المناطق على أربعة في المائة من المساحة الكاملة للبلاد وهي تعادل مساحةَ هولاندا تقريباً. ونتيجةً لهذا فإنّ مصرَ تُعتبر من أفقر الدول العربية دخلا من ناحية الدخل الفردي، بالرغم أنها من أكثرها تقدماً من الناحية العامة.

11. Précis

Précis passages in the early stages of the course could be structured by the teacher and treated as loose comprehension passages with broad questions being asked. Suggested guidance questions for the précis in Arabic of اليمن قطر عربي.

١ – أين تقع اليمن؟

٢ – ماذا يذكر الكاتب عن الحضارة اليمنية؟

٣ – مما تتكون اليمن؟

٤ – ماذا يزرع اليمنيون؟

٥ – كيف تختلف اليمن من منطقة إلى أخرى؟

٦ – صف الطقس اليمني.

٧ – صف العلم اليمني.

٨ – ما هي أهم المدن اليمنية القديمة ؟

2
Ethnic groups in the Middle East

3. Key vocabulary

As in chapter one, the key vocabulary section can be used to get students to skim read and select items of specific vocabulary. A few items of vocabulary should then be written up on the board or the overhead projector and the vocabulary can then be used as a starting point for discussion in Arabic of the topic covered in the chapter. The sort of questions which could be asked include:

– الأكراد :من هم الأكراد؟

– أين يسكنون اليوم؟

– شعب :ما معنى كلمة «شعب»؟

– من هي الشعوب الرئيسة في الوطن العربي؟

4. Written Arabic texts 1

(a) Answers to comprehension questions relating to يذكر علماء التاريخ.

1. Historians say that the Arabs are a Semitic people.
2. According to researchers, the ancestors of the Arabs lived in the southern end of the Arabian peninsula.
3. These people were forced to leave their country because of an increase in the population and adverse climatic changes.
4. No, they did not all leave at once.
5. The Akkadians, the Babylonians and the Assyrians went to Mesopotamia.
6. The Canaanites and the Phoenicians headed north.
7. Nomadic groups remained in the peninsula.
8. Their life of hardship enabled them to maintain their identity, independence, freedom and language.

5. Written Arabic texts 2

(a) Answers to comprehension questions relating to الأكراد.

1. The Kurds live in four countries in the Middle East: Turkey, Syria, Iraq and

Iran.

2. The total size of the Kurdish population is over 20 million.
3. The Kurds are first mentioned in writing before the advent of Islam.
4. Most of the Kurds embraced Islam in the time of Caliph Umar ibn al-Khattab.
5. Today Kurds embrace Islam or Christianity.
6. The Kurdish language is very different from Arabic.
7. Most Kurds work in the country as shepherds or poor farmers.
8. Some Kurds work in the towns in factories, and educated Kurds work as doctors, engineers, newspaper reporters and teachers, etc.
9. The Kurds encounter problems in Iran because Iran is an Islamic republic and the governmental position on nationalist movements is unclear.
10. The Kurds encounter problems in Syria because Syria is a dictatorship which does not accept non-Arab political parties.
11. Kurdish is still banned in schools in Turkey.
12. The Turkish government called the Kurds 'Mountain Turks'.
13. It gave them this name because the original homeland of the Turks is the high mountains in the east of Turkey.
14. Over the past twenty years the Kurds have been attacked by the Ba'th government.
15. In Halabja the army killed more than 5,000 men, women and children.
16. The future of the Kurds is not clear in Iran and Syria.
17. The future of the Kurds in Iraq depends on the general political situation in the country.
18. It is said that the future of the Kurds in Turkey may well be an improvement from the past.
19. The writer says this because Turkey is a democratic country with lots of people who support human rights and do not accept the government's former position of denying the existence of the Kurds within the country.

(b) Suggested translation of تاريخ الأكراد.

The history of the Kurds

The Kurds embraced Islam during the era of the Caliph Umar ibn al-Khattab, after Persia had been conquered and before the conversion to Islam of their neighbours, the Persians. The Kurds remained clients of the Islamic Caliphate until the final stages of the Umayyad era, when they rallied around the Abbasid banner. Abu Muslim al-Khurasani succeeded in defeating Nasr ibn Sabbar the Umayyad governor in Khurasan. He continued to pursue the scattered remnants of the Umayyad army until the Umayyad Caliphate was destroyed[1] and political power[2] passed to the Abbasids who [then] betrayed and killed Abu Muslim.[3] Under the Abbasid Caliphate the Kurds became semi-autonomous[4] and were even able to found a large state, the Marwanid State. However, the main task assumed by the Kurds[5] thereafter was that of resisting the Crusaders. Saladin was one of the most outstanding leaders in the Kurdish army which fought the Crusaders from the time of Imad al-Din Zanki, and his son Nur al-Din who succeeded him. Saladin founded a large state which comprised Egypt, Syria, the Hijaz, Yemen, Sudan and Mosul. He succeeded in defeating the Crusaders at Jerusalem, expelling them from the city[6] and destroying most of their castles on the coast. When the Islamic World was attacked by the Mongols, the Kurds took a noble stand in the face of this danger. When the forces of Genghis Khan reached the hills overlooking Hamadhan, the Kurds lured them to the battleground and defeated them, then[7] forced the Mongols into retreat. This was the first time that[8] the Mongols went into retreat and the Kurds subsequently stopped their advance on Baghdad. However the Mongols went back on the attack at the time of Hulagu, who was himself forced to change his course in order to avoid Kurdistan.

When Timur the Lame attempted to seize control of Kurdistan after his defeat of the Ottoman Sultan, the Kurds[9] opposed him so he attacked their country and set fire to many of their villages. His military instinct, however, told him that penetration of this country was not in his interest so he withdrew his armies to his base in Samarkand and Bukhara.

The Ottomans adopted a flexible policy towards the Kurds; the Ottoman Caliphate used the Kurds as a military force, so military affairs were placed more or less in their hands and they became the cavaliers of the army.

After the First World War the West, with the consent of Russia, carved up the remnants of the 'Sick Man [of Europe]'. Kurdistan was divided into four parts. Russia took a part, while the main portion was retained by Turkey; a the third portion came under English control, and France's share was the strip adjacent to Turkey in the South. The tragedy of the Kurds in the modern era [lit: the tragedy of the contemporary Kurds] had begun.

Notes

1. تم + verbal noun + pronoun suffix translates as the English passive, as here (cf. ch. 3, 7ai).
2. السياسة acts as a generic noun here, and is translated into English without the definite article.
3. In English, it is normal style to have two verbs followed by a single nominal object, as in the translation here: 'who betrayed and killed Abu Muslim'. In Arabic the norm is to have the first verb with a nominal object, followed by the second verb with a pronominal object, as in the original Arabic: الذين غدروا بأبي مسلم وقتلوه.

4. شِبه and its verbal counterparts are often translatable as 'semi-' in English (cf. ch. 1, 7c).
5. The verb is active in Arabic.
6. The pronoun ـه cannot be translated into English by a pronoun in this case. cf. also فيه and فيها where the pronoun stands for a previously mentioned place and is translated into English as 'there' (cf. ch. 1, 7f).
7. ف is sequential.
8. فيها . . . المرة الأولى التي 'the first time that...'
9. Note the use of the form كُرد to mean 'Kurds'. This can be regarded as a stylistic variant of أكْراد (cf. also تُرْك as well as أتْراك to mean 'Turks'), and is translated into English as a plural.

6. Written Arabic texts 3 (classical)

(a) **ii** Suggested translation of اعلم أنّ جميع العرب.

You should know that all the Arabs can be traced back to three lines, namely those of Adnan, Qahtan and Qada'a. Adnan was descended from Ismail [Ishmael] by common consent, however there is nothing to verify this apart from the names [lit: mention] of his forebears going back to Ismail. All the sons of Ismail apart from Adnan died out; so there are [now] none of them on the face of the earth. Qahtan is [also] said to be descended from Ismail and this is apparent from al-Bukhari's statement in his chapter on the relationship of Yemen to Ismail. Most people believe that Qahtan is Joktan[1] who is mentioned in the Torah as a descendent of Eber, and that Hadramawt is one of the people of Qahtan. With regard to Qada'a it is said that they are Himyarites; this was claimed by Ibn Ishaq, al-Kalbi and Ta'ifa. Evidence for this is found in the account of Ibn Luha'a on the authority of Uqba ibn Amir al-Jahni who said, 'Oh Prophet of God, who are we descended from?' He [the Prophet] said, 'You are descended from Qada'a ibn Malik.'

Note
1. Genesis, verse 10.

(b) Suggested translation of من الأخبار الواهية.

One of the improbable stories related by the historians is their account of the Tubba's,[1] the kings of Yemen and the Arabian peninsula, that they used to carry out raids from their villages in Yemen on North Africa and on the Berbers in the Maghrib; they also related that Ifriqish ibn Qays ibn Sayfi, one of their greatest early kings at, or a little before, the time of Moses, may peace be upon him, carried out a raid on North

Africa and massacred the Berbers, and that it was he who gave them this name when he heard their unintelligible speech and said, 'What is this gibberish [barbarity]?' This name was then taken up [from him] and they were called by it from then on. When Ifriqish left North Africa, he left a number of Himyaritic tribes behind, and they stayed there and intermarried with the people of the region. They included the Sinhaja and the Kutama; and on this basis al-Tabari, al-Jurjani, al-Mas'udi, Ibn al-Kalbi and al-Bili took the view that the Sinhaja and the Kutama were of Himyaritic stock. Berber genealogists, however, reject this [claim], and this [i.e. the latter explanation] is correct.

Note

1. تُبَّعُ, pl. تَبَابِعَة: title given to the ancient Himyaritic kings of Yemen.

(c) Suggested translation of فَأَمَّا أَجناس الأَكراد.

Regarding the Kurds, people have disagreed over their ethnic origins. Some say that they are descended from Rabi'a the son of Nazar the son of Mu'add the son of Adnan the son of Bakr the son of Wa'il, and that they became a separate ethnic group a long time ago and went to live in the mountains and valleys through force of circumstance. There they lived alongside the non-Arab and Persian communities who were settled in the towns and other inhabited areas. Their language then changed and became non-Arabic. Every branch of the Kurds has their own Kurdish dialect. Some people believe that they are descended from Mudar ibn Nazar and that they are also descended from Kurd ibn Mard ibn Sa'sa'a ibn Hawazin and that they branched off a long time ago because of battles between them and Ghassan. There are also others who believe that they are descended from Rabi'a and Mudar and sought shelter in the mountains in their search for water and fodder, and that they stopped speaking Arabic due to the influence of neighbouring peoples.

8. Aural Arabic texts 1

ii Answers to comprehension questions relating to حصاد الشهر, no. 26, side 2, item 6, من هم البربر وما هو أصلهم؟.

1. The term بربر is derived from the Greek word *barbaros*.
2. The Greeks used this term to describe people who did not speak Greek.
3. The Arabs described people who did not speak Arabic as أعاجم.
4. At the time that Rome established an empire the term بربر was used to describe all the people who inhabited Africa including the people of the Sahara.
5. Ultimately the term بربر came to be used to describe all the people who lived between the oasis of Siwa in the west of Egypt and Nouakchott, capital of Mauritania today, and between the tribes of Algeria in the mountains of Jarjura

and the north-west regions of Sudan.

6. According to some people the Berbers originally come from Yemen.

7. If this is the case the Berbers would belong to the Semitic race.

8. Some legends link the Berbers with the Hamitic race.

9. According to researchers the Berbers lived along the coast and in the desert including the areas immediately to the south of the desert at the time of the Arab conquest of North Africa.

10. There are three main groups of Berbers.

11. These groups are the Zanata, Masmuda and Sinhaja.

12. The first group can be found from Libya to the Rif in Morocco.

13. The second group speaks Shluh.

14. The Berbers mixed with the Arabs who came to conquer and then with the Beni Hilal in the fifth century AH.

15. According to the speaker it is not true that the Berbers can be divided into two groups: one which has maintained its original race and a second which has become Arabised.

16. The Berber groups can be distinguished by their language.

17. The Berbers speak four main languages: Amazigh and Shluh in Morocco and Mauritania and Tamashik which is spoken by the Tuareg and Zanga in Senegal.

18. The Berbers use Arabic for writing, literature, poetry, science and jurisprudence.

19. The Berbers describe themselves as 'Amazig' and this means 'noble'.

v Suggested structure translations relating to ؟من هم البربر وما هو أصلهم.

The relevant portion of the original Arabic text is quoted in curly brackets after the suggested translation. Notes relating to the translation are sometimes also provided after the translation.

١ – كلمة قاموس باللغة العربية [/بالعربية] مأخوذة من كلمة «اوكيانوس» اليونانية. {كلمة بربر مأخوذة أصلا من كلمة «بربروس» اليونانية}

٢ – تُطلق هذه العبارة عادة على الأجانب. {... التي أطلقها اليونان على الشعوب التي لم تكن تتكلم اللغة اليونانية}

٣ – كان البربر يزرعون القمح. {... الشعوب التي لم تكن تتكلم اللغة اليونانية}

It makes sense to think of يزرعون القمح as the complement (or object) of كان, just as مهندسا 'an engineer' is the complement (or object) of كان in the sentence كان هذا الرجل مهندسا 'this man was an engineer', or as غضبان كان هذا الرجل غضبان is the complement (or object) of كان in عليك كان البربر 'this man was angry with you'. The only difference in يزرعون القمح is that يزرعون itself also has an object (a subsidiary object in terms of the overall structure of the sentence) القمح. In these respects كان

is similar to أصبح. That is to say,كان البربر يزرعون القمح' (In the past) the Berbers used to grow wheat' parallels أصبح البربر يزرعون القمح 'The Berbers began to grow wheat' (lit. 'The Berbers became they-grow-wheat'). Note also that it is sometimes possible to translate adverbial phrases, such as 'In the past' in this example, by a combination of verbs in Arabic.

٤ – ما [هو] ذلك البناء المقابل لنا؟ {... الساحل الأفريقي المقابل لهم}

٥ – الظاهر أنه سكران. {والظاهر أنه لما اتّسعت روما ...}

Literally, 'The clear [thing] [is] that he is drunk'. Note that it is also possible to say من الظاهر انه سكران.

٦ – أريد أن أشتري البيت كله بما في ذلك الأثاث. {... جميع الشعوب التي تسكن أفريقيا بما في ذلك شعوب الصحراء}

٧ – هناك من يزعم أن أصل الأيرلانديين من شمال أفريقيا. {هناك من يقول إن أصل البربر من اليمن}

It is possible to use من in a non-question sense without any preceeding noun. In this case it normally translates into English as 'he who', 'she who', 'someone who', 'they who', 'people who', etc (cf. 9, 7a).

٨ – معنى هذا أنك لم تعمل العمل. {ومعنى هذا أن البربر يكونون شعبا ساميا أو شعوبا سامية}

٩ – والذي عليه المؤرّخون [هو] التالي. {والذي عليه الباحثون هو انه ... etc.}

١٠ – وصل الحلفاء إلى أوربا الشرقية مُحَرِّرين. {...جاء العرب إلى شمال أفريقيا فاتحين}

It would also be possible to say كمحررين The usage in the passage is what is known in traditional Arabic grammar as a *hal* (حال) clause (ch. 6, 7a).

١١ – كانت هذه المنطقة يسكنها الأرمن. {كانت المنطقة ... يسكنها البربر}

The phrase يسكنها الأرمن is the complement (or object) of كانت ; cf. also no. 3. Within this complement (or object) الأرمن is the subject of يسكنها. Literally the Arabic translates as: 'Was this region inhabits-it-the-Armenians'. This translates into idiomatic English as 'this region was/used to be inhabited by [the] Armenians'.

١٢ – وُلِد في القرن الأول للهجرة أي السابع للميلادِ {القرن الخامس للهجرة أي الحادي عشر للميلاد}

١٣ – يُزْعَم أن اكثر التركمن في العراق [قد] نسوا لغتهم. {ويُقال بأن هناك من البربر من لا يزالون يحتفظون بعنصرهم الأصلي}

١٤ – مع أنه يتكلّم اللغة العربية جيدا فأنه لا يعرف عربا كثارا. {ومع أن هذه المقولة شائعة فإنها ليست صحيحة إلى الحد الذي تلقاه من البعض}

It is quite common for initial prepositional phrases to be separated from the rest of the sentence by ف, فأنه etc. This is especially the case with phrases meaning 'despite', 'although' (ch. 10, 7b; ch. 17, 7bi).

١٥ - هذا ما يقوله البعض. {...إلى الحد الذي تلقاه من البعض}

١٦ - يملك عددا من الشركات كبيرا. {فالبربر يستعملون الآن عددا من اللغات كبيرا}

The phrase عددا من الشركات كبيرا is a variant of the more common كبيرا من الشركات.

١٧ - أهمّ المشاكل أربع. {أهم لغاتهم أربع}

١٨ - يستعملون اللغة الفرنسية لغة كتابة. {...استعمالهم اللغة العربية لغة كتابة وأدب وشعر وعلم وما إلى ذلك...}

١٩ - تشير إلى نفسها [/تصف نفسها] بأنها أفريقية متعربة. {والبربري يشير إلى نفسه وخاصة في المغرب بأنه « أمازغ » ومعناه النبيل}

9. Aural Arabic texts 2

i   Answers to comprehension questions relating to حصاد الشهر, no. 27, side 2, item 6, من هم الطوارق ؟.

1. The Tuareg are distinguished by a dark blue face covering which covers the whole of their face except for the eyes.
2. The listener's question was not answered the first time because he had not mentioned his name.
3. Nicola Ziadeh is a historian.
4. The skin colour of the Tuareg is white.
5. They belong to the larger ethnic group of the Berbers.
6. The Tuareg live in the area stretching from Touat in Algeria and Ghudamis (Ghadames) in Libya to al-Fazan and Timbuktu.
7. One group of Tuareg make their living by trading across the Sahara and protecting caravans which cross the Sahara. Another group of Tuareg make their living by raising cattle and camels and by agriculture.
8. There are two recognised groups of Tuareg.
9. The Tuareg have been around since the Roman Empire or even before that.
10. The Tuareg are called الملثمون because of the indigo-dyed veils they wear.
11. They were first given this name in the fifth century AH/eleventh century AD.
12. Ibn Yasin was the spiritual founder of the Almoravid state.
13. The Almoravid state was founded in the eleventh century AD.
14. The capital of this state was Marrakesh.
15. The origin of the name Tuareg is not yet known.

v   Suggested structure translations relating to من هم الطوارق ؟.

١ - اشتهر بتربية الإبل. {اشتهروا بغطاء الرأس}

٢ – كانت هذه الجماعة معروفة قبل دخول الإسلام إلى الهند. {هل كانوا معروفين قبل دخول الإسلام إلى الهند}

٣ – هل تستطيع [/هل يمكنك] أن توافيني بالمعلومات اللازمة؟ {يوافيك بجواب}

٤ – يغلب على النساء الشعر الطويل. {تغلب عليهم البشرة البيضاء}
Note that البشرة البيضاء/}الشعر الطويل} is the subject of this sentence in Arabic.

٥ – البربر من حيث السياسة قسمان [/من حيث السياسة البربر قسمان]. {وهم من حيث الاقتصاد والحياة الاجتماعية قسمان}

٦ – التهريب المصدر الرئيسي [/الرئيسي] للمال عندهم. {وكانت التجارة الصحراوية ... المصدر الرئيس للرزق عندهم}

٧ – يُعْرَف الشماليون بالبني عامر. {...فيما يُعْرَف الجنوبيون بتجمع أبسند وأيفورة}

٨ – يُطلق عليه «أبو أحمد». {يُطلق على الشماليين تجمع الهقر أو الأقر}

٩ – المعروف [هو] أن هذا الرجل لصّ [/سارق/سرّاق]. {والمعروف هو أن الطوارق كانوا موجودين ...}

١٠ – وُلِدت [/هي مولودة] في العشرينات إن لم يكن قبل ذلك. {...في عصر الإمبراطورية الرومانية إن لم يكن قبل ذلك}

١١ – كانت لابسة [/تلبس] فستانا مصبوغا باللون الأخضر. {ورجال الطوارق يُغَطُّون وجوههم بلثام من قماش مصبوغ باللون الأزرق}

١٢ – ومن هنا عُرف [/أصبح يُعْرَف] بالأسد. {ومن هنا يُسَمُّون الملثمين}

١٣ – قامت دولة المرابطين في القرن الخامس الهجري أي القرن الحادي عشر الميلادي. {...في قيام دولة المرابطين في المغرب في أواسط القرن الخامس الهجري أي القرن الحادي عشر الميلادي}

١٤ – ذلك أنه مجنون. {ذلك أن ابن ياسين ... قد اعتزل ...}

١٥ – يُرَجَّح أن الرباط كان في جبال كردستان. {اعتزل مع جماعة من أصحابه يُرَجّح أنه كان يقوم على جزيرة}
Note that the phrase أن الرباط كان في جبال كردستان is the subject of يرجج in the أنه كان يقوم على جزيرة is the subject of يرجج, just as in the example in the original text (ch. 2, 7c).

١٦ – خرج مع أصحابه وهم شيوعيون. {خرج مع جماعته من الملثمين وهم أهل الرباط}

١٧ – خان هذا الرجل كثيرون [/هذا الرجل خانه كثيرون]. {...وانضمّ اليهم كثيرون}

١٨ – ما هي [ما كانت هي] النتيجة النهائية لنشاطكم؟ {وكانت النتيجة النهائية لهذه الحركة إقامة دولة المرابطين}

١٩ – بنوا الجسر عند منعرج النهر [في الاتجاه] إلى الشرق. {ونشروا الإسلام في حوض نهر النيجر عند منعرجه في الاتجاه من الشمال إلى الجنوب}

٢٠ – بسبب استعمالهم للحشيش فإننا لا نحبّهم. {وبسبب استعمال جماعة ابن ياسين للثام فإن المؤرخين القدامى ...}

Note the usage استعمالهم للحشيش. It is also possible, but less usual, to say استعمالهم الحشيشَ where الحشيشَ is the object of استعمال, and therefore goes in the accusative.

٢١ – ما هو أصل تسمية هؤلاء الناس «أجانب»؟ {ما هو أصل تسمية هذه الجماعات الطوارق}

٢٢ – الذين يدرسون مثل هذه [/تلك] الأشياء أغبياء. {الذين بحثوا في هذا الأمر غير متفقين على المعنى}

٢٣ – تُشير إلى نفسها بأنها أفريقية مُتَعَرِّبة/مستعربة. {والبربري يشير إلى نفسه ... بأنه «أمازق»}

10. Written English texts

Suggested translation of 'The earliest account'.

أولُ ما ورد إلينا من ذكرِ الجزيرةِ العربيةِ والعربِ هو ما ذُكِرَ في البابِ العاشرِ لسفرِ التكوينِ حيثُ وردت أسماءُ الكثيرِ من شعوبِ الجزيرةِ ومناطقها . ومع ذلك فلا تُستعملُ لفظةُ «عرب» في هذا النصِ بل تظهرُ [هذه اللحظة] لأول مرةٍ في نقشٍ أشوريٍّ من سنة ثمانيمائة وثلاث وخمسينَ قبلَ الميلادِ حيثُ يُسجّلُ الملكُ شلَمانسرُ الثالثُ دحرَ القواتِ الأشوريّةَ لمؤامرةٍ دبّرها أمراءُ متمردون [/مؤامرةَ أمراءَ متمردين] ، ومن بينهم جندب العربي الذي أعطى قواتِ التحالفِ ألفَ جملٍ وهو عطاءٌ مُناسبٌ نَظَراً لكونه أميراً عربياً.

11. Précis

Suggested guidance questions for the précis in Arabic of تاريخ الأكراد.

١ – متى دخل الأكراد في الإسلام؟

٢ – ما هي الخطوط العريضة لتاريخ الأكراد في العهد الأموي؟

٣ – ما هي الخطوط العريضة لتاريخ الأكراد في العهد العباسي؟

٤ – ما هو دور الأكراد في محاربة الصليبيين؟

٥ – ما هو دور الأكراد في محاربة المغول؟

٦ – ما هي قصة تيمور لنك مع الأكراد؟

٧ – ما هي مكانة الأكراد في الدولة العثمانية؟

٨ – كيف بدأت مأساة الأكراد المعاصرين؟

3
The Middle East in antiquity

4. Written Arabic texts 1

(a) **ii** Answers to comprehension questions relating to اكتشاف آثار بلدة.

1. Umm al-Qaywayn is in the United Arab Emirates.
2. The settlement there is approximately 6,000 years old.
3. It possesses a walled tower.
4. This walled tower is probably the oldest of its type.
5. The archeological work on this settlement is being financed by the governmentt of Umm al-Qaywayn and General Motors.
6. Dan Potts is an Australian professor from the University of Sydney.
7. The name of the settlement is Tell Abraq.
8. It ceased to be inhabited in the first century AD.
9. The area of the settlement is four hectares.
10. Dan Potts considers the discovery of the settlement to be extremely important.
11. He says this is the case because it is the oldest and largest inhabited town to have been discovered on the southern coasts of the Persian Gulf.
12. The economic activity mentioned is trading between important towns in western and southern Asia.

(b) **i** Suggested structure translations relating to كشف أثري في الأردن.

The relevant portion of the original text is given in curly brackets.

١ – تمّ الكشفُ عن أقدم بناء/مبنى في العالم في الأردن . {تم الكشف عن كنيسة بيزنطية}

٢ – تعود الحكاية إلى القرن الرابع الهجري . {كنيسة بيزنطية ... تعود إلى القرن السادس الميلادي}

٣ – هو رئيس القسم التابع للأمم المتحدة . {معهد الآثار والأنثروبولوجيا

التابع لجامعة اليرموك}

٤ – قالت إنه تم الكشفُ عن المخطوطات الإسلامية في الثمانينات . {وأضاف أنه تم الكشف أيضا عن أجزاء من مبنى إداري}

ii Suggested translation of كشف أثري في الأردن.

A second mosaic-floored Byzantine church has been discovered on the ancient site of Basilla to the West of Ramtha in northern Jordan. The church, which dates back to the sixth century AD, was used in Umayyad, Abbasid and Ayyubid times.

According to Dr Zaydun al-Muhaysan, head of the team from the Institute of Archeology and Anthropology at the University of Yarmouk, which is undertaking the archeological dig on the site, the fact that a second church has been discovered on the same site is indicative of its large size[1,2] and its cultural importance during the classical and Islamic periods.

Dr al-Muhaysan added that parts of an administrative building were also discovered last season. This demonstrated the cultural stability of the local population. He also said that the team were currently carrying out a documentary study of irrigation and agricultural systems on the site.

Notes

1. Literally: 'archeological site'.
2. Notice that موقع is repeated a number of times in the Arabic text. In Arabic such word repetition (also called lexical-item repetition) across a text is considered good style. English style does not accept a high degree of word repetition; and in order to produce a good English style it is necessary to find alternative words having the same or roughly the same meanings – synonyms or near-synonyms – or to find an alternative formulation which gives the same basic sense, e.g. 'the local population' for سكان الموقع in paragraph 3. This issue is discussed in detail in chapter 18, section 7a.

5. Written Arabic texts 2

i Answers to comprehension questions relating to كشف أثري هام.

1. The French team have carried out archeological investigations in al-Shawaf in the Saqqara area in Egypt.
2. The team is being headed by the Egyptologist Dr Leclan.
3. The team leader is French.
4. The pyramid of one of the wives of King Bibi the First has been discovered.

5. The name of the pyramid's owner was confirmed by the discovery of a tablet with the Queen's name written in hieroglyphics near to the pyramid.
6. She had been forgotten by history as there is no mention of her in books on Pharaonic history up to now.
7. Advanced technological instruments were used in making this find.
8. Mr Farouq Husni is the Egyptian Minister of Culture.
9. The pyramids height is estimated to have been 30 metres.
10. Its base was constructed out of limestone.
11. Granite was also used in the construction of the pyramid.
12. They have found three pyramids.
13. It says, 'The beloved wife of the King'.
14. They reject this idea because, according to one of the King's ministers, she conspired against the King.
15. They were the daughters of the prince of Abydos and Nag Hammadi.
16. He is the head of the Archeological Department.
17. It is made up of engineers and restoration experts, together with two archeologists, Nabil Daniel and Issam Nabil.
18. They are continuing their excavations around the entrance to the pyramid, in an attempt to reach the burial chamber.

ii Types of questions for students to ask each other.

1. How many other pyramids belonging to other wives of King Bibi the First have been found?
2. What does the discovered tablet say?
3. What does this confirm?
4. Why do scientists not believe that King Bibi would have built one of the pyramids for his first wife?
5. What do we know about the second and third wives?
6. Who is Dr Sayyid Tawfiq?
7. What did the team present to Dr Tawfiq?
8. What did Dr Tawfiq say about the discovery to Mustafa al-Najjar?
9. Who is Mahmoud Abu al-Wafa?
10. How did archeological work on the pyramid begin?
11. What was the team trying to find?
12. What would this maybe reveal?

iii Constructions of grammatical interest.

Instances of apposition.
There are a large number of instances of apposition in this text. These generally present the title, the name, and then, if included, the profession of a person. In order, these include:

عالم المصريات الفرنسي الكبير / الدكتور / ليكلان

الملك / بيبي الأول / ثاني ملوك الأسرة السادسة

الدكتور / زاهي حواس / مدير عام لآثار الجيزة

السيد / فاروق حسني / وزير الثقافة

الملكات / زوجات الملك بيبي الأول

الدكتور / سيد توفيق / رئيس هيئة الآثار

مصطفى النجار / مندوب الأهرام

الأثري / محمود أبو الوفا / مدير منطقة سقارة

Impersonal passive.

There are two instances of impersonal passive in this text.

والتي أُعلن عن اكتشاف اثنين منها 'the discovery of two of which has been announced'

اللوحة التي عُثر عليها 'the tablet which was found'

Active sentences which should be translated as passive in English.

There are two active sentences in the text which should be translated as agentive passives in English.

هذه الملكة قد نسيها التاريخ 'this queen had been forgotten by history'

الهرم المكتشف توصلت إليه الأجهزة التكنولوجية المتقدمة 'the discovered pyramid was reached by advanced technological instruments'

i v Suggested structure translations relating to كشف أثري هام: هرم تحت رمال سقارة.

The relevant portion of the original text is given in curly in brackets.

١ – عثرت البعثة الألمانية على قرية لم تكن معروفةً من قبل . {وملكة لم تكن معروفة من قبل} and {كما عثرت على لوحة}

٢ – يمكن القول إن الملكة ماتت/تُوُفِّيت عام/في عام أربعة آلاف قبل الميلاد . {ويمكن القول إن هذه الملكة قد نسيها التاريخ}

٣ – قَدَّم رئيس الوزارة تقريراً عاجلاً . {وقدم الدكتور زاهي حواس ... تقريراً عاجلاً}

٤ – يُقَدَّر عمقُ البحيرة بنحو أربعين متراً . {وقدر ارتفاعه بنحو ٣٠ مترا}

٥ – يُعَدُّ هذا الاكتشافُ/الكشفُ إضافةً غيرَ هامةٍ للتاريخ اليمني . {يعد هذا الكشف إضافة هامة للتاريخ المصري القديم}

٦ – رافَقَ البعثةَ الألمانيةَ الآثاريُّ/الأثريُّ المصريُّ المشهورُ . {ويرافقهم الأثريان نبيل دانيل وعصام نبيل}

٧ – ربما تُفْضِي النصوصُ القديمةُ بأسـرار تَتَعَلَّق بالحكومة البـريطانيـة . {ربما تفضي بأسـرار أو نصـوص}

6. Written Arabic texts 3 (classical)

(a) Suggested translation of ذكر الأهرام والبـرابي.

They are one of the wonders mentioned throughout the course of time. People talk about them at length, ponder them, and ask why they were first built. They say that all the sciences which emerged before the flood were taken from Hurmus the First [= Hermes Trismegistes of Greek tradition] who lived in the farthest part of Upper Egypt; he was called Akhanukh [= Enoch of the Bible], he is also Idris, peace be upon him. He was the first person to discuss the movements of the planets and the sublime substances. He was also the first to build temples and exalt God on high within them. He warned people about the flood. He was fearful that learning would disappear and that crafts would be destroyed, so he built the pyramids and the temples and had pictures drawn of all the trades and tools inside them. He also had the various sciences depicted in them so that they would remain for ever.

It is said that the centre of learning and power in Egypt was the town of Memphis – twelve miles away from Fustat. When Alexandria was built, people moved there and it became the centre of learning and power until the coming of Islam. Then Amr ibn al-'As, may God be pleased with him, laid out the city of Fustat, the capital of Egypt until the present day.

The pyramids are constructed from hard chiselled stone; they are extremely high, round, wide at the bottom and narrow at the top, and conical. They have no doors, and it is not known how they were built.

According to one account, an Egyptian king before the Flood saw something which terrified him, and impelled him to build those pyramids which are on the west bank of the Nile as a store for the sciences and the bodies of kings, and to ask the astrologers, 'Is there any part of them which can be opened?' They informed him that they could be opened on the northern side; they showed him the place they could be opened from, and how much it would cost to have it opened. So he ordered that the amount of money which they told him it would cost should be placed in that spot. He applied himself to the task of building, and finished in 60 years. Then he wrote on the pyramids, 'We constructed these pyramids in 60 years. Let whoever wishes to, destroy them in 600 years – for destruction is easier than construction.'

(b) Suggested translation of بناء الأهرام.

He was asked about the construction of the pyramids. He replied that they were tombs for kings. When their king died, his body was placed in a stone trough; in Egypt and Syria this is called a *juruun*. It was closed over him; then the pyramid was built [for him] up to the height which they wanted for the foundation [more lit: a part of the pyramid was built for him to the extent that they wanted in the way of the height of the foundation]. The trough was then carried and placed in the middle of the pyramid, and a vaulted structure was constructed over it. They then built up the building to the height which you see and the pyramid door was attached underneath the pyramid; then a path to the door was dug underground and an arched prolate vault [i.e. a vaulted funnel] was constructed. The length of the prolate vault under the ground was 100 cubits or more. Every one of these pyramids had an entrance door as I have described. He was asked, 'How were these smooth pyramids built? What did they use to go up and build them? What did they use to carry these huge stones, a single one of which[1] people of our day would only be able to move with [great] effort, if at all?' He replied, 'The people used to build the pyramid in the form of steps like a staircase. When they finished, they smoothed it from top to bottom. This was their technique. In addition[2] they had strength, patience, and a [sense of] religious obedience[3] to their kings.'

Notes

1. No راجع (referential pronoun) in this relative clause; one would expect منها (cf. ch. 4, 7e).
2. مع هذا normally means that the following clause contrasts with, or contradicts, the preceding clause. Here it clearly reinforces the preceding clause.
3. Note the word order here طاعة للوكهم ديانية where the adjective follows an intervening prepositional phrase, cf. عددا من اللغات ... كبيرا in the text من هم البربر وما هو أصلهم؟ and sentence no. 16 in the corresponding structure translation exercise 'He owns a large number of businesses' (ch. 2, 8av).

In addition to the above notes, consider the frequent use of the sequential conjunction ثم, and relatively infrequent use of و to conjoin clauses and sentences. Note also the use of the imperfect for the past tense in the first half of the passage. Consider the lack of punctuation.

8. Aural Arabic texts 1

i Answers to comprehension questions relating to حصاد الشهر, no. 28, side 2, item 2, ‏ما الفرق بين قرطاج وقرطاجنة؟‏.

1. The person who asked the question comes from Morocco.
2. The immediate origin of the form قرطاج is an Arabisation of a French expression.
3. The form قرطاجنة is found in the east.
4. According to traditional sources Carthage was founded in 814 BC.
5. The name of the Princess of Tyre was Dodo.
6. The Princess's brother usurped her right to rule.
7. She fled as a result.
8. The original meaning of 'Carthage' is 'the new town'.
9. Archeologists suggest that Carthage was founded at the end of the eighth century BC.
10. The main interests of the Carthaginians was industry and trade.
11. The eastern and western limits of the Carthaginian state were from Libya to Tangiers.
12. The wars between Rome and Carthage continued for one and a half centuries.
13. Carthage was destroyed in 146 BC.
14. The most common Arabic form for Carthage is قرطاجة.
15. The other Carthage was founded by the Phoenicians.
16. The Phoenicians founded this city after they settled in North Africa.
17. They set out from North Africa.
18. The other Carthage is on the south-eastern coast of Spain.

iv Suggested structure translations relating to ‏ما الفرق بين قرطاج وقرطاجنة؟‏.

The relevant portion of the original Arabic text is quoted in curly brackets after the suggested translation. Notes relating to the translation are sometimes also provided.

‏١ – هل هتان الكلمتان اسمان لفكرة واحدة؟ {هل قرطاج وقرطاجنة اسمان لمدينة واحدة؟}‏

‏٢ – اجاب على هذا السؤال رئيس الوزراء. {يجيب على هذا السؤال الدكتور نيقولا الزيادة المؤرّخ المعروف}‏

Note that Arabic word order *verb–object–subject*, or *verb–prepositional~ phrase–subject* (as here) typically translates the English passive with agent (X is done by Y).

‏٣ – هذا تعريب للمصطلح الانجليزي. {هو تعريب للفظ الفرنسي}‏

Arabic ل is often used to translate English 'of' when the Arabic phrase involves a verbal noun (such as تعريب).

٤ – ما هي الصيغة الأخرى الواردة في بداية الكتاب؟ {أما الصيغة الأخرى الواردة في السؤال ...}

Literally, 'the other form the-appearing in the question'. Note that it is possible in Arabic to expand (add to) adjectives by adding prepositional phrases. In English this requires turning the adjective into a relative clause; so 'the occurring form', but 'the form which occurs in the question', *not* 'the occurring form in the question'.

٥ – تمّ إنشاء الدولة بعد الحرب. {تم إنشاءها سنة ثمان مائة وأربع عشرة قبل الميلاد}

The verb تمّ + *verbal noun* is often used to translate English agentless passives (passives without 'by'-phrase), especially to give a sense of formality and to convey the idea that some effort was involved in the process (cf. section 7ai).

٦ – تركوا بيوتهم خشية من أن يقتلَهم الجيش. {فرّت من مدينتها خشية من أن يبطش بها اخوها}

The clause أن يقتلهم الجيش functions like a noun, and could be replaced by a noun/noun phrase, such as عنف الجيش 'the violence of the army'.

٧ – تزوّج بعد موت أبيه بثلاث سنين/سنوات. {... بعد تاريخ الرواية الصورية بقرن تقريبا}

٨ – عُنُوا بالمال اكثر من عنايتهم بالصدق. {عني أهلها بالصناعة والتجارة أكثر من عنايتهم بالفن والأدب}

All prepositions in Arabic must be followed by a noun or a pronoun. Therefore عناية (the verbal noun from عني) is added after من.

٩ – يملك الأرض الممتدة من هنا إلى البحر. {الساحل الافريقي الممتد من ليبيا حتى طنجة.} cf. question 4.

١٠ – من الطبيعي أن تغضب. {فكان من الطبيعي أن تتنافس روما وقرطاجة}

Cf. also من اللازم أن 'it is necessary that', من الممكن أن 'it is possible that', من الغريب أن 'it is strange that' (cf. ch. 2, 7c).

١١ – الكلمة الأولى هي الأغلب. {...وإن كانت الأولى هي الأغلب}

Where both the subject and the predicate (the other bit) of the sentence are definite it is usual to separate them by a pronoun. That is to say it is normal to say الكلمة الأولى هي الأغلب rather than الكلمة الأولى الأغلب (cf. ch. 14, 7b).

١٢ – أعرف امرأة أخرى اسمها مريم. {ثمة مكان آخر كان اسمه قرطاجنة}

١٣ – الذين يقولون هذا لا يفهمون المشكلة. {لعل الذين بنوا قرطاجنة الثانية هم اصلا من قرطاج التونسية}

It is possible to use الذي etc. without any preceding noun (cf. ch. 9, 7a). In this case it normally translates into English as 'he who', 'the one who', 'that which', 'those who', etc.

9. Aural Arabic texts 2

ii Answers to comprehension questions relating to حصاد الشهر, no. 26, side 2, item 2, ما هي أقدم مدينة في العالم؟.

1. Yes, there are a large number of historical cities worldwide.
2. The listener's name is Surur Ahmad Surur.
3. The man who answers the question is Fu'ad Haddad.
4. The oldest city for which there is archeological evidence is Jericho.
5. This city was inhabited from 8,000 BC.
6. The city is situated on the west bank of the river Jordan.
7. In the Mesolithic era the city was settled by groups of hunters.
8. Jericho began to acquire the characteristics of a city after 1,000 years.
9. The inhabitants built their houses of baked brick.
10. They built their city wall in 6,800 BC.
11. They also built a watch tower.
12. The Canaanites arrived in the middle of the Bronze Age.
13. The Canaanites originally came from the Arabian peninsula.
14. Researchers have a good idea about life at this time because the inhabitants used to bury their dead with many household items.
15. Tell Al-Salihiyya lies south-east of Damascus.
16. It dates back to 4,000 BC.
17. Damascus became the capital of Aramea in the eleventh century BC.
18. Tell El-Amarna is in Egypt.
19. Tuhtamis the Third conquered Damascus in 1,500 BC.

v Suggested structure translations relating to ما هي أقدم مدينة في العالم؟.

The relevant portion of the original Arabic text is quoted in curly brackets after the suggested translation. Notes relating to the translation are sometimes also provided.

١ – المدن الجميلة في اليمن الجنوبية غير كثيرةٍ/ليست كثيرةً. {المدن التاريخية في العالم كثيرة}

Cf. المشاكل قليلة 'there are few/not many problems'; مشاكلنا قليلة 'we don't have/haven't' got many problems'.

٢ – تعود هذه الكتابات إلى العهد الفرعوني. {... آثارا تاريخية تعود إلى قرون خَلت}

٣ – ما [هو] اسم تلك القرية الواقعة على [نهر] النيل التي زاروها السنة الماضية؟ {...مدينة أريحا الواقعة على الضفة الغربية من نهر الأردن}

Where English has a definite noun followed by a prepositional phrase (such as 'that village on the Nile') it is common for Arabic to have a noun followed by an expanded adjectival phrase (an adjective, such as the active participle واقع, followed by a prepositional phrase, such النيـل [نهر] على).

٤ – هل تقصـد المكان الذي سكنها الأقبـاط ؟ {وكـان يسكنهـا جـمـاعـات من الصيادين}

٥ – مـا لبث أن بدأ البدو يرحلون إلى المدن. {ومـا لبـثت بعـد ذلك أن أصبحت لها معالم المدينة}

Note that أنْ مـا لبث is followed by a perfect verb. أن بعـد and أن قبـل are also followed by a perfect verb if they refer to simple facts in the past.

٦ – أصبحت لهذه القرية بعضُ معالم المدينة. [... أصبحت لها معـالم المدينة] The sentence المدينة معـالم بعض القرية لهذه would mean 'This village has some of the characteristics of a/the town' (note the generic use of الـ in المدينـة to refer to towns generally). The verb أصبـح in Arabic can be followed by a noun مهندس 'an engineer', or by an adjective غريبا أصبح 'he became strange', as can the verb 'become' in English. Unlike 'become' however, أصبح can also be followed by a verb/verb phrase شيء كل يفهم اصبح 'he finally understood everything', lit. 'he became he understands everything'; similarly, it can be followed by a prepositional phrase, مـن قـريبـا أصبـح المدينة 'he got close to the city', lit. 'he became close to the city'. In اصبحت المدينة معـالم بعضُ is the the phrase المدينة معـالم بعض القرية لهذه the subject, أصبحت is the verb, and القرية لهذه is a prepositional phrase following أصبحت.

٧ – تبلغ مساحة الملعب خمسة كيلومـترات مُربَّـعة. {بـاغـت مسـاحـتها حوالى عشرة فدادين}

Formal written Arabic prefers sentences containing verbs if possible, and verbs such as بـلغ are sometimes used where they would appear unnecessary in English; cf. بغـداد جنوب البصرة تقع 'Basra is south of Baghdad' (cf. ch. 1, 7d).

٨ – لماذا عملوا التمثال من البرونز ؟ {وبـنـوا للسور برجا من الأحجار القوية للمراقبة}

٩ – مـا [هي] أول دولة ظهرت فيها الرأسمـالية ؟ {فـهي أول مكان يظهر فيه انتقال الانسان من حالة البداوة والصيد إلى حالة الثبات والاستقرار}

Although the English translation of دولة/مكان أول is definite, i.e. 'the first place/country', the Arabic form is indefinite, and is therefore not followed by الذي/التي.

١٠- اشترى لابنه سيارة امريكية غالية جدا. {بنوا سكان أريحا لمدينتهم أول سور}

Arabic allows greater word-order variation than English, and it is not uncommon for a prepositional phrase, such as لابنه, to be placed before an object, such as سـيـارة أمـريكيـة غـاليـة جدا. This is particularly the case where the object is long and the prepositional phrase short (as in the translation sentence), or where the object is itself followed by a related phrase (as in the sentence in the original text, where أول سـور is followed by لحماية ممتلكاتهم).

١١ - من الغريب أنهم كانوا يسكنون [في] بيوت من الأحجار . {ومن الطريف أنهم كانوا يدفنون موتاهم ومعهم حوائج وأشياء كثيرة من أمور البيت}
Note that when what follows the initial phrase (here من الغريب) is a fact, this following element is introduced by أنَّ + *noun* (in the accusative). When what follows the initial phrase is a possibility, the following element is introduced by أنْ + *subjunctive verb*, e.g. من الممكن أن يذهبـوا 'it is possible they will go/they may go'.

١٢- تسكن [في] «ستوكبـورت» الواقعـة جنوب «مـانتشسـتـر». {وتُظهر الحفريات في تل الصالحية الواقع جنوب شرقي دمشق}

١٣ - [قـد] جاءت أول اشـارة إلى هذه المدينـة في كتـاب «دومـزداي». {وقـد جاءت أقدم إشارة إلى مدينة دمشق من مكتبة تل العمارنة}

١٤ - أخضع المنطقة كلها المصريون. {وقالت إنها إحدى المدن الكبرى التي أخضعها الملك تهتميس الثالث إلى حكمه}

10. Written English texts
Suggested translation of 'The sphinx'.

أبو الهول

أشـهـرُ رجل أسدٍ [/إنَّ أشـهـرَ رجل أسدٍ] في مـصـرَ هو الرجلُ الأسدُ في الجيـزة [/يُعتبرُ أشهرُ رجلِ أسدٍ في مصرَ الرجلُ الأسدُ في الجيـزة]، والمعـروفُ باللغـة [/في اللغة] العـربيـة باسمِ «أبـو الهـول». نُحت هذا الرجلُ الأسدُ من حجرٍ واحدٍ وبُني خلالَ الأسرةِ [/السُلالةِ] الرابعـة ، ويقولُ نقشٌ في المعبدِ الموجودِ بـين كفّي أبو الهول يعودُ تاريخُه إلى الأسرةِ [/السلالةِ] الثامنة عشرةَ إن الرجلَ الأسدَ يمثّلُ إلهَ الشـمسِ هرمـخـيس . وقـد تمّ حفـر أبو الهـول وترميمُ رأسِه في السـنواتِ الأولى مـن القرنِ العشرينَ. ورأسُ أبو

الهول عبارةٌ عن صورةٍ ملكيةٍ ويبدو أنّ قصدَ هذا التمثال هو تجسيدُ قوةِ الفرعونِ الحاكمِ . ووُضع أبو الهول في مكانِهِ لكي يحرسَ مـدخلَ وادي النيلِ والمعابدَ المنتشرةَ [/الموجودةَ] في المنطقةِ المجاورةِ .

11. Précis

Suggested guidance questions for the précis in Arabic of علمـاء أوروبا وأمـريكا يشاركون في المؤتمر الدولي لترميم أبو الهول.

١ – ما هو هدف المؤتمر؟

٢ – من هم اللاعبون الرئيسيون في المؤتمر وتنظيمه؟

٣ – ماذا شملت أعمال ترميم المرحلة الأولى ومن قام بهذه الأعمال؟

٤ – ما هي الدراسات والإجراءات التي ستتم في المستقبل من أجل صيانة ابو الهول؟

٥ – ما هو هدف المظلة التي يذكرها النص؟

4
The rise of Islam

3. Key vocabulary

The key vocabulary section in this chapter can be used as an introduction to discussion of the use and significance of certain terms. What epithets are used for the Prophet? What epithets are used for relatives of the Prophet? What epithets are used for the four Rightly Guided Caliphs? Which religious terms are peculiar to Islam? Which are general?

4. Written Arabic texts 1

(a) Additional exercise: suggested use of text أركان الإسلام.

This text can be used to introduce a general discussion on Islam. Additional questions could be asked to the ones given in the coursebook. These could compare the precepts of Islam with those of Judaism or Christianity and include, for example:

– إذا كان هناك أركان للمسيحية فماذا اشتملت هذه الأركان؟

– كيف تختلف الأديان الثلاثة – الإسلام والمسيحية واليهودية – عن بعض؟

(b) Answers to comprehension questions relating to الإسلام والحضارة الإسلامية.

1. Islam appeared at the beginning of the seventh century AD.
2. Islam appeared in the Hijaz region of the Arabian peninsula.
3. The fundamental principal of Islam is the unity of God.
4. Yes, Muslims do accept the validity of the Christian and Jewish prophetic figures.
5. Muslims do not accept that Jesus is the son of God because this does not accord with the Islamic view of the oneness of God.
6. The Prophet Muhammad spent most of his life in the towns of Mecca and Medina.
7. Muhammad's original profession was that of trader.

8. The two aspects of his religious mission were as a religious caller to Islam and a political leader.
9. The borders of the Islamic empire were from Spain in the west to India and China in the east.
10. This was the largest empire in the world to date.
11. Islamic civilisation developed in these countries.
12. The Muslims adopted all the good aspects of other civilisations to be part of their civilisation.
13. Islam may be regarded as an integral system because it does not distinguish religious aspects from other aspects of life.
14. Islam is a social, economic and political system in addition to being a religious system.
15. This is in order to help Muslims in all matters.
16. Regarding marriage Muslims must marry according to the Islamic way: a Muslim man may marry a non-Muslim woman, but a Muslim woman may not marry a non-Muslim man.
17. In the Islamic world an industrial enterprise must accord with the Islamic sharia.
18. When a political decision is made it must be in line with general and particular Islamic thought.
19. Islamic practice helps those without power or wealth.
20. This makes for a society based on security, safety and happiness.

(c) Suggested translation of الإسلام‎ I.

> The word 'Islam' is derived from the verb *aslama*, and means complete submission to God, to what He enjoins and what He prohibits. There are two types of Islam. The first is obligatory, and includes everything in the universe – the sun, the moon, the planets, plants, animals and man. All these things submit to God Almighty, in that they submit to the laws which He has laid down for the natural world. In relation to man, for example, these laws include the need for food, drink, sleep, and so on. Similarly with the sun, the moon and the planets; they all move in accordance with a precise and specific system which they do not deviate from.
>
> The second type of Islam is termed voluntary Islam. This consists in man's submission to God in all that he does by his own free will. This type of Islam is specific to man alone. The starting point is man's belief and trust firstly in God, secondly in His angels, thirdly in His books, fourthly in His Messengers, fifthly in fate – both good and evil – as decreed by God Almighty, and sixthly in the Last Day. This type of Islam also requires man's adherence to the pillars of Islam, of which there are five: firstly the two testimonies of faith, namely 'I testify that there is no god but God, and I testify Muhammad is the Messenger of God', secondly ritual prayer, thirdly alms-giving, fourthly the fast of

Ramadan, and fifthly the pilgrimage to Mecca. Man should also follow everything which God has enjoined, and desist from everything which God has prohibited.

5. Written Arabic texts 2

(a) Suggested translation of أمـا بـعـد، إن القـرآن الكريم هـو مـعـجـزة الإسـلام العظمى.

The Noble Qur'an is the greatest miracle of Islam, because of the eloquence, rhetoric, rules and wisdom contained within it. Its eloquence was the original reason why many of the pre-Islamic Arabs came to believe in Islam. They saw in it that which they could not find even among their most remarkable orators. As one of the leaders of the Quraysh said, 'It displays grace and beauty; it surpasses and is not surpassed.'

The miraculous nature of the Quranic rhetoric remained clear to the first generations of Arab Muslims and to those who immediately followed them. Subsequently, however, the Arabs began to intermarry with non-Arabs, and grammatical errors [lit: ungrammaticality and foreignism] gradually began to creep into people's [lit: the Arabs'] speech. Brilliant grammarians were therefore forced to deduce the rules of Arabic grammar, and to develop the linguistic sciences, in order to help people to speak correctly, and to understand the Holy Qur'an as it was understood by those who lived at the time of its revelation.

(b) Answers to comprehension questions relating to مـنـذ هذا الـيـوم.

1. The boy became a sheikh because he had memorised the Qur'an.
2. The boy was nine when he began to be called 'sheikh'.
3. The sayyid called the boy 'sheikh' in front of his parents, when he was pleased with him, and when he wanted to please him.
4. On other occasions he would call him 'laddy'.
5. The boy's physical appearance is described as short, thin, pale and miserable.
6. This description is considered relevant at this point in the story because his appearance contrasts with what would be expected of a sheikh.
7. The boy liked being called sheikh at first.
8. He was waiting to have the true trappings of a sheikh.
9. Then he would wear a turban, a jubbah and a qaftan.
10. He felt fed up of waiting.
11. He then tired of being called 'sheikh'.
12. He felt that life was full of unfairness and lies.

6. Written Arabic texts 3 (classical)

Suggested translation of (صلعم) قال رسول الله .

The Messenger of God said, 'While I was sleeping, he [i.e. the Angel Gabriel] came to me with a saddle cloth of silk brocade which had a book in it. "Read!", he said. "I cannot read", I replied. Then he throttled me with it until I thought that I would die [lit: that (it was) death]; then he released me and said, "Read!"' [He said,'] "I cannot read", I replied. Then he throttled me with it until I thought that I would die, then he released me, and said, "Read." [He said,] "What should I read?", I replied. I only said this to make sure he didn't do the same thing to me again. He said,

> "Read in the name of your Lord who created,
> Created man from a blood clot.
> Read, and your Lord is the most generous,
> Who has taught with the pen,
> Taught man what he did not know."

[He said, '] So I read it. Then he finished and went away; and when I awoke, it was as if I had a book written in my heart.[' He said,'] I went out [of the cave], and when I reached the heart of the mountain, I heard a voice from heaven say, "Oh Muhammad, you are the Messenger of God, and I am Gabriel." [' He said, '] I raised my head to heaven and looked; and there was Gabriel in the form of a pure man with his feet on the horizon of the sky saying, "Oh Muhammad, you are the Messenger of God, and I am Gabriel." I stood staring at him unable to go forward or go back. I began to turn my face away from him towards the [other] horizons of the sky, but I could not look anywhere in the sky without also seeing him, so I remained standing, unable to go forward or back. Finally, Khadija sent her messengers to look for me. They reached the highest part of Mecca and returned to her with me [still] was standing on that spot. Then Gabriel left me and I left him, and returned to my family. I came to Khadija and sat by her side drawing close to her. She said, "Oh Father of Qasim, where were you? By God, I sent my messengers to look for you and they got as far as the highest part of Mecca and returned to me." Then I told her what I had seen. Then she said, "Tell the good news, my cousin, and be firm. For by Him in whose hands lies the soul of Khadija, I hope that you will become the prophet of this community. The she got up and gathered her clothes around her and set off for Waraqa ibn Nawfal, her paternal cousin. Waraqa had become a Christian and had read the scriptures and listened to the people of the Torah and the Bible. She told him what the

Messenger of God had told her he had seen and heard and Waraqa said,
"Most Holy, Most Holy. By the One in whose hands lies the soul of
Waraqa, if you have told me the truth, Khadija, the Greatest Law [i.e.
the Archangel Gabriel] came to him who [also] came to Moses. He is
indeed the prophet of this community. Say to him that he should be
resolute."'

8. Aural Arabic texts 1

(b) i Complete transcription of حصاد الشهر no. 8, side 1, item 1, the
introduction to سورة مريم.

لكننا نستهله بتلاوة مباركة من آي الذكر الحكيم، الشيخ محمد رفعت،
الذي تُوفي منذ ما يزيد عن ثلاثين عاما، لا يزال يُعتبر حتى الآن شيخ
المُقرئين ، إذ إنّ هذا المُقرئ الكفيف حباه الله صوتا نادرا لم يكد يحْظى
به قارئ آخر، وقيل إنه سجّل القرآن كله في القاهرة ومن أندر
تسجيلاته تسجيل فريد في نوعه في حوزة هيئة الإذاعة البريطانية.
سيداتي وسادتي من آيات الله البينات يتلو علينا الشيخ محمد رفعت
ما يتيسر له من سورة مريم.

ii Answers to comprehension questions relating to the introduction to سورة مريم.

1. Shaikh Muhammad Rif'at died more than thirty years ago.
2. He is still considered to be the Sheikh of Qur'anic recitation.
3. He was blind.
4. God blessed him with a rare voice.
5. In Cairo he is said to have recorded the whole of the Qur'an.
6. The BBC has a copy of the recording in its possession.

9. Aural Arabic texts 2

i   Answers to comprehension questions relating to حصاد الشهر no. 12, side 2,
item 4, مساعدة الغرب على فهم الإسلام.

1. Yahya al-Mu'allim is a Saudi writer.
2. His book, مكارم الأخلاق في القرآن الكريم, was printed twice in the Arab
world.
3. He has now decided to publish it in English.
4. The radio programme in which he discusses the project is called مع الأسرة
العربية.
5. Yahya Mu'allim's English-speaking friends suggested that they translated it into
English.

6. He agreed to this.
7. Tariq Ihsan is from Pakistan.
8. Hala al-Sulh is from Lebanon.
9. Yahya al-Mu'allim took the two translations and summarised them in one book.
10. The new book is being printed in Saudi Arabia and in London.

ii Complete transcription of مساعدة الغرب على فهم الإسلام.

«مكارم الأخلاق في القرآن الكريم» عنوان كتاب من تأليف الكاتب
السعودي يحيى المعلم ، وقد أراد بعد نفاد طبعتين من هذا الكتاب في
العالم العربي طبعه بالإنجليزية. تحدث عن ذلك إلى عفاف جلال في
برنامج «مع الأسرة العربية» .

– هذا كتاب كنت ألّفته باللغة العربية وعنوانه «مكارم الأخلاق في
القرآن الكريم» ، وقد طُبع مرتين ونفدت الطبعتان ، وعرض عليّ بعض
الأصدقاء من من يجيدون اللغة الإنجليزية أن يترجموه هم إلى اللغة
الإنجليزية فوافقت على ذلك وقد ترجمه شخصان أحدهما طارق إحسان
من باكستان والآخر السيدة حالة الصلح من لبنان . وقد جمعت
الترجمتين ولخّصتهما في كتاب واحد أو في نسخة واحدة وهما الآن
تحت الطبع في السعودية من جهة وفي لندن بالاتفاق مع إحدى دور
النشر في لندن .

– ما السبب في اختيار هذا الكتاب بالذات؟

– هذا الكتاب يعرض صوراً من الأخلاق الفاضلة التي يدعو إليها
القرآن . ومن هنا جاءت أهمية هذا الكتاب من جهة للمسلمين بصفة
عامة ومن هنا أيضا جاءت أهميته – أهمية ترجمته – لمن يتكلم اللغة
الإنجليزية سواءً من المسلمين أو غير المسلمين من المتحدثين باللغة
الإنجليزية في أنحاء العالم . وأعتقد أن ترجمة هذا الكتاب ونشره ...
ونشره باللغة الإنجليزية سيحقق هدفاً طيباً وهو إظهار محاسن الإسلام
ومكارم الأخلاق التي يدعو إليها الإسلام وما يتمتع بهذا الدين الحنيف
من ميزات .

10. Written English texts

(a) Suggested translation of 'A complete way of life'.

طريقةٌ كاملةٌ للحياة

ليس الإسلامُ دينًا في المعنى العادي المُشَوَّه للفظة ينحصرُ نطاقُه في حياةِ الإنسانِ الخاصةِ بل هو طريقةٌ كاملةٌ للحياةِ تعالجُ كلَ مضاميرِ الوجودِ الإنساني. ويهدي الإسلامُ الإنسانَ في مضاميرِ الحياةِ كلها – من ضمنها الفردية والاجتماعية [/الفردية منها والاجتماعية]، والمادية والأخلاقية، والاقتصادية والسياسية، والقانونية والحضارية، والوطنية والدولية. فيُوصي القرآنُ الفردَ بأنْ يعتنق الإسلامَ [/يدخل في الإسلام] من غيرِ تَحَفُّظٍ وأن يتبعَ هدايةَ اللهِ في كلِ مجالاتِ الحياةِ.

(b) Suggested translation of 'Simplicity, rationalism and practicalism'.

البساطة والمعقولية والتطبيقية

الأسلامُ [/إن الإسلامَ] دينٌ يخلو من الأساطيرِ الوهميةِ، فتعاليمُه بسيطةٌ وسهلةُ الفهمِ لا تستندُ إلى المعتقداتِ الخرافيةِ والمفاهيمِ غيرِ العقليةِ. أما أحكامُ [/أصولُ] هذا الدينِ فوحدةُ اللهِ ونبوةُ محمدٍ [/الرسولِ محمدٍ] – صلى اللهُ عليهِ وسلم – والحياةُ الآخرةُ وتقومُ هذه الأحكامُ [/الأصولُ] على العقلِ والمنطقِ السليمِ. وتنجمُ تعاليمُ الإسلامِ بأكملها [/كلها/كافةً] عن هذه المعتقداتِ الأساسيةِ وهي تعاليمُ سهلةٌ وواضحةٌ. و لا يوجدُ في الإسلامِ كَهَنَةٌ [في مناصبَ عاليةٍ/متفاوتةٍ] ولا أفكارُ مجرَّدةٌ غامضةٌ ولا طقوسُ وشعائرُ معقدةٌ. فيجبُ على كلِ مسلمٍ أن يقتربَ من كتابِ اللهِ مباشرةً وأن يطبّقَ ما يأمرُ به تطبيقاً عملياً.

Note
One of the problems in this text is that a number of synonymous terms
in English are likely to be translated by the same phrase in Arabic, e.g.
'without any', 'is free from'. The translator has to attempt to find at
least an acceptable degree of lexical variation in the Arabic.

11. Précis
Suggested guidance questions for the précis in Arabic of ١٠. آلاف بريطانية دخلن
دين الإسلام.

١ – كم عدد البريطانيات اللواتي دخلن دين الإسلام في السنوات الأخيرة؟

٢ – في رأي الكاتب ما هي الأزمة التي تواجه المجتمعات الغربية ومنها
المجتمع البريطاني؟

٣ – ما هي الافتراءات حول الإسلام في الفكر الغربي المعاصر؟

٤ – ماذا يمنح الدين الإسلامي والشريعة الإسلامية للمرأة؟

٥ – ما هي الوظائف التي تشغلها معتنقات الإسلام البريطانيات؟

٦ – برأي الكاتب ما هو سبب تحلل الأسرة الغربية في الوقت الحاضر؟

٧ – ما هي الإغراءات التي تقوم بها جماعات نسائية فيما يخص مكانة المرأة
في المجتمع البريطاني؟

5
Arabic language

4. Written Arabic texts 1

(a) **i** Answers to comprehension questions relating to من تاريخ الأدب العربي.

1. According to the writer the terms Mudar, Rabi'a, Adnan, Qahtan and Himyar are now used to denote the geographical regions where these people lived.
2. Before Islam, the language of the Quraysh was spoken in the Hijaz.
3. The term Mudar is used to denote the Arabs who used to speak the language of the Quraysh.
4. The Romans used to claim that they had fled from Troy to Italy.
5. Some Greeks claim that they are descended from the Phoenicians.
6. The author claims that 'we are now Arabs from the cultural point of view whatever our lineage may be in reality' because the language used by the Arabs is the language of the Quraysh and that has been the only language used by [the Egyptians] for centuries.

iv Suggested translation of من تاريخ الأدب العربي.

> In my second book, I observed that [when] we use the terms Mudar, Rabi'a, Adnan, Qahtan and Himyar, we do not have the [same] meanings in mind as [understood by] the genealogists; they are simply terms which have become widely used. People have become familiar with them, and we [now] use them to mean geographical regions. We do not know Adnan, Qahtan, Mudar or Rabi'a; we only know the Hijaz, Najd, Yemen and Iraq. We know those places which were settled by the Arabs, and we know that the language of the Quraysh before Islam existed in the Hijaz and Najd. If we mention Mudar, then we only mean those Arabs who spoke this language and who used it as an aspect of their cultural life. Who can claim that they know of a true historical link between the Romans and the Trojans? Nonetheless, the Romans used to claim that they had emigrated from Troy to Italy. There

is a little of this in all the stories which peoples adopt in order to link their lineage with [that of] ancient peoples; thus, some Greeks claimed that they were of Phoenician descent, while others claimed to be of Egyptian descent. We are now Arabs from the cultural point of view whatever our lineage may be in reality – whether we are connected to the ancient Egyptians, the Greeks, or the Turks, or to any of those ethnic groups which invaded Egypt and settled there. None of this detracts from the [actual] scientific fact that our language is the Arabic language of the Quraysh. We have known no other natural language for centuries.

(b) Answers to comprehension questions relating to ومن المفيد.

1. The period of cultural flourishing is mentioned.
2. Not everyone spoke فصحى during this period because regional dialects were spoken in rural and urban areas.
3. The classical language came to be used by writers and poets.
4. The vernacular language was used in everyday life.
5. Social and cultural distance served to increase the disparity between the classical and colloquial languages.

5. Written Arabic texts 2

(a) **ii** Suggested translation of اللغة العربية – أو لغة الضاد كما تدعى.

The Arabic language, or the language of *Dad* as it is called, is one of the most ancient languages in the world. During its long history it has been subject to the same influences as any language which aspires to be a means of communication and thought. Thus pre-Islamic Arabic was different from Islamic Arabic, which was different from Umayyad Arabic and Abbasid Arabic. The language incorporated new terms in the fields of religion, society and the arts, drawing on figurative usages in the Qur'an and *hadith*, on the esoteric vocabulary of Sufism, and on the technical terminology of Islamic philosophy. Through all these channels it also borrowed Greek words which mitigated the harshness of some of its own terms, substituting for them other terms which were easier to pronounce. Urban life also gave rise to a certain softness which manifested itself in the romantic love poetry of the urban centres of Syria and Iraq as well as the desert areas of Najd and the Hijaz. This language was then modified – or so it is claimed – to a greater or lesser extent, to give rise to that form of poetry and song which has a colloquial Arabic flavour.

Colloquial Arabic is a linguistic term for a specific level of language which belongs to the common people, who are the overwhelming majority of any nation. This level is not bound by rules of grammar, and makes no use of the case-endings which are a feature of the official, or formal, level of language. The Arabic term for colloquial Arabic, *'ammiyya*, is derived from the term *'amma* or *'awamm*, meaning common people. Over time this word developed into a technical term, meaning the level of language used by the overwhelming majority of the people. It was only in the modern era, however, that the word acquired a scholarly status, with the appearance of universities and the emergence of lexical definition as a scholarly activity.

(b) Suggested translation of ‫ولم يكن عمي صغيرا‬.

My uncle was not young. He was several years older than me, and he used to travel to Cairo on his own and go to the Azhar, where he studied. I was only a girl who had not yet learnt [to sort out] my letters. My father used to put me the pencil between my fingers, and make me write on the slate blackboard: *a, b, c, d*. Sometimes he would make me repeat after him the rules of Arabic script,[1] 'The Arabic *a* has nothing above it, the Arabic *b* has a dot under it, the Arabic *c* has a dot in the middle, the Arabic *d* has nothing above it.' He would shake his head and recite the Alfiyya of Ibn Malik,[2] just as he would recite the Qur'an. I would also shake my head as I stood behind him, and repeat verbatim what he said.

When the holiday came to an end, my uncle would get on his donkey, and I would put on my head my big basket, which was full of eggs, cheese and unleavened bread, on top of which were his books and his clothes; and I would walk along behind him until we got to the delta railway station. All the way, my uncle would talk to me about his room in *al-Qal'a* at the end of Muhammad Ali Street, about the Azhar, about *al-Ataba* the green, about the tramway, about the people in Cairo, and he would sing in a sweet voice swaying as he rode on the donkey, 'On the seas I didn't left[3] you, on the land you left me [i.e. I stood by you when when times were hard, but you betrayed me even when times were easy].'

Notes
1. Phrase added in an attempt to make the text more comprehensible to the supposed general English-speaking reader who has no background in Arabic script.
2. A famous traditional Arabic grammar book, written in verse and summarising the grammar of Arabic in 1,000 lines (hence the name ‫ألفية‬).

3. An attempt to convey the ungrammaticality of the Arabic original in the English.

(c) Translation of colloquial elements of سكة السلامة into standard Arabic.

In this section ask the students for the standard equivalent of the Egyptian Arabic words and phrases given in the dialogue. For example:

«دلوقت» معناها «الآن»، «كويس» معناها «جيد»، «ايه» معناها «ما» أو «ماذا»، «فين» معناها «أين»، «دا» معناها «هذا».

Discuss why colloquial elements are used for the dialogue but not for the setting of the scene. What effect does this have?

6. Written Arabic texts 3 (classical)

(a) ii Suggested translation of الجمهور من أهل الرواة.

> All the *rawis* agree that the first person to codify the grammar [of Arabic] was the Commander of the Faithful, Ali ibn Abi Talib, may God honour him. Abu al-Aswad al-Du'ali, may God have mercy upon him, said, 'I went to the Commander of the Faithful, peace be upon him, and saw that he had his head bowed in contemplation. So I said to him, "What are you thinking about, Commander of the Faithful?" He said, "In your town I heard a grammatical error, so I want to produce a book on the rules of Arabic." I said to him, "If you do that you will preserve the Arabic language for us." Then I returned to him after a few days and he gave me a piece of paper on which was written, "In the name of God, the Merciful, the Compassionate. All speech is composed of nouns, verbs and particles. The noun describes the named item, the verb describes the movement of the named item, and the particle is that which has meaning but is neither noun nor verb."'

(b) Suggested translation of إنّ أبا الأسود الدؤلي دخل إلى ابنته.

> Abu al-Aswad al-Du'ali went to his daughter in Basra and she said to him, 'Father, how hot it is!' (but she put the word أشد into the nominative) and he thought she was asking him which was the hottest period, so he told her, 'The month of Najir.' (meaning the month of Sifr. In the Pre-Islamic period, the months were called by these names.) Then she said to him, 'Father, I was only telling you something, not asking you!' So he went to the Commander of the Faithful, Ali ibn Abi Talib, peace be upon him, and said to him, 'Commander of the Faithful, the language of the Arabs is disappearing because of mixing with non-Arabs, and if much more time passes it will vanish

altogether.' He said, 'How can that be?' So he told him what his daughter had said. The Commander of the Faithful then ordered him to buy one dirham's worth of paper and he dictated to him, 'All speech is made up of nouns, verbs and particles which have meaning.' (This is what is said at the beginning of Sibawayhi's *Book*.[1]) Then he codified all the basic rules of [Arabic] grammar. The grammarians then transmitted them and divided them into their various subsidiary aspects. Abu al-Faraj al-Isfahani said, 'I learnt this from Abu Ja'far when I was young, and I wrote it down from memory. This may not be excatly what was said [lit: The words increase and decrease], but this is its meaning.'

Note
1. Sibawayhi (750-793? AD) was one of the first Arab grammarians, and the dominant figure in Arabic grammar. The book which he wrote is known as كتاب سيبويه, or simply الكتاب, in Arabic.

8. Aural Arabic texts 1

i   Answers to comprehension questions relating to حصاد الشهر, no. 36, side 2, item 6, أصول اللهجات العربية.

1. The standard Arabic meaning of وبس is فقط.
2. Dialects of Arabic are said to have arisen from a linguistic conflict between Arabic and Greek [Byzantine], Persian, Berber, Coptic, Romance.
3. The dialect of Egypt is taken as an example in this passage.
4. Arabic was introduced into this country with the Islamic conquest of Egypt.
5. At that time the predominant languages in the country were Greek and Coptic.
6. The official language of the ruler was Greek.
7. Coptic came to be restricted to the church and Christian families.
8. Elements of Turkish entered this dialect during Ottoman rule.
9. Elements of French, English and Italian entered this dialect at a later stage.
10. People who have had little education are said to speak عامية قاع المجتمع.

ii Complete transcription of أصول اللهجات العربية.

نشأت اللهجات المحلية المعروفة باسم العامية في البلاد العربية المختلفة نتيجةً للصراع اللغوي بين اللغة العربية لغة الفتح العربي الإسلامي لهذه البلاد من ناحية واللغات التي كانت سائدة فيها في ذلك الوقت من ناحية أخرى كالرومية أي اليونانية أو الرومانية القديمة والفارسية والقبطية والبربرية والرومانثية المتطورة عن اللاتينية. وهكذا، وإذا أخذنا مصر نموذجًا لما نقول فسنجد أن دخول اللغة العربية إلى مصر

مع الفتح العربي الإسلامي أحدث صراعًا لغويًا بينها وبين اللغتين الرئيسيتين السائدتين وهما الرومانية اللغة الرسمية للحاكم والقبطية التي هي امتداد للغات الفرعونية القديمة. وهي لغة الشعب والكنيسة. وهكذا نشأ خليط لغوي يضمّ مفردات وتراكيب وعناصر من اللغات الثلاث العربية والرومانية والقبطية يستعمله الناس بنسب متفاوتة بينما بدأ سُلّم العربية في الصعود على المستوى الرسمي وانحصار سُلّم الرومانية والقبطية التي أصبحت مقصورة على الكنيسة وبعض الأسر المسيحية المحافظة على التمسك بها.

ثم أُتيح لهذه العامية المصرية المزيدُ من التفاعل والاحتكاك والثراء والغنى من خلال لغات أجنبية كثيرة وافدة على مصر أهمها التركية من خلال السيطرة العثمانية لعدة قرون ثم اللغات التي حملها المماليك المجلوبون إلى مصر من بلاد وسط آسيا فاللغة الفرنسية فالإنجليزية فالإيطالية. وعبر التركية كانت هناك المفردات الفارسية التي انتقلت أولا إلى التركية، وأصبحت عامية المتكلمين في مصر الآن مزيجاً من هذا كله نستطيع أن نحلله وأن نردّه إلى عناصره الأولية من كل هذه اللغات وأن نرى فيه نسبة واضحة من العربية ثم نسباً متباينة من اللغات الأخرى، وهذا هو ما يُفسّر لنا وجود مفردات في العامية المصرية مثل «أورمة» و«شورمة» و«أسطة» و«برنيطة» و«أجزخانة» و«مرسي» و«بنجور» و«بنسوار» و«رفري» و«نجريت» و«هنزبول» و«جورن» و«ماجور» و«فدان» و«تليس» و«أليت» و«تزّ» و«جرسون» و«اسبتاليا» و«شفخانة» و«ضلمه» و«اسبداج» و«ازيّك» و«عشان» و«معلهش» وغيرها من ألوف الكلمات التي تتردد يومياً على ألسنة المتكلمين. ويبقى أن نُشير إلى حقيقة واضحة في هذا المجال وهي أنه كلما كان المتكلم على درجة من التعليم والثقافة كلما شاعت في عاميته أي لغته في الحديث اليومي نسبة أكبر من مفردات العربية الفصحى، وكلما حُرم هذا القدر من التعليم والثقافة كلما كانت عاميته بعيدة تماماً عن التأثر بالعربية الفصيحة وانطبق عليها ما يُسمّى بعامية الأميين أو عامية قاع المجتمع.

iii Suggested translation of paragraph one of أصول اللهجات العربية.

Local dialects, known as العامية 'colloquial', developed in different Arab countries as a result of a linguistic conflict between Arabic, the language of the Arab–Islamic conquest, on the one hand, and indigenous languages of the countries at that time, on the other hand. These included old Greek or Byzantine, Persian, Coptic, Berber and Romance which had developed from Latin. Thus, if we take Egypt as an example, we see that the introduction of Arabic into Egypt with the Arab–Islamic conquest created a linguistic conflict between Arabic and the two main languages, namely Greek which was the official language of the ruler, and Coptic which was descended from ancient Pharaonic and which is the language of the people and the church. In this way a linguistic mixture emerged comprising lexical items, structures and elements from the three languages, Arabic, Greek and Coptic which were used to differing degrees by the people. Meanwhile Arabic began to rise in importance at the official level while Greek and Coptic began to lose importance, Coptic becoming confined to the church and to some Christian families who continued to use it.

9. Aural Arabic texts 2

(b) Complete transcription of حصاد الشهر, no. 5, side 1, item 7, كلمات عربية في اللغة الإسبانية.

الأندلس: لا شك أن سماع اسمها يدغدغ مشاعر كل عربي بعظمة أمجاد أسلافه. ولا تقتصر آثار العرب فيها على الفن المعماري بل تشمل أيضًا اللغة الإسبانية. فوجود الكلمات المأخوذة من أصل عربي ما يزال ماثلاً، ليس في اللغة فحسب بل كذلك في أسماء الأنهار والمدن والأماكن. وقد أكد ذلك في برنامج «لكل سؤال جواب» الدكتور جرير أبو حيدر فحلّل لمستمعي البرنامج أسماء كثيرة من بينها اسم نهر كبير يمرّ بمدينة قرطبة ثم اشبيلية ويجعل من الأخيرة ميناء نهريًا اسمه باللغة الإسبانية Guadalquivir والاسم يتألف من كلمتين عربيتين هما على التوالي «وادي» أو «الوادي» و«الكبير». وهكذا يكون الاسم العربي للنهر «الوادي الكبير». وكلمة «وادي» هذه ما تزال ظاهرة في أسماء أنهار وأماكن كثيرة في إسبانيا، فهناك مقاطعة في إسبانيا تُعرَف باسم Guadalajara وعاصمتها مدِينة تُعرف بنفس الاسم. وهذا الاسم بدوره كلمتان عربيتان في الأصل هما «واد» أو «وادي الحجارة». وربما يجدر بنا أن نذكر هنا أن المدينة الثانية بين مدن المكسيك في أميـركا الوسطى تُعرف أيضًا باسم Guadalajara.

وهناك الكثيـر من الكلمات التي يمكن أن نستـدلّ على أصلها العربي في اللغة الإسبانية لأنها تبتدئ بلفظة al وهي تقابل «ال التعريف» باللغة العربية. ومن هذه الكلمات على سبيل المثل almacen

المَأخوذة من كلمة «المخزن» العربية. وهذه كلمة قد وجدت طريقها إلى اللغة الفرنسية أيضًا في كلمة magasin التي تعني «مخزن» كما نجد أثرًا لها في اللغة الإيطالية في فعل immagazzinari الذي يعني «خَزَنَ» أو «خَزْن». وكلمة alferez وهي رتبة عسكرية في الجيش الإسباني مأخوذة من كلمة «الفارس» العربية. واسم القطن الذي أدخله العرب كما يبدو إلى إسبانيا هو في اللغة الإسبانية algodon. والزيت والزيتون في اللغة الإسبانية هما على التوالي aceite و aceituna أو aceitunas بصيغة الجمع. وإنْ تكن عند الإسبان كلمة أخرى للزيتون مأخوذة من أصل لاتيني وهي كلمة oliva أو olivas. ومع أن الكلمات الإسبانية من أصل عربي تُعدّ بالمئات فإن البعض منها قد سقط مؤخّرًا من الاستعمال وإن كانت القواميس ما تزال تُثبِته وتُشير إلى مصدره.

10. Written English texts
Suggested translation of 'In an Arabic-speaking diglossic community'.

تُعَدُّ اللغةُ المستعمـلةُ في البيـت في المجتمـعات الناطقة باللغة العربيةِ[1] لهـجةً من اللهـجـاتِ العـربيـة المحليـة – وقـد تـوجَدَ اختلافاتٌ كبيرةٌ جدا بـين لهجةٍ عربيةٍ وأُخرى قد تصلُ إلى حدِ عدمِ التفاهمِ المتبادلِ، ولكن لا يُوجَدُ إلا فرقٌ قليلٌ بـين المتحدثِ المثقفِ والمتحدثِ غيرِ المثقفِ.[2] ومع ذلك فإذا احتاج المرءُ إلى أنْ يُلقي مـحـاضـرةً في الجامـعـةِ أو خطبـةً في المسجـدِ[3] فـمن المتوقعِ أن يستخدمَ اللغةَ العربيةَ الفصحى[4] فتـختلفُ هذه اللغةُ[5] عن اللهـجـةِ العاميةِ المحليةِ اختلافاً جذرياً[6] حيثُ[7] أنّها تُدرَّسُ في المدارسِ كما تُدرَّسُ اللغاتُ الأجنبيةُ في المجتمعاتِ الناطقةِ باللغةِ الإنجليزيةِ. وكذلك تُعتبَرُ اللغةُ التي يدرسُها الطفلُ عندما يتعلمُ القراءةَ والكتابةَ لغةً عربيةً فصحى وليس لهجةً عاميةً محليةً.[8]

Notes
1. Since all Arabic-speaking communities are diglossic, there is no need to translate 'diglossic' here. 'Diglossia' could be translated as الازدواجية اللغوية (cf. passage starting من المفيد, Written Arabic texts 1, section 4b, this chapter). However, no adjective can be simply constructed from

this phrase.

2. An interpretation – i.e. 'the [highly] educated speaker, and the not [highly] educated speaker' – rather than a translation. مثقف is used to mean someone who is highly educated. A more literal translation would be المتحدث الأكثر ثقافةً والمتحدث الأقلّ ثقافةً. The problem with this, apart from its wordiness, is that the primary meaning of ثقافة is 'culture', while 'education' is the secondary meaning. This contrasts with مثقف, where the primary meaning is '[highly] educated', and the secondary meaning is 'cultured' (cf. Wehr).

3. مسجد used here instead of جامع to avoid an unmotivated repetition جامعة – جامع.

4. اللغة الفصيحة and اللغة الفصحى mean the same thing. There is, however, a debate in the Arab world about which form is more correct.

5. The phrase النوع اللغوي is not used to describe a linguistic variety. The easiest way to relay this idea is to exploit the distinction between لغة and لهجة. In traditional thinking, at least, a لغة is a language which is standardly written down; thus standard Arabic is a لغة; so is English. A لهجة, on the other hand, is not standardly written down; thus a colloquial Arabic dialect, or a non-written 'local language' (such as Nubian in Egypt) is a لهجة, not a لغة. There is probably some regional variation in different parts of the Arab world in these respects. Also, some speakers might now choose to describe the colloquial dialects as لغات for various reasons such as their emergence in writing; e.g. in dialogue in prose fiction.

6. The phrase 'on all levels' could be translated by the cliché على كل الأصعدة (note that على كل المستويات is not common usage). However, an even more common usage is اختلاف جذري, which can be here included as a cognate accusative (المفعول المطلق). The cognate accusative is very common in Arabic, and stylistically highly regarded (cf. ch. 17, 7aii).

7. The obvious choice of translation for 'and felt to be so different from the vernacular that it is taught' would be something like ومن المتفق عليه أنها تجتلف عن اللهجة العامية اختلافا يصل إلى حد أنها تُدرّس. The problem with this is the repetition of the verb اختلف, which is used in the previous phrase (and even the repetition of the cognate accusative). Unfortunately, there is no other obvious verb in Arabic to use. An alternative (though not an ideal one) is effectively to reduce the phrase 'and felt to be so different from the vernacular' to 'to the degree/such that it is taught', i.e. حيث أنها تُدرّس.

8. Note that لغة is here translated as an indefinite; a literal back-translation into English of the phrase لغة عربية فصحى وليس لهجة عامية محلية yields 'a standard Arabic language and not a colloquial dialect'. The logic of this is that *the* language which children is taught is *a* language, this language being *a* standard Arabic language and not *a* colloquial dialect.

11. Précis

(a) Suggested guidance questions for the précis in Arabic of كلمـات عـربيـة فـي اللغة الإسبانية.

١ – ما هي أسباب دخول بعض الكلمات العربية في اللغة الإسبانية؟

٢ – ما هي أهم هذه الكلمات؟

٣ – هل تُستعمل اليوم كل الكلمات الإسبانية من أصل عربي، ولماذا؟

(b) Suggested guidance questions for the précis in Arabic of الرواية التمثيلية العربية

١ – ما رأي الكاتب في استعمال اللغة العامية في الروايات التمثيلية؟

٢ – ما رأي الكاتب في استعمال اللغة الفصحى في الروايات التمثيلية؟

٣ – ما هي «العقدة» التي يذكرها الكاتب؟

٤ – إلى أي درجة قد وجد الكاتب حلا لهذه العقدة أو هذه المشكلة؟

6
The Arab–Israeli conflict

4. Written Arabic texts 1

(c) Suggested structure translations relating to بدأت مـشكلة تدفق المهـاجـرين
اليهود.

١ – تدفق اللاجئون إلى العاصمة السودانية الخرطوم.

٢ – أثار تعليقُهُ غضبي.

٣ – أعلنتْ معارضتَها التامةَ للخطة.

٤ – هذه التنازلاتُ من شأنها أنْ تساعدَ عمليةَ السلامِ.

٥ – وصلوا كلُهم في الأشهرِ الثلاثةِ الأخيرةِ.

٦ – تقعُ دمشقُ جنوبَ حلبَ.

٧ – لا يفهمُ معظمُ السكانِ المشكلةَ.

٨ – نقلت جريدةُ النهارِ عنه أنّه سيكونُ هناك زيادةٌ كبيرةٌ في سعرِ النفط.
Note dummy pronoun. Generic noun = singular definite in Arabic.

٩ – من الرجلُ المتوقعةُ استقالتُه.

(i) رأيتُ الرجلَ المتوقعةَ استقالتُه Compare also:

(ii) وصل مع الرجلِ المتوقعةِ استقالتُه

١٠ – وصل هذه السنةَ.

١١ – وصلت قادمةً من روسيا.

١٢ – عليك أنْ تفكّر في ذلك/فيه.

١٣ – سوف أقابلُ القادمين الجددَ من السواحِ الأجانبِ.

(d) Suggested translation of قلق عميق بسبب الهجرة السوفياتية.

Palestinian leaders urge Arabs to prevent settlement of new immigrants

Yesterday Palestinian leaders from the Occupied Territories urged Arab states to stop Israel settling thousands of Soviet Jewish emigrants on the occupied West Bank and Gaza Strip.

Reuters newsagency released a copy of a memorandum sent to Western consulate generals in Jerusalem in which twenty-six leaders from the West Bank, Gaza and East Jerusalem expressed their extreme anxiety regarding the expected mass immigration of Soviet Jews to Israel. The memorandum was signed by the prominent Palestinian leader Faisal Husseini, the Mufti of Jerusalem Sheikh Sa'd ad-Din al-'Ilmi and twenty-four doctors, academics, workers, journalists and trade union leaders.

The memorandum noted the Israeli Prime Minister Yitzak Shamir's statement regarding the need for a 'Greater Israel' in order to accommodate Soviet Jews and called for steps to be taken to ensure that no immigrants to Israel were settled [or: 'no settlement took place'] in the Occupied Territories including East Jerusalem. The memorandum criticised the United States for imposing restrictions on the entry of Soviet Jews which then forced those who wanted to emigrate to go to Israel. It also noted that this mass immigration is taking place at a time when Israel is pursuing a policy of emptying the Occupied Territories of its inhabitants by expelling Palestinians who are not registered in the Israeli census and by refusing to reunite Palestinian families.

5. Written Arabic texts 2

(a) **ii** Suggested structure translations relating to « ١٥ أيار » وأتى يوم.

١ – قالتْ بصوت يهدرُ بالغضب

When they function generically, nouns such as *rage*, *sorrow*, *joy*, *men*, etc. do not take the definite article in English; in Arabic, however, they always take the definite article.

٢ – تصرفَ الجنودُ كالمجانينَ (cf. note on generic nouns above)

٣ – مشينا عبرَ المدينة حفاةً

٤ – تبعدُ المدينةُ عن النيل عدةَ كيلومترات

Where possible, verbal clauses (clauses which take an initial verb) are preferred over nominal clauses (clauses which take an initial noun) in Arabic.

٥ – كانوا كلُهم ، أغنياءَ وفقراءَ ، يُحِسُّونَ بالبردِ

٦ – ملكَ عليها الرئيسُ أحساسَها

Word order: where a verb takes a preposition and the object of the preposition is a personal pronoun, the prepositional phrase precedes any non-pronominal object.

٧ – قدمتْ لنا أمّكم وهي تنوحُ بأعوامها الستينَ المناديلَ

The prepositional phrase precedes the subject *and* the non-pronominal object (cf. 5 above). The حال clause can interrupt the verb and its non-pronominal object.

iii Suggested translation of « ١٥ أيار » يـوم وأتى.

> The day of April 15th arrived after a bitter wait. At 12 o' clock exactly your father kicked me as I lay deep in sleep, and said in a voice filled with brave hope, 'Get up! Watch the Arab armies make their way into Palestine!' I rushed out of bed like a lunatic, and we made our way barefoot across the hills in the middle of the night and down to the road, which was a full kilometre from the village. All of us, young and old, panted as we ran like madmen. The headlights of the cars could be seen from afar, as they made their way up to Ras al-Naqura. When we reached the road we felt cold, but your father's shouting took possession of our very being. He began to run after the cars like a young child – calling out to them, shouting in a hoarse voice, panting – but still running on after the convoy of cars like a young child. We ran beside him, shouting with him. The good soldiers looked at us from beneath their helmets stiffly, silently. We were panting, while your father – at fifty years old – ran alongside, taking cigarettes out of his pocket and throwing them at the soldiers. He went on shouting at them and we went on running beside him like a small flock of goats.
>
> Suddenly the cars were no more. We returned home, exhausted, panting and wheezing. Your father was absolutely silent. We too were unable to speak; and when a passing car lit up his face, we could see that his cheeks were wet with tears.

(b) Suggested translation of نسافر كالناس

We travel like other people

> We travel like other people, but we do not return to anything. As if travel
> Is the road of the clouds. We have buried our loved ones in the darkness of the clouds, and between the trunks of the trees.
> We said to our wives, 'Give birth to us for hundreds of years, so we can complete this journey,

To an hour of a country, and a metre of the absurd.'

We travel in the carts of the Psalms; we sleep in the tent of the Prophets; and we emerge from the words of the Gypsies.

We measure space with the beak of a hoopoe, or we sing to keep our minds off the distance. And we wash the moonlight.

How long your road is! So, dream of seven women so you can carry this long road

On your back. Shake the date-palms for them, so that you can learn what their names are, and which mother will give birth to the child of Galilee.

Ours is a land of words; speak, speak so I can rest my path on a stone of stones.

Ours is a land of words; speak, speak so we can learn of an end to this travelling!

6. Written Arabic texts 3 (classical)

Suggested translation of قال ابن أبي زيد.

Ibn Abi Zaid said, 'The Berbers in North Africa apostacised twelve times and the message of Islam did not become firmly established amongst them until the rule of Musa ibn Nusair and subsequent times.' This is what is meant by the account which is related on the authority of Umar that Africa is divided according to the hearts of its people, alluding to the great number of tribes and clans there which prompted them to lack submissiveness and obedience. Neither Iraq nor Syria wre like this at that time; their protecting powers[1] had been Persia and Byzantium, and the mass of the population lived in administrative and garrison towns. When the Muslims defeated the Persians and Byzantines and wrested power from them [lit: from their hands] there was no one left to resist or dissent. The tribes of the Berbers in North Africa are innumerable [/ are too many to count]. They are all nomads and are organised into [lit: they are people of] clans and tribes. Whenever one tribe is wiped out another takes its place and its religion of dissension and apostasy. The Arabs spent a long time establishing their state in [north-east] Africa and the Maghrib. It was the same in Syria at the time of the Children of Israel. There were innumerable groups of Philistines, Canaanites, Children of Esau, Midianites, Lotians, Byzantines, Greeks, Amalekites, Akrikish, and Nabateans in the areas of the Peninsula and Mosul. It was difficult for the children of Israel to establish their state and consolidate their power, and their authority broke down time and time again. They were rent by discord, and they disagreed with their ruler and rose up against him. For the rest of their days, they had no firm government until they were defeated by the Persians, then the Greeks, then finally the Romans at the time of the diaspora. God has control over His affairs.

Note

1. The Arabic is an abbreviation of الدولة الحامية.

8. Aural Arabic texts 1

ii   Complete transcription of BBC Arabic Service news broadcast from Sept. 26, 1988.

أنباؤنا هذه سياداتي وسادتي تأتيكم من لندن:

اندلعت اشتباكات جديدة بين قوات الأمن الإسرائيلية والفلسطينيين في الأراضي المحتلة حيث يُنفّذ إضراب عام. وفي قطاع غزة أُصيب شخصان بأعيرة بلاستيكية أطلقها الجنود الإسرائيليون. وتفيد الأنباء أن أشخاصا آخرين قد جرحوا خلال الاشتباكات التي جرت في الضفة الغربية. وقد فرض الجيش الإسرائيلي حظر التجول على كثير من المدن ومخيمات اللاجئين في الأراضي المحتلة. ويُنفّذ الإضراب العام لمساندة السجناء العرب المحتجزين في معسكر الاعتقال الإسرائيلي في صحراء النقب.

تقول وكالة غوث وتشغيل اللاجئين الفلسطينيين التابعة للامم المتحدة إن عدد الفلسطينيين الذين أُصيبوا برصاص الجيش الإسرائيلي في قطاع غزة المحتل قد ارتفع إلى مستويات لا يمكن القبول بها في الأسابيع القليلة الماضية. وعبّرت الوكالة عن قلقها بشأن السماح رسميا بإطلاق العيارات البلاستيكية على المتظاهرين وهو الإجراء الذي أعلن عنه في شهر أغسطس/آب. وقال مسؤول في الوكالة إن عدد الفلسطينيين الذين يتمّ معالجتهم من إصابات بالعيارات البلاستسكية والحية قد ازداد سبعة أضعاف في المتوسط عما كان في الماضي. وقدمت الوكالة شكوى رسمية إلى السلطات الإسرائيلية بشأن سلوك إحدى وحدات الجيش في قطاع غزة.

9. Aural Arabic texts 2

i   Complete transcription of BBC Arabic Service news broadcast from Oct. 31, 1991.

مؤتمر إحلال السلام في الشرق الأوسط يبدأ يومه الثاني في مادريد، وقد ألقى إسحاق شامير رئيس وزراء إسرائيل كلمة إسرائيل وقال

فـيـهـا إن بـلاده ملتـزمـة بالتـفـاوض للتـوصل إلى اتفّاق ووصف هذا الاجتماع بأنه حدث تاريخي ومناسبة يرقبها الإسرائيليون بلهفة وتوقع. ثم ألقى كامل أبو جابر وزير الخارجية الأردني كلمة دعا فيها إلى إحلال سلام كامل وعادل. هذا وسيستمع المؤتمر بعد حوالى نصف الساعة إلى كلمة الدكتور حيدر عبد الشافي من الوفد الأردني الفلسطيني المشترك كما سيستمع بعد ذلك إلى كلمة الوفد اللبناني ثم إلى كلمة الوفد السوري. هذا ولم تتفّق الوفود المشتـركة في مـؤتمر مـادريد على مكان إجراء المحادثات الثنائية وهي المرحلة الثانية من المؤتمر. القوات الإسرائيلية تواصل قصف مناطق في جنوب لبنان.

ii Answers to comprehension questions relating to second half of news broadcast from Oct. 31, 1991.

1. According to Shamir the conference provides an opportunity to end violence and terrorism.
2. According to Shamir the conference provides an opportunity to begin dialogue, peaceful co-existence and the realisation of peace.
3. According to Shamir a cause for regret would be if the speeches concentrated on objections.
4. This is because this would be the quickest way to a dilemma.
5. According to the BBC's Jerusalem correspondent Shamir hinted at no changes in this opposition to the idea of land for peace.
6. Shamir called on the Arab leaders to renounce their holy war against Israel.
7. According to Shamir the basic reason for the continuation of the Arab–Israeli conflict is their rejection of the legitimacy of the Israeli state.
8. Shamir suggested to Arab leaders that the next round of peace talks be held in Jerusalem.
9. He also said that Israel would be ready to hold negotiations in Syria, Lebanon or Jordan.
10. Ronny Milo said that Israel would be ready to hold negotiations outside the Middle East if circumstances so dictated.
11. He suggested Washington.
12. The BBC correspondent in Madrid described the speech by Kamel Abu Jaber as calm.
13. The BBC correspondent described Jordanian policy in the region as moderate.
14. Kamel Abu Jaber said that the principle of land for peace had the most reasonable principles and slogans.
15. Kamel Abu Jaber said that the Palestinians should be allowed to decide their fate on the land of their forefathers.

10. Written English texts
(a) Suggested translation of 'Arabs express their fears'.

العرب يعبّرون عن مخاوفهم

قد بدأ [/يبدأ] الفلسطينيون والحكوماتُ العربيةُ في الإعراب عن قلقهم وسخطهم الحقيقيين إزاء هجرة اليهود الواسعة من الاتحـاد السـوفـيـاتي إلى إسـرائيلَ. وهذا [/هو] أقلُ مـا يستطيعـون عملَه نظراً للتقديرات الإسرائيلية المُبالَغ فيها [والمتـزايدة] والتي يؤكّدُ آخـرُها أن مـا بين مـائة الف ومـائةٍ وعشرين الفَ يهوديٍ سيهاجرون إلى إسرائيلَ خلال السنوات الخـمس أو السـبع القـادمـة [/خـلال الخـمس أو السـبع سنوات القادمة]. وقد صرّح شامير في الخامس عشرَ من يناير/كانون الثاني أن لهـؤلاء المهـاجـرين الحقَ في الإسـتـيطان أَينمـا [/حيـثمـا] يريدون إما داخلَ إسرائيلَ نفسها [/داخلَ حدود إسرائيلَ المعترف بها دوليا] وإما [/أو] في الأراضي المحتلة [عامَ ١٩٦٧].

والذي يخشـاهُ [/يخـشى منه] العربُ بصـفة عـامـة والأردنيـون بصـفـة خـاصـةٍ [هو] أنّ إسـرائيلَ قد تتـذرعُ بهذه الهجـرة الواسـعـة لطرد أهالي الأراضي المحتلة إلى الخارج وخـاصةً إلى الأردنِ كي تفسحَ المجالَ للقادمـين الجدد. وجاء أولُ تعبيرٍ رسميٍ عن الاعتراضِ العربيِ في تصريح أدلى بـه وزيرُ الخـارجيـة الأردنيُ مـروان القـاسم. ودعت الأردنُ وسوريا في بيانٍ مشتركٍ أصدرتاه في الثلاثين من يناير/كانون الثاني إلى عـقـد قـمـة عـربيـة لمناقشـة مـا سمّتاه بـ«الطمـوحات التوسعيةِ الإسرائيليةِ، كما أنّ مصرَ وهي [/والتي] تُعتبر الصديقةَ العربيـةَ الوحيـدةَ لإسـرائيلَ قد أدانت هي الأخرى هجرةَ اليهودِ السوفياتِ إلى إسرائيلَ.

(b) Suggested translation of 'Amnesty International accuses'.

منظمة العفو الدولي تتهم

اتـهـمتْ منـظـمـةُ الـعـفـو الـدولـي فـي تقـريـرٍ نشـرتْهُ فـي ٣ ينـايـر الحكـومـةَ الإسـرائـيـلـيـةَ بـأنّـها تُشـجّعُ قـوات أمـنـها بصـورةٍ مبـاشرةٍ على قتـل الفلسطـينـيـينَ فـي الضفـة الغربـية وقطـاع غزةَ . ويَـدعو تقـريـرُ منـظمـة العفـو الدولـي إلى استعـراضٍ عـاجلٍ للإرشـادات التـي تَسـمـحُ للجنـود الإسـرائـيـلـيين بإطلاق النار كمـا يدعو إلى تحـقـيـقٍ قانونيٍ [/ قضائيٍ] فـيـما سمـته بالانتهاكات «الـواسعـة النطـاق والخطـيـرة» لحقوق الإنسـان التـي ارتكبتْها قـواتُ الأمـنِ الإسرائـيلـية مُنذُ بداية الانتفاضة [/ منذُ أنْ بدأت الانتفاضة] .

ويَـقـولُ الـتقـريـرُ إنّ خمسَ مائـةٍ وستيـنَ فلسطـيـنيـاً قد قُتـلوا بالـرصـاص مُنذُ بدايـةِ [/ خـلالَ] الانتـفـاضـة – ومن الملحـوظ أنّ هذا الـتـقـديـرَ أدنى من الـتـقـاديـر المستقلة الأخـرى – ويتسـاءلُ الـتـقـريـرُ عـن النسـبـة العـالـيـة للأطـفـال الـقـتـلى والانتـهـاكـات المتكررة للإرشـادات الرسـمـيـة المتـعـلقـة بإطلاق النـار وعن التحـقـيـق غـيـر الكافـي [/ النـاقصِ] . وتقـولُ المنظمـةُ فـي هذه الانتهاكاتِ إنّه فـي عددٍ عـالٍ من الحالات قدْ قُتـل الفلسطينيـون وهم لا يشتركـونَ فـي أعمالِ العنف كمـا تعبـرُ عنْ شكِّها فـي أنّ الأطـفـالَ الراشـقـينَ الجنـودَ بالحـجـارةِ يُهدّدونَهم تهديداً يُبـرّرُ إطلاقَ النار عليهِم .

11. Précis

i Answers to comprehension questions relating to بداية النضال وليست نهايته.

1. The historical events which the writer mentions are, in order: the partition of Palestine in 1947, three major wars and hundreds of minor scirmishes, the Camp David Agreement in 1979, the subsequent boycott of Egypt, the Gaza–Jericho Agreement, the Madrid Conference, the Palestinian rejection of violence in the Palestine National Council session in Algeria in 1988 and their acceptance of UN Resolution 242 which implicitly recognises the existence of Israel.

2. The writer says that the Palestinians should accept the Oslo Accords because it is an initial step towards a more permanent solution, and because, by not accepting earlier agreements, the Palestinians now find themselves being offered less than they were offered at earlier stages.
3. The writer says that the Palestinians should look towards Africa because there there has been human tragedy which ended after a long and bloody conflict in the signing of agreements.
4. The writer says that the Accords are new insofar as they agree to Palestinian autonomy.
5. The political figures mentioned in the text have all been involved with the Palestinian–Israeli conflict and accords in some form or other. They include Anwar Sadat who is mentioned for his pivotal role in the Camp David Accords, Arafat for his role in the present accords and his appearance in the UN in 1988, Rabin for his exchange of letters with Arafat, and Abu Jihad who should be remembered.

ii In writing a précis in Arabic consider the questions provided in section i. of this exercise. Consider also the writer's attitude to the Accords, to Palestine and to the various historical figures mentioned.

7
Iraqi invasion of Kuwait

4. Written Arabic texts 1

(a) **i** Answers to comprehension questions relating to القوات العراقية تهاجم الكويت.

1. The Iraqi forces invaded Kuwait in the early hours of Thursday morning.
2. That day Iraq announced that the regime of the Emir, Sheikh Jabir al-Ahmad al-Sabah, had been overthrown and that a provisional government had been established in its place.
3. The immediate reaction of the Arab states to these events was to maintain silence.
4. The United State mobilised its naval fleets in the region, and announced the freezing of Iraqi and Kuwaiti assets in American banks.
5. The Iraqi invasion was condemned by the United Nations Security Council.
6. The Iraqi Revolutionary Command Council said that it had responded to a call from the Provisional Government of Free Kuwait.
7. The Council said that Iraqi forces would withdraw from Kuwaiti territory as soon as stability was restored and an appropriate request was received from the Kuwaiti government.
8. [Agence] France Presse reported that a 'Provisional Government of Free Kuwait' had announced the overthrow of the regime of the Emir Sheikh Jabir al-Sabah and the dissolution of parliament.

ii Suggested translation of القوات العراقية تهاجم الكويت.

Iraqi forces attack Kuwait, occupy Emir's palace
Kuwaiti forces resist, call on friends to intervene to protect Kuwait
Security Council and United States call on Iraq to withdraw

The Arab world was stunned in the early hours of Thursday morning by the intervention of Iraqi forces in Kuwait, and the announcement by

Iraq that the regime of the Emir, Sheikh Jabir al-Ahmad al-Sabah, had been overthrown and a provisional government established in its place. There are still conflicting reports about the fate of the Emir.

Up until Thursday afternoon Arab states maintained silence concerning these events, as various Arab leaders pursued intense diplomatic contacts. Meanwhile, the United States mobilised its naval fleets in the region, and announced the freezing of Iraqi and Kuwaiti assets in American banks. The Bush administration also called for an immediate withdrawal of Iraqi forces. This call was echoed by Moscow, and the Iraqi invasion was also condemned by the United Nations Security Council.

A statement issued by the Iraqi Revolutionary Command Council announcing the overthrow of the Kuwaiti government said that the Council had decided to 'respond to a request for cooperation from the Provisional Government of Free Kuwait'.

The statement went on to say that Iraqi forces would withdraw from Kuwaiti territory 'as soon as stability is restored and an appropriate request is received from the Kuwaiti government.' The statement added that it was possible that Iraqi forces would remain on Kuwaiti soil for no more than 'a few days or a few weeks'.

Meanwhile a spokesman for Kuwait International Airport announced that the airport had been closed to international air-traffic on Thursday a few hours after the entry of Iraqi troops on Kuwaiti soil.

According to the Kuwaiti Ministry of Defence Iraqi forces crossed the northern border of Kuwait and occupied positions on Kuwaiti soil. France Press reported that a 'Provisional Government of Free Kuwait' had announced the overthrow of the regime of the Emir Sheikh Jabir al-Sabah and the dissolution of parliament.

(b) Suggested translation of دخلت امس قوات الحلفاء مدينة الكويت.

Yesterday allied forces entered Kuwait City which had remained under Iraqi occupation since 2nd August. Eye-witnesses said that Kuwaiti flags were raised on the roofs of buildings, while Kuwaiti citizens expressed their joy, in spite of the situation the city is in due to a complete lack of public services.

Although President Saddam Hussein announced the withdrawal of his troops from Kuwait, the Alliance considered this to be 'unacceptable', and George Bush said that 'the war will continue'. Military reports claimed that French, American and British troops had crossed the Euphrates and reached the town of Nasiriyya to the north of Basra in order to cut off all bridges and roads which would allow for the withdrawal of Republican Guard forces stationed in southern Iraq and of other forces withdrawing from Kuwait.

Yesterday, thousands of Iraqi troops surrendered in Kuwait abandoning their weapons without any any significant resistence. The one exception to this was a tank battle at Kuwait airport between Iraqi and Allied forces which took place with the arrival of an advance party of Egyptian forces.

The Emir of Kuwait, Sheikh Jabir al-Ahmad imposed martial law on his country for a period of three months starting from yesterday, and appointed the Crown Prince, Sheikh Sa'd al-'Abdullah, ruler [under martial law].

5. Written Arabic texts 2

Suggested translation of خرج مروان من دكان الرجل السمـين.

Marwan left the shop of the fat man who was in charge of smuggling people from Basra to Kuwait. He found himself in the crowded, covered street which smelt of dates and large straw baskets. He did not have any clear idea what to do next. There, inside the shop, the last threads[1] of hope which, for many years, had held everything inside him together,[2] had been severed. The last words uttered by the fat man were decisive and final; [indeed,] he had felt that they were made of lead.[3]

– Fifteen dinars, don't you understand?

– But …

– Please! Please! Don't start wailing! You all come here and start wailing like widows! … Brother, my God … no one is forcing you to stay here. Why don't you go and ask someone else. Basra is full of smugglers!

Of course he would go and ask someone else. Hasan, who had worked in Kuwait for four years, had told him that the smuggling of a person from Basra to Kuwait should cost no more than five dinars, and that when he presented himself to the smuggler he would have to be bigger than a man and more than a hero, otherwise the smuggler would laugh at him, trick him, exploit the fact that he was only sixteen years old and [generally] make a laughing stock[4] out of him.

Notes

1. Metaphor in Arabic and English.
2. Metaphor in Arabic and English.
3. Simile in Arabic and English.
4. ألعوبة 'plaything, toy'.
5. General note: tense subordination is well exemplified in the final paragraph of this passage which takes the perspective of the young Palestinian.

6. Written Arabic texts 3 (classical)

i Suggested translation of حدثنا القاسم بن الحسن.

> Al-Qasim ibn al-Hasan told me on the authority of al-Hasan ibn al-Rabi' on the authority of Ibn al-Mubarak on the authority of Haya ibn Shurayj that when Umar ibn al-Khattab, may God be pleased with him, sent commanders of the army he counselled them to fear Almighty God. Then he said at the binding of the banners, 'In the name of God and with God's help go forth with God's support in victory and continue in the path of [lit: and in sticking to] right and perserverance. Fight in God's path those who do not believe in God. Do not act unjustly. Do not become fearful at the encounter. Do not treat harshly in strength. Do not dissipate your strength at the beginning [of the battle]. Do not kill old men, women or children. Be wary of killing them when the two armies meet, with the fervour of the advance, and in launching attacks. Do not be greedy in taking booty, declare the *jihad* (Holy War) above the trappings of this world and rejoice in the gains made through the allegiance which you have sworn. That is the great victory.'
>
> The people of Aktham ibn Sayfi sought his advice in fighting a tribe. He said, 'Lessen any disagreements between your commanders. Know that much shouting leads to failure and makes men incapable of fighting. Proceed with caution, for the more resolute of two groups is the confident one, and many a time haste is followed by delay. Wear armour for battle and take up arms at night, for it better conceals wails. There is no group of people who disagree with this viewpoint.'

ii Additional exercise: The teacher could also use this text as a discussion piece. Ask questions along the following lines:

١ – بماذا أوصى عمر بن الخطاب أمراء الجيوش الإسلامية؟

٢ – ما هو « أدب الحرب »؟

٣ – ما رأيك في أدب الحرب؟

8. Aural Arabic texts 1

i Answers to comprehension questions relating to BBC Arabic Service news broadcast from Nov. 16, 1990.

1. Yevgeny Primakov is the Soviet special envoy in the Middle East.
2. He called for more time before the Security Council decides to use force to oust Iraqi forces from Kuwait.
3. This would enable President Hussein to withdraw his forces and save face.
4. The Americans launched a new satelliteto observe Iraqi troop movements.
5. This new satellite was carried on the space shuttle Atlantis.

6. Six other American satellites are observing the area.
7. Iraq condemned the military exercises conducted by American and Saudi forces as an escalation which could engulf the whole region in war.
8. The Iraqi Thawrah newspaper described the military exercises as provocation designed to put more pressure on Iraq.
9. It accused the United States of making up excuses to go to war.
10. The military exercises were called Operation Imminent Thunder.
11. The exercises will last six days.
12. One thousand planes took part in the exercises.
13. The function of these planes was to provide cover for troops attacking from the sea.

iii Complete transcription of BBC Arabic Service news broadcast from Nov. 16, 1990.

الأنباء بالتفصيل من لندن . دعى يذغيني بريماكوف المبعوث
السوفياتي الخاص بالشرق الأوسط إلى مزيد من التمهل قبل أن يُقدِم
مجلس الأمن الدولي على التخويل باستخدام القوة لإخراج القوات
العراقية من الكويت . وقال إن هذه المهلة يمكن أن تُستغَل في إيجاد
صيغة تحفظ ماء الوجه تمكّن الرئيس العراقي صدام حسين من سحب
قواته . ولكنه قال إنه إذا لم يستجب الرئيس العراقي لذلك فسيتعيّن
على مجلس الأمن الدولي الموافقة على اتخاذ إجراء عسكري كما
سينبغي تنفيذه على الفور . وصرّح المبعوث السوفياتي لصحيفة النيو
يورك تايمز بأنه يعتقد أن الرئيس صدام حسين يفكّر الآن بطريقة أكثر
واقعية وإذا أمكن إيجاد تحرك ما بشأن مطالبته بربط مشاكل الشرق
الأوسط معا فإن ذلك سيسمح له باتخاذ قرار بالانسحاب من الكويت .
هذا وتفيد الأنباء بأن الولايات المتحدة أطلقت قمرا صناعيا جديدا
للتجسس لرصد تحركات القوات العراقية . وذُكر أن القمر الصناعي
حُمل على متن مكوك الفضاء « أطلنتس » وذلك في آخر مهمة عسكرية
له، إذ ستحل محله في المستقبل صواريخ غير مأهولة . وقالت القوات
الجوية الأمريكية إن تأخير إطلاق المكوك في الأسبوع الماضي يرجع إلى
مشاكل تقنية . ولكن مراسل هيئة الإذاعة البريطانية للشؤون العلمية
يقول إنه يُعتقد أن تعديلات قد أُجريت على القمر الصناعي لتمكينه من
جمع مزيد من المعلومات التي تتعلق بالخليج . ومن الجدير بالذكر أنه
يوجد ستة أقمار أمريكية أخرى تراقب المنطقة .
ندّد العراق بالتدريبات العسكرية التي تجريها القوات الأمريكية

والسعودية في الخليج باعتبارها تصعيدا يمكن أن يغرق المنطقة في جحيم . فقد قالت صحيفة الثورة البغدادية الناطقة بلسان حزب البعث بالعراق إن هذه التدريبات التي ستستغرق ستة أيام إنما هي استفزاز يهدف إلى ممارسة مزيد من الضغط على العراق. واتهمت الصحيفة الولايات المتحدة بتلفيق الذرائع من أجل شن حرب . وتشترك في هذه التدريبات التي أطلق عليها اسم الرعد الوشيك ألف طائرة توفر غطاءًا للجنود وهم يقومون بهجوم من البحر على شواطئ السعودية قرب حدود الكويت.

9. Aural Arabic texts 2
ii Complete transcription of BBC Arabic Service news broadcast from Jan. 21, 1991.

إلى تفاصيل الأنباء من لندن: قالت إذاعة بغداد إن طياري القوات المتحالفة الأسرى سيُنقلون إلى ما سمّته بمنشآت علمية واقتصادية في العراق. وقالت الإذاعة إن هذا القرار اتُخذ لأن قصف القوات المتحالفة لأهداف اقتصادية داخل المدن والقرى العراقية أحدث إصابات بين المدنيين وأضافت قائلة ان عدد الطيارين الذين أسروا يزيد على عشرين. أعربت كل من الولايات المتحدة وبريطانيا عن قلقهما من معاملة العراق للأسرى . وقد استُدعى القائم بالأعمال العراقي في واشنطن إلى وزارة الخارجية وسُلّم مذكرة احتجاج تضمّنت شكوى من سوء معاملة الأسرى على ما يبدو وذُكِّر بأن ذلك يُعدّ جريمة حرب بموجب معاهدة جينيف. أما في لندن فقد دعى دوغلاس هورد وزير خارجية بريطانيا العراق أيضا إلى مراعاة معاهدة جينيف التي قال إنها وُجدت لضمان حسن معاملة أسرى الحرب دون تحفّظات.

هذا وقالت وزارة الخارجية البريطانية إنها سوف تستدعي السفير العراقي في لندن إليها بعد قليل. وجاء في بيان صادر عن الوزارة انه سيُبلّغ بأن بريطانيا تتوقع من العراق أن يطبّق بنود معاهدة جينيف بحذافيرها. قالت القوات المتحالفة إنها تمكّنت من صد هجمات صاروخية عراقية على المملكة العربية السعودية ليلة أمس باستعمال صواريخ «باتريوت». وقال المتحدثون الرسميون الاميريكيون والسعوديون إنه أطلقت أربعة صواريخ من طراز « اسكاد » على العاصمة

السعودية الرياض وإنها دُمّرت جميعا بوابل من صواريخ «باتريوت». وهذه هي أول مرة يشنّ العراق فيها هجوما صاروخيا على الرياض. ويقول مراسل لهيئة الإذاعة البريطانية هناك إن الانفجارات هزّت أجواء المدينة حيث أطلقت صواريخ الدفاع الجوي لاعتراض صواريخ «اسكاد». وقد دخل سكان المدينة إلى الملاجئ وارتدوا الأقنعة الواقية من الغاز وقد انفجر صاروخ واحد من طراز «باتريوت» على ما يبدو على الأرض وألحق أضرارا كبيرة بأحد المباني ، إلا أنه لم تحدث إصابات خطيرة بين الأفراد. ويقول المسؤولون الاميريكيون إنه أطلقت ستة صواريخ عراقية أخرى على المنطقة الشرقية من المملكة العربية السعودية في موجتين وإن بعضها صُوّب نحو مدينة الظهران. وقالوا أيضا إن خمسة منها أُسقطت بينما سقط الآخر في البحر. هذا ولم يظهر ما يدل على أن أي من الصواريخ العراقية كان يحمل متفجرات كميائية. وهذا هو ثاني هجوم بالصواريخ تتعرض له المملكة العربية السعودية إذ كان قد أسقط صاروخ عراقي واحد من طراز «اسكاد» في الهجوم الأول الذي حدث يوم الجمعة الماضي.

10. Written English texts

(a) Suggested translation of 'The invasion of Kuwait has its roots'.

تعودُ أسبابُ غزو الكويت إلى الحرب العراقية-الإيرانية إذ أراد صدام حسين إعادة فرض سيطرته على مضيق شط العرب الذي سُلم قسرًا للشاه في مؤتمر الجزائر عام ألف وتسعمائة وخمسة وسبعين، ولكنه هُزم وتكبدَ خسائرَ ماليةً وديونًا للدول الغنية مثلَ الكويت والسعودية تتراوح بين ستةَ عشرَ وواحدٍ وعشرينَ بليونَ جنيهٍ إسترلينيٍ.

ولقد أدى غزو الكويت إلى سهولة الوصول إلى جزيرتي وربة وبوبيان المتنازع عليهما وبهذا قد استطاع صدام حسين أن يحصل على مدخلٍ أفضلَ لمياه الخليج وأن يُلغيَ ديونَه الكويتية.

(b) Suggested translation of 'Talks between Iraq and Kuwait collapse'.

١ أغسطس/آب :   تنهارُ المحادثاتُ بين العراق والكويت . يحتشدُ الجنودُ العراقيونَ على الحدودِ الكويتية . تعبرُ الولاياتُ المتحدةُ عن قلقها.

٢ اغسطس/آب :   تعبرُ القواتُ العراقيةُ الحدودَ الكويتيةَ في الساعةِ الثانيةِ بالتوقيتِ المحلي وتستولي بسرعةٍ على البلادِ . يهربُ الأميرُ وأسرتُهُ الممتدةُ إلى السعودية . تقفلُ «حكومةٌ مؤقتةٌ حرةٌ» جديدةٌ كلَّ الموانيِ والمطارَ وتمنعُ السفرَ إلى الخارجِ وتفرضُ حظرَ التجول وتقطعُ الاتصالاتِ الهاتفيةَ واللاسلكيةَ مع العالمِ الخارجي . يدينُ الرئيسُ بوش الغزوَ العراقيَ قائلاً إنه «اعتداءٌ لا مبررَ له إطلاقاً» ويُجمِّدُ الودائعَ العراقيةَ والكويتيةَ في الولاياتِ المتحدةِ ويبعثُ بالمزيدِ من السفنِ الحربيةِ الامريكيةِ إلى الخليجِ . ويقول بوش للصحفيينَ إنه لا يُفكِّرُ في التدخلِ العسكري . تُجمِّدُ بريطانيا الودائعَ الكويتيةَ في المملكةِ المتحدةِ [و]البالغةَ قيمتُها بلايين الدولاراتِ . يُعلنُ الجيشُ العراقيُ عن تحريكِ جميعِ القواتِ الاحتياطيةِ . تدعو الكويتُ مجلسَ الامنِ للامم المتحدةِ للانعقادِ فيُصدرُ المجلسُ قرارَ رقم ٦٦٠. الداعي إلى انسحابٍ عراقيٍ فوريٍ. تشتركُ إيران وسوريا في الإدانةِ وتدعو سوريا إلى انعقادِ قمةٍ عربيةٍ طارئةٍ . أما بقيةُ الدولِ العربيةِ فتلتزمُ الصمتَ المذهولَ .

11. Précis
Suggested guidance questions for the précis in Arabic of مائة طائرة للهجوم على العراق!

١ – ما رأي الكاتب في هجوم الحلفاء على العراق ؟

٢ – لماذا يذكر الكاتب إسرائيل والصرب ؟

٣ – على قول الكاتب ماذا يفيد صدام حسين ؟

٤ – كيف يرى الكاتب قول بعض الدول العربية «بأن الحلفاء لقنوا العراق درسا لن ينساه» ؟

٥ – كيف يخلص الكاتب مقاله ؟

8
Climate and environment

4. Written Arabic texts 1
(c) **ii** Answers to comprehension questions relating to بعد « صدمة » المطر.

1. Very heavy rains fell in Cairo the day before yesterday.
2. This happened during Ramadan.
3. The population of Cairo heard claps of thunder for the first time this winter.
4. An improvement in the weather is expected from today.
5. The inhabitants of the whole of Egypt have been affected.
6. The whole of Egypt was affected.
7. According to the head of the meteorological office the rains were caused by unsettled weather conditions resulting in a build-up of middle- and low-level clouds and thunder clouds.
8. In Alexandria the rains continued for twelve hours, and in Mersa Matruh for eleven hours.
9. Khalid Izz al-Din is a representative of الأهرام.
10. Cairo was hit by rains at sunset the day before yesterday.
11. Middle and Upper Egypt were then affected by the rains.
12. The clouds in these areas are described as low level.
13. In Sohag strong winds caused trees to be uprooted and windows to be smashed.
14. In al-Buhayra communications were severed between villages and towns, and shacks and huts were uprooted.
15. On the Cairo–Alexandria road there were two accidents.
16. Said Nabawi said that rains had continued for forty-eight hours and the water level in some places had been raised by approximately one metre and had resulted in falls of large amounts of rock.
17. The governor in South Sinai province ordered a doubling of efforts to reconnect regions in the shortest possible time.
18. This was necessary because floods had resulted in the closure of the Nuwaybi'–Nafaq road and the closure of all roads leading to Abu Radis and Ras al-Naqab.

19. The rains are said to have been dark in colour.
20. Some people thought the colour was due to the black clouds in the Gulf.
21. The head of the meteorological office considered the colour to be due to dirt particles suspended in the air.
22. The improvement in the weather will be quick starting in the west and gradually heading inland, but in the east the situation will remain unstable. There will be a small amount of low-level cloud which may increase around midday with the possibility of light rainfall in some areas. The temperature will be lower than usual.

5. Written Arabic texts 2

(a) Suggested translation of بـسـبـب ضوضاء القاهرة.

Cairo chaos: 62% on sedatives, 33% with high blood pressure, 14% loss of productivity

From the point of view of traffic management, Cairo lags further behind international standards than any other city in the world. One is struck by bridges stretching across narrow streets such as al-Azhar Street, or the May Fifteenth Street in Zamalek, the uncontrolled movement of pedestrians and road traffic, pedestrian behaviour which refuses to acknowledge any rule of the road, car drivers who use their horns with gay abandon, and engines whose raucous screams proclaim the fact that their projected life came to an end years ago.

This week marked the publication of a study of current noise levels in the principal streets of Cairo, which are used by approximately 1m. cars. The results of the study confirm that the noise exceeds danger levels. According to the figures, 62% of the population take tranquillisers and sleeping pills because of the noise, and the blood pressure of those who suffer from the noise has risen by 33% while productivity has fallen by 14% annually. Some of the areas studied exceeded the permitted international level by an average of 10 times.

This study has been produced mainly by scientists from the National Research Centre funded by the Scientific Research Academy together with a group from the Institute of Building Research headed by Dr. Adil al-Milwani, head of the Department of Acoustics, while the Cairo Engineering Authority is in charge of examining the relationship between noise levels and air pollution from [car] exhausts. The research team is also being assisted by a consultancy team which includes Major General Awad al-Kurdi, Director of the General Traffic Administration, Major General Mustafa Baili, head of Cairo Traffic Authority, and Major General Lutfi Ayub, head of Giza Traffic Authority.

(b) **i** Answers to comprehension questions relating to باحث أمريكي يؤكد.

1. Professor Heathway is an American professor of geology at the University of Rolla.
2. The Professor is working with Egyptian scientists in Egypt.
3. This team has been working on restoration of the Sphinx after pollution damage.
4. The Sphinx represents the body of a lion and the face of a man (of the Pharoah Khafra').
5. The Sphinx was built over four thousand years ago.
6. The Sphinx is in a dilapidated state today.
7. The key factors which caused the Sphinx to be in its present condition are natural and human, with pollution being one of the most important factors.
8. The stone from which the Sphinx was sculptured was quarried from the place where it stands.
9. This stone is approximately 70 million years old.
10. The Sphinx stands only four metres above the level of ground water today. Due to capilliary action the water rises to the body of the Sphinx and dissolves the salt in the lime stone changing this salt into crystals. These crystals collect on the surface of the statue which in turn leads to cracking and breaking up of the surface of the statue.

ii Suggested structure translations relating to باحث أمريكي.

١ – قابل الوزراء من أجل توقيع الاتفاق.

٢ – أخي عضو في المعهد الأمريكي-اليمني.

٣ – أما البناء الأثري فلا بد من إنقاذه هذه السنة.

٤ – قد انتهى البروفسور الجديد مؤخرا من كتابه.

٥ – يقع مستوى المياه الجوفية بخمسة أمتار تحت البيت فقط.

(c) **i** Answers to comprehension questions relating to التجميد.

1. It is said that it is common knowledge that oil is difficult to remove from water.
2. Because oil is a liquid it is difficult to control it in sea water.
3. Experts in the oil industry said that there is a new method for cleaning up oil pollution.
4. This new method was invented by Daniel Snow.
5. He works at the Langley Centre for Research.
6. Liquid nitrogen is used in this new cleaning method.
7. The cleaning method works by freezing the oil in the water and changing it into hard granules and spheres.
8. Using this new method salvage teams will be able to scoop up the oil and

remove it from the sea.

9. Specialists in water pollution believe it will be possible to freeze many different types of chemical waste which leak into the sea.

10. The inventor believes the method will require special ships which have the technology to spray liquid nitrogen through hosepipes with mouths beneath the level of the floating oil.

11. The cleaning-up operation will take place directly beneath the surface of the polluted water, so that it will be confined to the level of pollution.

12. The oil will be removed from the sea by wide hosepipes and put into ships with large holds or cisterns.

13. The salvaged oil could then be used to produce appropriate petro-chemical products.

iii Suggested translation of التجميد.

Freezing: treatment for water pollution

Once again the world is faced with[1] the problem of the spillage of massive amounts[2] of crude oil into the sea. As everyone knows,[3] it is very difficult to remove traces of oil from water, despite[4] the recent production[5] of a number of chemical solutions designed to break up the oil.[6] One thing which makes cleaning up almost impossible is the fact that oil is a liquid which is extremely difficult to control[7] in sea water.[8] There are, however, positive signs of a new and effective[9] method for dealing[10] with this type of disaster.

Sources in the oil industry say that a reseacher [/one of the researchers] at the Langley Centre for Research has devised [/invented /designed] a quick and easy method to eliminate oil pollution; this method involves the use of liquid nitrogen sprays in order to freeze the oil in the water and change it into hard granules and spheres. In this way, the salvage teams[11] will be able to scoop up the leaking oil and separate it from the sea water. Specialists in [combating] water pollution believe that it will be possible to use liquid nitrogen to freeze many different types of chemical waste which [may] leak into the sea.

The originator of this idea, the researcher Daniel Snow, suggests that this process will require special ships which have the technology to spray liquid nitrogen through hosepipes with mouths below the level of the floating oil: that is to say, the cleaning operation should be carried out directly beneath the surface of the polluted water. Accordingly, freezing is limited to the polluted layer itself. This method of freezing puts a limit on the [lit: continuous] expansion of chemical poisons to wide areas [of sea] or other large bodies of water. The frozen oil mass can then be scooped up or pumped through wide hosepipes into ships with large holds or cisterns. The treated water can then be pumped back[12] into the sea. In addition [to that], it will be possible to re-refine[12] the salvaged oil to produce appropriate [/suitable] petro-chemical products.[13]

Notes

1. This is an interpretation which assumes that نعود reflects outside events in the world, and is not simply an attempt to link this article with previous material in the magazine.

2. It is not possible to say in English 'disasters of spillage of crude oil'. This same basic idea can, however, be relayed by the phrase, 'problems of spillage of ... crude oil'. The phrase 'massive amounts of' is added to compensate for the loss of forcefulness in translating كوارث as 'problems'.

3. The main-clause phrase والكل يعرف is translated into English as a subordinate clause, 'As everyone knows' in order to downplay the importance of this information, with the consequent upgrading to a main clause in the English of the information given by the phrase أن إزالة أثر النفط من المياه أمر صعب جدا.

4. The order of elements in the English is somewhat problematic. The Arabic sentence هذا على الرغم من إنتاج عدد من المحاييل الكيمياوية المضادة has been translated as a subordinate phrase, beginning 'despite'. This is partly because the phrase 'This is despite ...' is unidiomatic (unusual) in English, but also because the information contained in the Arabic sentence هذا على الرغم من إنتاج عدد من المحاييل الكيمياوية المضادة does not have enough independence from what has gone before to warrant a separate sentence in English. If the phrase 'as everyone knows' were not in the translation, it would be possible to recast this sentence along the lines, 'Despite the production of a number of chemicals designed to break up the oil, it is very difficult to remove traces of oil from water'. This would put the key bit of new information 'it is very difficult to remove traces of oil from water' at the end of the sentence, which is the most natural place for it in English. The presence of the two subordinate elements 'As everyone knows', and 'despite the production of a number of chemicals designed to break up the oil', however, makes this kind of solution problematic, since it would require these two subordinate elements to occur in close succession at the beginning of the sentence (e.g. 'As everyone knows, despite the production of a number of chemicals designed to break up the oil, it is very difficlt to remove traces of oil from water'). Such a use of two subordinate elements at the start of a sentence in English is felt to be stylistically inelegant.

5. The Arabic إنتاج can be interpreted either in a continuous sense, i.e. these solutions are currently being produced, or in a dynamic sense, i.e. these solutions have come to be produced. In English 'production' in this context gives a generally dynamic sense. One possibility in translating إنتاج is to make this dynamic sense more explicit, and important, by adding the word 'recent' (as in this version). An alternative would be to adopt the continuous interpretation and translate إنتاج as 'existence'.

6. مضاد is typically translated into English as 'anti-'. 'Anti-', however, requires something to follow it, e.g. 'anti-freeze', 'antibiotics', etc. In this case therefore, it is necessary to translate مضادة by an extended phrase in English interpreting the intended sense of the original.

7. The obvious translation of احتواؤها is 'contain'. 'Contain', however, seems to be used largely of solid physical objects (although it is also possible to say things like 'The police were unable to contain the riots, which subsequently spread to other districts'). 'Control', while less precise than 'contain', is a fairly idiomatic alternative.

8. 'Sea water' is a standard cliché in English.

9. 'New and effective' is better than 'effective and new', for rhythmic reasons. An alternative translation would be 'effective new', which again seems preferable to 'new effective' for rhythmic reasons.

10. It is sufficient to translate تنفع لمواجهة as 'for dealing' in English.

11. lit: men

12. إعادة followed by a verbal noun means to do again that which is indicated in the main verbal noun. It is often translated into English as 'X back' or 're-(X)' or 'do X again'.

13. i.e. a limited range of chemical products.

iv Additional exercise: comparison of translations of التجميد.
This passage presents a number of problems from a translation point of view, some of which are dealt with in the notes. Students could be asked to compare their versions with the suggested translation given above.

6. Written Arabic texts 3 (classical)
Suggested translation of وليس بمكة ماء جار.

There is only a small amount of running water in Mekka and this was diverted from a spring under the direction of one of the governors. It was completed in the days of al-Muqtadir and was let into a channel which had been constructed for this purpose and which led to a canal which had been made at the Bani Shayba gate. Most of their water came from the sky [as rainwater] and filled the cisterns and pools which were

built there. Its use was controlled [and monopolised] by those who
were in charge of the *waqf* properties in Mekka. They do not have any
wells containing drinkable water; the well with the best water is
Zamzam but you always cannot drink from this. The only fruiting trees
in the whole of Mekka are desert trees. If you cross the Holy Sanctuary
there are numerous springs, wells, walls and wadis with vegetables,
grains and palm trees. It is said that in Fakh there are numerous
scattered palm trees and this forms part of the Holy Sanctuary, but I
have not seen them.

8. Aural Arabic texts 1

i Transcription of BBC Arabic Service news broadcast from Jan. 22, 1991 from
بالأزمة القائمة في الخليج to الرابعة بتوقيت غرينيتش.

الرابعة بتوقيت غرينيتش. سيداتي وسادتي السلام عليكم ورحمة
الله وبركاته نشرة الأخبار يقرأها عليكم حسن أبو العلاء وهذا موجزها.
الولايات المتحدة تقول إن القوات العراقية في الكويت قامت
بتدمير بعض آبار وصهاريج تخزين النفط إلى الشمال مباشرة من
الحدود السعودية. ويُقال إن النيران لا تزال مشتعلة. استمرار الهجوم
الجوي الذي تشنّه القوات المتحالفة. وفي المملكة العربية السعودية
أطلقت القوات الأمريكية مزيدا من صواريخ «باتريوت» بعد الاشتباه
في شن هجوم بصواريخ اسكاد العراقية على الظهران. الدبلوماسيون
الغربيون يقولون إن مبعوثا من الرئيس بوش يقوم بزيارة العاصمة
الأردنية عمان. وصول رئيس الوزراء الباكستاني إلى إيران في مساع
دبلوماسية أخرى تتعلق بالأزمة القائمة في الخليج.

ii Transcription from الأنباء بالتفصيل من لندن to end.

الأنباء بالتفصيل من لندن:
قال متحدث عسكري أميركي في المملكة العربية السعودية إن العراق
يقوم بتدمير منشآت النفط في الكويت المحتلة. وقال متحدث إن
الصور التي التُقطت من الجو تظهر أن العراق فجر آبار النفط
وصهاريج التخزين في حقل نفط الوفرة في جنوب الكويت على الحدود
مع المملكة العربية السعودية. ولم يذكر المتحدث أي تفاصيل أخرى.
وجدير بالذكر أن شركة «تيكساكو» الأميركية تقوم بتشغيل حقل
الوفرة نيابة عن الحكومة الكويتية، وهو الحقل الوحيد الذي تقوم

شركة أجنبية بتشغيله في البلاد .

وكان العراق قد هدد في السابق بتدمير المنشآت النفطية الكويتية وتعتقد الدول المتحالفة بأنه جرى تلغيم منشآت النفط هناك . ويقول مراسل هيئة الإذاعة البريطانية لشؤون الدفاع في المملكة العربية السعودية إن من أكبر مخاوف القوات المتحالفة قيام العراق بتدمير منشآت النفط ويقول مراسلنا إنه بصرف النظر عن عملية التدمير في حد ذاتها فإن حرق آبار النفط له قيمة من الناحية العسكرية نظرا لأن انبعاث الدخان في سماء المعركة يمكن أن يعيق الهجمات الجوية للقوات المتحالفة.

ويقول علماء البيئة إن انبعاث الدخان بصورة مكثفة من آبار النفط يمكن أن يحجب ضوء الشمس مما يؤدّي إلى تبريد سطح الأرض في المنطقة المتأثرة بالدخان . هذا وقد اتسم رد فعل الحكومة البريطانية بالتحفظ لما ذُكر من قيام القوات العراقية بتدمير المنشآت النفطية الكويتية . وقال متحدث بريطاني إن النيران ربما اشتعلت في المنشآت النفطية بطريق الخطأ ولكن إشعال النار في المنشآت النفطية الكويتية ربما يكون مقدمة لانسحاب القوات العراقية من المنطقة أو محاولة لإعاقة الهجمات الجوية التي تشنها القوات المتحالفة.

9. Aural Arabic texts 2

i Answers to comprehension questions relating to حصاد الشهر, no. 7, side 1,
item 2, مشاريع التنمية الاقتصادية الكبرى في العالم ١: الري.

1. Dr Tony Allan is from the University of London.
2. What is extraordinary about Libya's attitude to the project discussed in this passage is that it is prepared to spend its entire annual GNP in one year on a single project.
3. In general, the project aims to extract water from the desert and take it to where it is required in northern regions with the greatest agricultural potential.
4. John Wright suggests that the project may at first sight appear to contradict the laws of nature.
5. The most dramatic water source was discovered at the Kufra Oasis.
6. The somewhat poetic assessment of the amount of water potentially available here is that it is equal to the amount of water which flows from the Nile over two hundred years.
7. The Libyan government started these projects in the 1970s.
8. The project faced technical problems and had difficulties in finding the

necessary workforce which could live and work in an isolated area.

9. Agricultural production in a remote area in the country is described as illogical.

10. In recent years the water table in Tripoli and its outskirts has dropped alarmingly.

11. According to John Wright the water will be collected from around 300 artesian wells in Tazarbo.

12. Srir is located between al-Kufra and Jiyala.

13. The water will travel through the pipes by gravitational forces.

14. The pipes are four metres in diameter.

ii Transcription of مشاريع التنمية الاقتصادية الكبرى في العالم ١: الري from واستهلّ هذه السلسلة.

واستهلّ هذه السلسلة بالحديث عن شبكة أنابيب الماء في الجماهيرية الليبية، وهي موضوع عددنا الحالي وقد وصف لنا الدكتور Tony Allan من جامعة لندن هذا المشروع بقوله: «لا أعرف بلداً في العالم مستعداً كالجماهيرية الليبية لإنفاق ما يعادل ثروته خلال سنة بأكملها على مشروع واحد» إنه مشروع استنباط الماء من الصحراء وضخه إلى حيث تشتدّ الحاجة إليه في الأقاليم الشمالية ذات الإمكانات الزراعية الكبرى، وقد وصفه John Wright من هيئة الإذاعة البريطانية بأنه مشروع عظيم وطموح، قد يبدو لأول وهلة مناقضاً لقانون الطبيعة، ففي الجماهيرية الليبية ثروات ضخمة جداً من المياه العذبة وإن لم يتمّ استغلالها حتى هذا الوقت، وقد أُكتشفت مصادر الماء في مواقع قصية من البلاد ولعل أروع هذه الاكتشافات واحة الكُفرى، وقد وُصف الماء في هذه البقعة وصفاً شعرياً قد لا يكون دقيقاً بأنه يُعادل ما تدفّق عبر نهر النيل خلال قرنين من الزمن، ثم مضى برنامجنا «أضواء» يقول على لسان John Wright «إن نظام الحكم الثوري في الجماهيرية قد باشر العمل في السبعينات في عدة مشاريع زراعية طموحة تعتمد على استغلال مصادر المياه القصية تلك، وإن كانت هذه المشاريع سليمة من وجهة نظرية معيّنة إلا أنها صادفت مشكلات تقنية عديدة وصعوبات جمة في إيجاد الإيدى العاملة الضرورية القادرة على العيش والعمل في بقاع معزولة، ومن الصعوبات التي لا يسهل تذليلها صعوبة النقل والمواصلات، فمن غير المنطقي إنتاج زراعة من الدرجة الأولى في بقعة قصية من البلاد ومن ثَمة نقل ذلك الإنتاج عبر آلاف الكيلومترات من الطرق الصحروية لتسويقه في بنغازي بكُلفة أكبر من سائر المنتجات

الزراعية المتوفرة في الأسواق العالمية».

يخطط الليبيون حالياً إلى جلب المياه من مصادرها الطبيعية تحت الأرض عبر الصحارى الجنوبية الشرقية إلى المراكز السكانية الرئيسية في شمال البلاد، ولا سيما في طرابلس وضواحيها حيث بلغ انخفاض منسوب الماء المتوفر فيها خلال السنوات الأخيرة حداً يدعو إلى الفزع، ولكن ما الذي تنطوي عليه عملية جلب الماء من عمق الصحراء إلى سواحل الجماهيرية على البحر الأبيض المتوسط، John Wright يواصل الحديث:

«سيتم تجميع المياه من حوالى ثلاث مائة بئر أرتوازي في تزربو، وهي واحة صغيرة تقع في الشمال الشرقي من الكفرى وكذلك في السرير التي تتوسط المسافة ما بين الكفرى وجياله ومتى تم ضخ الماء إلى السطح فسيتدفق بقوة الجاذبية عبر أنابيب من الفلاذ والأسمنت المسلّح يبلغ قطرها أربعة أمتار أي ما يُساوي قطر نفقٍ للسكك الحديدية يتسع لقطار واحد، وسيتدفق الماء من الآبار في تزربو والسرير عبر صحراء إجدابية لمسافة تبلغ قرابة خمس مائة كيلومتر، ومن تلك النقطة سيتم توزيع الماء شمالاً إلى بنغازي والمناطق المحيطة بالمدينة وغرباً إلى المراكز الصناعية والسكانية النامية على حدود خليج سرت الجنوبية».

10. Written English texts
(a) Suggested translation of 'I lived in the marshes of Southern Iraq'.

عشتُ في الأهوارِ بجنوبِ العراقِ من نهاية عامٍ ألفٍ وتسعمائةٍ وواحدٍ وخمسينَ حتى شهرِ يونيو/تموز عامَ ألفٍ وتسعمائةٍ وسبعةٍ وعشرينَ، وكنتُ أبقى هناك لفترات تمتدُّ أحياناً إلى سبعةِ أشهر. وكانت السنةُ الوحيدةُ التي لم أزرْ فيها الأهوارَ هي سنةُ ألفٍ وتسعمائةٍ وسبعةٍ وخمسينَ. وبالرغم من أنني كنتُ أتنقّلُ باستمرارٍ في تلكَ[1] الفترةِ إلا أن هذا الكتابَ ليس كتاباً عن رحلاتي،[2] فالمنطقةُ التي تجوّلتُ فيها كانت صغيرةً نسبياً. ولا أدّعي أن هذا الكتابَ هو دراسةٌ تفصيليةٌ[3] عن سكانِ الأهوارِ الذين عشتُ معهم فلستُ خبيراً في الأنثروبوليجيا ولا متخصّصاً في أيِ مجالٍ. ففي الحقيقةِ قضيتُ هذه السنواتِ

في الأهوار لأنني استمتعتُ[5] بعيشي[6] هناك، وعشتُ خلالَ تلك الفترةِ مع سكانِ الأهوار وكأنني واحدٌ منهم وألفتُ طريقةَ حياتِهم إلى حدٍ ما وذلك أمرٌ طبيعيٌ. وقد حاولتُ مستعيداً[7] ذكرياتي الجميلةَ[8] ومذكّراتي اليوميةَ التي كتبتُها في تلك الفترةِ أن أرسمَ صورةً[9] عامةً للأهوار وسكانها. وبسبب الاضطرابات السياسية الأخيرة أُغلِقت هذه المنطقةُ للزوّار وقد يتمُّ[10] تجفيفُها قريباً فتزولُ طريقةُ حياةٍ دامتْ آلافَ السنينَ إذا تمّ ذلك.[11]

Notes

1. The phrase في تلك الفترة is added to provide a greater sense of connection with what has gone before in the Arabic. Arabic typically favours more explicit connection of this kind within texts than does English. Note also that in English one would tend to say 'in this period'; cf. later in this text 'I spent these years in the Marshes'. In Arabic تلك is preferred because the time being referred to is in the non-recent past.

2. رحلات is typically (and classically) used for 'travel', as in 'travel book'; cf. رحلات ابن بطوطة.

3. تفصيلي is preferred to مفصّل in this context.

4. The phrase في الحقيقة is added to provide an explicit contrast in the Arabic, where the English has an implied contrast. This is also an example of Arabic using more explicit forms of connection.

5. استمتع and تمتّع both mean 'to enjoy', but تمتّع refers more to physical pleasures (cf. مُتْعَة, which can also have sexual connotations), while استمتع refers to more abstract enjoyment.

6. عيش gives a greater sense of 'everyday living', or 'way of living' than حياة (cf. Wehr).

7. استعاد 'to recall, recollect' is a verb typically used with ذكريات.

8. الجميلة has been added to provide balance with the following phrase, by giving this first phrase just as the following مذكراتي اليومية a noun–adjective pattern.

9. رسم صورة is a typical phrase in Arabic to relay what is meant by 'give a picture' (in this sense) in English.

10. The use of قد followed by the imperfect gives a sense of 'might', 'possibly', rather than 'probably', as in the original. It might, however, be felt that a more strictly accurate translation would be preferable here.

11. The placing of إذا تم ذلك at the end of the sentence allows the phrase قد يتم تجفيف الاهوار to follow فتزول ... immediately, thereby

emphasising that the disappearance of this way of life would be a consequence of the draining of the Marshes. The use of ‫...فـ‬ before ‫تزول‬ also presents the information contained in the ‫تزول‬-clause as a consequence of what has previously been said.

(b) Suggested translation of 'Wet and windy conditions will spread'.

الجزر   البريطانية

سـتـنـتـشـرُ الأمـطارُ والـريـاحُ في الجزر الـبـريـطانـيـة في الصبـاحِ، وسـتـتـوجـهُ الأمطارُ إلى إيرلندا وويلز تدفـعُها ريـاحٌ شبـهُ عاتيـةٍ مـن الجنـوب أو الجنـوب الـغـربيِ، وأمـا إنجلتـرا وإسكتلندا فلن تنزلَ فـيـهـمـا الأمطارُ في بداية النهارِ وستكونُ هناك فـتـراتٌ مُشْمـسةٌ مـتـقطِّعة وتصحو السماءُ مـن الغـربِ بـالـغةً إيرلندا في وقتِ الظهرِ.

فـفـي الـوقتِ ذاتـه سـتـمـتـدُ الأمطارُ إلـى إنجلتـرا وإسكتلندا مـتـوجـهـةً شرقاً ولـيـسَ مـن المتوقعِ أنْ تصحو السماءُ قبـلَ غـروبِ الشمسِ وبـعـدَ العصرِ سـتـتـوسعُ ريـاحٌ شبـهُ عاصفيةٍ مـن الجنـوبِ.

11. Précis

The précis in Arabic of ‫كارثة إنسانية‬ should be structured around a selection of the comprehension questions listed in section 11.i. of the textbook.

9
Social issues and development

4. Written Arabic texts 1

(a) Answers to comprehension questions relating to معظم سكان افريقيا.

1. In Cairo next Wednesday a meeting on environmental pollution and African security will take place.
2. It will take place at the headquarters of the Arab League.
3. The conference will be convened by the African *Bagwashi* Group.
4. According to the head of this party, around 25 African states will participate in the conference.
5. In general they will discuss political, economic and social security for the Black Continent and, most importantly, environmental problems.
6. The UN says that environmental problems threaten security for a large number of African states.
7. The conference will last for four days.
8. The five major problems to be discussed are: the population explosion, the disappearance of the forests, the lack of water, desertification, and the burial of nuclear and [other] dangerous waste in Africa.
9. Dr Ahmad Abd al-Wahhab is a famous professor in agricultural pollution of the environment and one of the participants of the conference.
10. He is of Egyptian nationality.
11. According to him, the population explosion may not be seen as an environmental problem.
12. UN reports say that the size of the population is predicted to be 872m. in 2000.
13. This makes the population explosion an environmental problem because most of the population live below the poverty level, and food production is only increasing by 2.5%.
14. Nineteen African countries have an average population increase of 3%.
15. In terms of the overall size of the continent's population this means the continent's population will double in 23 years or less.
16. 86% of the world's population live in developing countries.

17. The average life span of people in Africa is predicted to be 70 in the year 2000.
18. The disappearance of the forests is described as reaching dangerous proportions.
19. The forests provide a cover which protects the earth and helps improve environmental conditions, maintain the fertility of the earth and retain water. It also protects plants and animals and microscopic beings.
20. According to reports, half the continent's population use the wood from the forests as fuel.
21. 15m. feddans of the forests is disappearing every year.
22. Two thirds of the forests has already disappeared.
23. Lack of sufficient water leads to desertification and water pollution.
24. Water is polluted from factory discharge and sewage works.
25. Water pollution threatens human, plant and animal life.
26. The percentage of people in developing countries who cannot find clean water to drink is 61% in rural areas and 26% in urban areas.
27. As a result of water pollution people.contract many indigenous diseases.
28. The principle reason behind the emigration of 10m. people from their home countries is desertification.
29. Another problem which threatens the entire continent is the burial of dangerous material.
30. More than 4,000 tons of this came from Italy to Nigeria.
31. The Organisation of African States took notice of this danger.
32. The OAS now demands the cancellation of contracts to bury dangerous waste in Africa.

(b) **ii** Answers to comprehension questions relating to العالم يحتفل اليوم.

1. Twenty-six years ago the United Nations announced the Day of the Child.
2. More than 40,000 children are dying of starvation every day.
3. According to UNICEF reports, hundreds of millions of children in Africa will not be healthy when they grow up because of the emaciation, illness and physical weakness they have suffered.
4. The rights of children are being infringed mainly as a result of political factors.
5. Iranian children have been forced to go to war.
6. Palestinian children suffer from neglect and dispersion.
7. Lebanese children suffer from psychological trauma.
8. The picture of children in the world is made worse by the phenomenon of selling children to work in domestic service, and the presence of gangs which kidnap children to sell as slaves in India and Brazil.
9. Children in the developed world suffer from psychological trauma.
10. UNICEF has set aside $48m. this year for the advancement of women.
11. $285m. has been set aside to help children who have been the victims of armed conflict and other circumstances.

12. There is now a pressing need to hold an international conference to formulate an International Declaration for the Protection of Children's Rights along the lines of the International Declaration of Human Rights and the International Declaration of Women's Rights.

iii Additional translation exercise. Our suggested translation of the passage runs as follows.

The world celebrates the day of tortured childhood

Egypt and the world are today celebrating the Day of the Child. This is the anniversary of the declaration of the rights of children announced by the United Nations 26 years ago.

Celebrations of the Day of the Child are taking place in the midst of difficult circumstances for children of the developing world: more than 40,000 children in countries of the developing world die of starvation every day, while UNICEF reports that hundreds of millions of African children who are suffering from drought, although still alive, will not be in good health when the grow up because of the emaciation, illness and physical weakness they have suffered.

The rights of children are also abused in our world as a result of political factors: in Iran we find children being forced into the front line in its war against Iraq; Palestinian children suffer from neglect and dispersion in the Occupied Territories; and Lebanese children suffer from psychological trauma.

There is another aspect to the lack of children's rights in a number of countries in Asia and Latin America where children are put to work in physically demanding jobs at a young age.

One of the things that makes the picture more gloomy for children in the world is the phenomenon of selling children, particularly girls, to work in domestic service, and the presence of gangs which kidnap children to sell them as slaves in India and Brazil. Similarly we find that children in the developed world suffer from psychological trauma because of the personal problems of their parents.

The executive bureau of the United Nations fund for the care of mothers and children, UNICEF, takes an interest in mothers in order to help their children. UNICEF has allocated more than 48.5 million dollars this year for the advancement of women.

UNICEF has also allocated 275 million dollars to help children who have been the victims of armed conflict and other circumstances in the world.

Thus, there is now a pressing need to hold an international conference to formulate an International Declaration for the Protection of Children's Rights along the lines of the International Declaration of Human Rights and the International Declaration of Women's Rights.

(c) Suggested translation of رجل قبل الأوان.

One million Egyptian children employed illegally
A man before his time

The expression 'child proletariat' has an odd ring to it. It does, however, precisely describe a social fact and a strange world whose features have an almost tragic quality; a world full of sorrow and toil, and frustrated joys. This is the world of children who begin their working lives before they have completed their education, even before they have experienced the dreams of childhood.

Egypt is not alone amongst poor countries in possessing a child proletariat[1] which plays a key role in all areas of economic activity. In Egypt, however, the problem of child labour has reached such serious proportions that it has come to attract the attention of government, opposition and the general public alike. For the number of working children under the age of 12 has risen to 1,014,000, or 7% of the total national workforce. This figure does not take into account hundreds of thousands of other children employed in the agricultural sector, for whom no statistics are yet available, and who, therefore, fall outside government considerations.

Why do these children go out to work? And why do certain experts support child labour, despite the fact that this exposes children to the dangers of injury at work and to innumerable psychological traumas? These and other related questions are the subject of studies currently being undertaken for the Egyptian government by a number of experts in research centres and universities. These studies may well take an extremely long time to complete, since it is generally accepted that child labour is not only very complicated as a social issue, but is also inextricably bound up with various other social and economic problems; indeed, in the opinion of many observers, it is itself a direct outcome of these problems.

Note
1. Literally: 'In Egypt as in many poor countries of the world a "child proletariat" appears.'

6. Written Arabic texts 3 (classical)

Suggested translation of وقال زيد بن جَبَلة.

Zayd ibn Jabala said, 'No poor person is poorer than a rich person who feels immune from poverty.' He also said on the authority of Ali ibn Abi Talib, may God honour him, 'Anything less than 4,000 dirhams is just about sufficient, whilst anything above that is treasure.' It is also said, 'The grave is better than poverty.' It is also said, 'Whenever children have preceded money the possessor of them will be poor.' A Basran was once asked, 'Why isn't your capital increasing?' He said, 'Because I had children before I had money, while other people have money before they have children.' It is said that children are the weevils of money. A Medinan was asked, 'How are you?' He said, 'How would a man be whose money has been used up but whose lifestyle remains the same?' It is also said, 'Wealth in exile is home, but poverty at home is exile.'

Muhammad ibn Yahya told me, mentioning an *isnad*, 'One of the prophets complained to God of extreme poverty, but God spoke to him and said, "This is how I determined your affairs to be. Do you want me to remake the world for your sake?"'

Abu Hatim said, 'Al-'Utbi told me he had heard Yunis ibn Habib say, "The people of the desert were never completely lacking in water; and eventually the rain came [to them], and wealth was subsequently restored to the people of wealth."'

Al-Asma'i said, 'I saw an extremely beautiful Bedouin woman asking for a favour. I said to her, "Servant girl of God, why are you asking for this when you possess such beauty!" She said, "God has decreed, so what can I do?" I asked her, "Where does your living come from?" She said, "The people of the Hajj; we sweep up for them and clean their clothes." So I said, "And if the Hajj disappeared, then where would you get your living from?" She looked at me and said, "Oh hard-headed one, if we lived only from what we knew about we would not live at all!"'

8. Aural Arabic texts 1

i   Complete transcription of حصاد الشهر, no. 12, side 2, item 1, discussion with طه حسين.

ثم انتقلت الندوة إلى الخوض في إجابات عن أسئلة أخرى، أسئلة لم تخلو في ذلك الزمن من سؤال لعلّه ما زال إلى يومنا هذا يُثير الحيرة في عدد كبير منا، هاكم سؤال مثلما طُرح في ذلك الزمن:

ما سبب العداء بين الزوجة وأم الزوج وهل ذلك عند شعوب معينة

أم في جميع العالم؟ هذا هو السؤال الذي ورد إلينا من السيد عبد الله
صادق الاوداوي من الكويت ولعلّه يواجه مشكلة الحماة. فهو يُريد أن
يعرف سبب العداء بين الزوجة والحماة وهل هذا مقتصر على البلد
الذي هو فيه أم يشمل جميع بلاد العالم. الدكتور طه بيك :

أظن أن هذا ليس مقصورا على شعب بعينه، فنحن نعرفه في
شعوب مختلفة، قد عرفناه عند العرب القدماء، وفي الشعر المروي في
الحماسة قالت له عرسه يوم لتسمعني مثلا فإن لنا في أمنا أربة ولو
... لا أدري ماذا ثم ... ولو غوتني في نار مؤججة ثم استطاعت لزادت
فوقها حطبة . ونعرف مثلا أن في فرنسا كاتبا عظيما مشهورا هو
François Mauriac قد وضع قصة من أروع ما كُتب في هذا العصر وهي
Génitrix أو الوالدة ، يصوّر فيها ما يكون من العداء بين أم الزوج وبين
الزوجة، وأكبر الظن أن سبب هذا العداء بين الحماة وزوجة ابنها أو
العكس يأتي من أن الأم تحب دائما أن تستأثر بحب ابنها وأن تخلص لها
نفسه وحياته، والأمهات العاقلات وحدهن هن اللاتي يحببن أبناءهن
ويقرّرن في أنفسهن أن الحب ليس استئثارا وإنما هو التضحية ، وهذا
يردنا إلى ما كنا نتحدث فيه آنفا من الشجاعة والقلب والعقل ففي هذا
تدخل العناصر المختلفة عنصر الحب الذي يأتي من القلب وعنصر
التقدير والحكم الذي يأتي من العقل فالأم التي تؤثر ابنها على نفسها
تتركه يسعد بحياته الزوجية دون أن تنغّص عليه من أمره ولا من أمر
زوجه شيئا ولكن الأم التي تؤثر نفسها بالخير وتريد أن تستأثر بكل
شيء، هي التي تنغّص على ابنها أو على ابنتها الحياة لأنّها لا تحس أنّ
ابنها يخلص لها من دون زوج.

ii Answers to comprehension questions relating to the discussion with طه حسين.

1. The two parts of the question put to Dr Taha Hussein are: what is the reason for animosity between a wife and her mother-in-law; and is this animosity restricted to certain peoples or is it found throughout the world?
2. The questioner comes from Kuwait.
3. Taha Hussein demonstrates that this problem is not restricted to one part of the world through looking at literature. He says that we know of animosity of this type from ancient Arabic poetry. We also have the book *Génitrix* written by François Mauriac in which animosity between the mother-in-law and her daughter-in-law is described.

4. According to Taha Hussein the most probable reason for animosity between the mother-in-law and her daughter-in-law is that the mother wants to monopolise the love of her son.
5. Sensible mothers view love not as a monopoly but as a sacrifice.
6. Taha Hussein was earlier talking about courage, the heart and the mind.
7. Love stems from the heart.
8. Appraisal and wisdom stem from the mind.

9. Aural Arabic texts 2

i Complete transcription of المجاعة، حصاد الشهر no. 19, side 1, item 2.

المجاعـة المؤلمة التي ضربت أطنابها في إثيـوبيا والأقطار المجاورة لها حركت من شدتها الضمـير العـالمي. ومن الطبيـعي أن اهتمـام النـاس خارج المناطق المنكوبة انصبّ حول المشكلة وليس على أسبابها الجذرية. وفي الـوقت الذي مـا زال فيـه الإنسـان عاجزا عن الحيلولة دون وقـوع الزلازل والأعاصير والبراكين لأنه يعتبرها كوارث طبيـعية نجد علماء يعتقدون بأنّه يجب على الإنسان الا ينظر إلى أحداث من قبيل الفيضان والقحط على أنها كـوارث طبيـعية. فـهناك عـالم غـربي هو Lloyd Timberlake ألّف كتابا عن الكوارث الطبيـعيـة تسـاءل في عنوانه «هل هي من صُنـع الطبيـعة أم الإنسان؟». هاكم إجابة على سـؤاله هذاك بعد أن نقلها إلى المستمعين برنامجنا «على مسرح الحياة».

إن المجاعة الرهيبة الحديثة في إثيوبيا أحد الأمثلة على أن كثيرا من الكوارث التي تبـدو في الظاهر من صنع الطبيـعـة إنما هي في الحقيـقة من صنع الإنسان. ويُضيف قـائـلا إنه حدث شُحّ في المطر في السـنوات الثلاث الماضيـة، ولكن الأهالي هناك أجهدوا الأرض بزرعها أكثر من اللازم كمـا قامـوا بقطع الكثيـر من الأشجـار في المرتفعـات الوسطى في البـلاد مما تسـبب في ضيـاع هذا المطر القليل وعـدم امتصـاص التربة له، وبالتالي لم يستطع الأهالي إنتاج أي مـحصـول على الإطلاق. ثم مـضى برنامـجنا يقول إن تآكل التـربة يحصل بفعل عـوامل التعـرية من أمطار ورياح وحرارة عالية طبيـعية ويحدث هذا التآكل في أشد درجـاته في الأراضي المزروعة التي تفقد تربتها الفوقية بسـهولة أكبر من الأراضي التي تغطيها نبـاتات طبيـعية فهذا الغطاء النبـاتي الطبيـعي يحـتفظ برطوبة بدرجة أكبـر، ولكنّ تآكل التـربة وفقدها في مرتفعات إثيوبيا شكّل شكلا كارثة حيث أن التربة المفقودة في

بعض المناطق وصلت إلى مائتي طن للهكتار الواحد سنويا وذلك في
مقابل أحد عشر طنا للهكتار وهو المعدَّل المقبول عالميا، إلا أن هناك
وجهة نظر أخرى: هناك رأي يقول ، ولكن لم تثبت صحته تماما بعد ، إن
فقد أو إزالة غطاء النباتات الطبيعي في المناطق الشبه القاحلة مثل
إثيوبيا يمكن أن يؤثر على المناخ حيث أنه يؤدي إلى نقص في هبوب
الرياح الجالبة للمطر. ولكن متى وصل تآكل التربة إلى درجة معينة
فإن المطر لو جاء لن يقضي على القحط أو المجاعة فقد هطلت في
إثيوبيا أمطار غزيرة لحوالى أسبوع ، كل ما فعلته هذه الأمطار هو أنها
كسحت المزروعات والتربة الفوقية في الحقول المرتفعة إلى الحقول
الأكثر انخفاضا على جانب التل ، كما أن هناك ناحية أخرى تتعلق
بالأشجار: في بداية هذا القرن تم تشجير مناطق كثيرة من إثيوبيا،
تصل مساحتها إلى أربعين بالمائة، أما اليوم فهذه المساحات لا تزيد عن
اثنين بالمائة، ولكن التآكل لا يقتصر على منطقة معينة ففي
الثلاثينيات من هذا القرن حدث تآكل في السهول الشمالية من
الولايات المتحدة الأمريكية تسبب في إفقار ملايين الفلاحين ، بل إنه
دفع ببعضهم إلى حافة الموت جوعا.

يقول الدكتور Roy Morgan خبير البيئة إن ما حدث في الولايات
المتحدة ما هو إلا مثل من أمثلة عديدة لما حدث في العالم على مر
العصور ، لقد كان السبب الرئيسي فيه هو امتداد الزحف الزراعي
إلى أراض ليست مناسبة للزراعة وخاصة إذا كانت أراض لا تصلح إلا
للري فقط. لقد تسبب ذلك في زيادة عوامل التعرية وخاصة تلك التي
تسببها الرياح.

iii In the English summary of this text, (most of) the following points should be
mentioned:

(a) The recent drought in East Africa has stunned the world.
(b) Scientists say disasters such as floods and drought should no longer be
regarded as 'natural' disasters.
(c) Many 'natural' disasters are in fact manmade.
(d) The cutting of trees to make way for agriculture has caused a drop in rainfall.
(e) Soil erosion takes place more in agricultural areas than in areas with natural
vegetation.
(f) Erosion in some areas of Ethiopia has reached 200 tons per hectare annually.

(g) Removal of natural vegetation has climatic effects and may lead to a drop in rain-carrying clouds.

(h) In eroded areas rain does not end the effects of drought. In Ethiopia a week of rains removed agriculture and top soil from the hills to the lower slopes.

(i) Early this century a forestation project in Ethiopia covered 40% of the country with trees. Today the forested area is only 2%.

(j) Erosion is not confined to specific regions. Erosion took place in the plains of North America in the 1930s resulting in the impoverishment of millions of farmers.

10. Written English texts
Suggested translation of 'Cairo poor swell in former land of plenty'.

فقراء القاهرة يتكاثرون
في بلاد [/أرض] الخيرات سابقاً

فَقَدَ والدُ أحمدَ عملَه في مصنعٍ منذُ سنتين، أما الآنَ فيستأجرُ كشكاً صغيرا حيث يكسبُ حوالي ثلاثين جنيها مصريا شهرياً (أو ما يعادلُ [/أي] اثني عشرَ جنيها استرلينيا في السوقِ السوداء) وهو يبيعُ السجائرَ والصابونَ والبسكويتَ. ويقولُ أحمدُ إنّ والدَه يستطيعُ بهذه الطريقةِ أنْ يكسبَ القليلَ من المالِ، «ولكنّ أبي يدخّنُ كلَ يومٍ علبتينِ على الأقلِ من سجائرِ الكشك مما يُقللُ [من] الأرباحِ بكثيرٍ».

أما أحمدُ [نفسُه] فيعملُ فراشاً يومينِ في الأسبوعِ. وتزيدُ أجورُه دخلَ الأسرةِ ثلاثةَ أضعافٍ وتمكّنُه من القيامِ بالدراساتِ العليا في المدرسةِ الفنيةِ المحليةِ. ويقولُ «لو لا المالُ الذي أكسبُه، لما سمحَ لي أبي بالذهابِ إلى المدرسةِ».

ينظرُ أحمدُ إلى التعليمِ على أنّه الوسيلةُ الوحيدةُ ليجدَ عملاً في الخارجِ فيتزوجَ البنتَ التي خطبها منذُ أكثرَ من سنةٍ، وهو من أبناءِ منطقةِ شبرا الواقعةِ في شمالِ العاصمةِ المصريةِ والبالغُ عددُ سكانها أكثرَ من أربعةِ ملايينِ نسمةٍ حيثُ يُعتبرُ من أكثرِ الأحياءِ ازدحاماً في العالمِ برمّتهِ، وتُعَدُّ هذه

الكثافةُ السكانيةُ الهائلةُ نتيجةً من نتائجِ الانفجارِ السكاني العجيبِ الحاصل في مـصـرَ والذي هو السـببُ الرئيسيُ في الأزمةِ الاقتصاديةِ الحالية .

11. Précis
Suggested guidance questions for the précis in Arabic of تزوج حتى لا تموت.

١ – ماذا تؤكد الدراسة التي أجريت حول الانتحار ؟

٢ – من هو الدكتور سامي عبد القوي؟

٣ – لماذا وجد الباحث صعوبة في إيجاد الكثير من محاولي الانتحار كعينة للدراسة؟

٤ – ما هو الدافع الأساسي للانتحار ؟

٥ – ما هي المشاكل الرئيسية التي تؤدّي الى محاولات الانتحار ؟

٦ – ما هو دور الآباء في محاولة الانتحار بين الشباب؟

٧ – ماذا يعوق الشباب من تحقيق أهدافهم؟

٨ – ما هي السمات الشخصية الرئيسية لمحاولي الانتحار ؟

٩ – لماذا يواجه محاولو الانتحار مشاكلهم بشكل سلبي؟

١٠-لماذا يقول الباحث إن محاولة الانتحار مجرد صرخة استغاثة؟

10
Gender

4. Written Arabic texts 1

(b) **ii** Answers to comprehension questions relating to المرأة المسلمة تعيش عصر الصحوة الإسلامية.

1. Dr Zeinab Ismet Rashid is a leading proponent of girls' teaching in al-Azhar.
2. According to Dr Rashid, Islam has given women human, civilian, economic and social rights.
3. According to Islam, the other شروع سماوية are Judaism and Christianity.
4. According to Dr Rashid, Islam has given women the following specific rights: the right to live, the right to inherit, to right to possessions, the right to dispose of her wealth as she wishes, and the right to express her opinion about who she should marry.
5. The rights of women in Islamic societies compare very favourably with the rights of women in other societies. Dr Rashid says that women do not enjoy the type of rights mentioned in 4. above in many non-Islamic societies.

(c) Suggested paraphrase of تُعتبر الأمية مشكلة إنسانية.

Millions of people are illiterate. Illiteracy is intricately bound with poverty, illness and ignorance. The UN announced 1990 as the year of eradication of illiteracy. According to UNESCO figures one in four adults in the world is illiterate, and while illiteracy is found in the developed as well as the developing world, most illiterate people are found in the developing world, particularly in Africa where more than half the population cannot read or write. Two thirds of illiterate people are women.

Poverty and illiteracy are related; however, in Sri Lanka, which is a very poor country, the level of literacy is very high.

In the developed world illiterate people may be able to identify letters and figures but will lack basic reading and writing skills.

5. Written Arabic texts 2

(a) Suggested translation of المرأة العربية ... دعوة إلى التغيير.

Arab women: a call for change

The debate over the role of women in Arab society has been raging for over a hundred years. Since the days of figures such as Muhammad Abdu and Jamal al-Din al-Afghani, the same questions have been raised by religious scholars and social reformers alike.

In this book Nadia Hijab considers why the role of women in Arab society – both as mothers and as producers – remains problematic. She comes to the conclusion that as with many other issues the resolution of this question awaits the resolution of the continuing debate concerning the role of Islam in Arab society.

In the second part of the book the author goes on to consider the possible effects on the structure of Arab society of the integration of women on an equal basis with men in all areas of employment. She concludes that the liberation of Arab women depends on the liberation of Arab society from the bonds of tradition, and that reformers must concentrate on changing social, political and economic structures.

(b) Suggested translation of وانفتح أمامي عالم واسع جديد.

A whole [lit: wide] new world opened up before me. At first I felt afraid, but soon I applied myself with voracity once the obsession with learning took its hold. Science revealed to me the secret of humanity and nullified the huge distinctions my mother had tried to make between me and my brother.

Science confirmed to me that women are like men and that men are like animals. Women have a heart, a brain and muscles just like men. Animals have a heart, a brain and muscles just like human beings. There are no essential differences between them; there are simply differences of form, while the fundamental and essential features are the same.

There is a man in the depths of [every] woman, and [every] man hides a woman in his depths. Women have the members of men, some of which are visible, others of which are concealed, and men have female hormones in their blood.

Human beings have a savage wild animal locked within the cage[1] of their chest, and there is a human being within [all] animals. Human beings have a tail: a short, docked tail in a small section at the base of their spinal column, and animals have a heart which beats, and tears which flow.

I took delight in this new world which placed women alongside men and men alongside animals. I took delight in science and felt that it was a strong, powerful, just god which knew the secrets of everything, and I [both] believed in it and embraced it.

Note
1. Metaphor in Arabic and English.

(c) **i** Answers to comprehension questions relating to القمة النسائية.

1. The women's summit was held in Geneva.
2. The wives of sixty-four rulers from around the world took part in the summit.
3. The summit is described as a noteworthy event.
4. The increase in poverty of women in rural areas was discussed at the summit.
5. Poverty affects children adversely both emotionally and educationally.
6. Young people are badly affected by poverty and often become violent and negative.
7. The living conditions of rural women forms an obstacle to rural development.
8. Husbands of rural women tend to work abroad.
9. This doubles the responsibilities of women.
10. Women produce 50–70% of the food. The question of food relief is conditional upon an improvement in women's conditions.
11. Had the UN invited world leaders to the summit instead of their wives there would have been:
    • Long preparation time due to the other commitments of world leaders.
    • Long-winded preparation of work programme.
    • Huge insurance costs for participants.
    • Marginalisation of the principal issue. Participants would have used the opportunity to arrange bilateral meetings on the margins of the conference. The spotlight would have been moved from the main hall to side rooms and backstage.
12. The matters which would have been discussed include:
    • Collapse of the Soviet Union.
    • Help to new republics.
    • Commercial protection.
13. The writer considers the main importance of the women's summit to be that it has made the world aware of a problem which would have otherwise remained neglected.

ii Linking phrases found in القمة النسائية include:

‒ ويصعب الحديث عن
‒ وعلاوة على ...

– يضاف إلى ذلك

– وإذا أخذنا في الاعتبار

– ومن الطبيعي

– ولذلك

– طبعا

– ولا مبالغة في القول

Once students have made lists of linking phrases used in the text they could produce a short essay of their own on a topic relating to gender issues in the Middle East in which they use cohesive words and phrases culled from القمة النسائية.

6. Written Arabic texts 3 (classical)
(a) Suggested translation of حُكِي أنَّ امرأة.

> It is said that a woman went before a judge to bring out a lawsuit against her husband over a son. The woman said, 'May God help you, this is my son. My belly has been a drinking vessel for him, my lap a courtyard, and my breast a milkskin. I have watched over him when he has got up and protected him when he has slept. I have done this for [several] years, and now that his weaning has come to an end, and his limbs have become strong and his qualities fine, his father wants [lit: has wanted/has come to want] to take him from me and send him far away from me.' The judge said to the man, 'You have heard what your wife has to say, what reply do you have?' He said, 'She has told the truth, but I carried him inside me before she carried him inside her, and I bore him before she bore [i.e. gave brith to] him. I want to teach him knowledge and make him understand wisdom.' The judge said, 'What do you say in response to what he says, woman?' 'He has spoken truthfully', the woman replied, 'but he carried him when he was light [lit: weak], while I carried him when he was heavy, and he bore him in accordance with his desire, while I bore him against my will.' The judge was deeply impressed by what the woman said and told the man, 'Give her her son. She is more deserving of him than you are.'

(b) Suggested translation of عيسى بن يونس قال.

> Isa ibn Yunus said, 'One of our sheikhs told us, "I heard Samra ibn Jundub say on the pulpit of Basra, "The Prophet of God, may God bless him and grant him salvation, said, "Woman was created from no more than a crooked rib, and if you strive to straighten it, you will break it, so be satisfied with her as she is and live with her."" '

One of the poets said,

> She is the crooked rib you cannot straighten.
>> If you straighten her ribs you will break them.
> Have you ever come across sturdiness[1] and strength in a young man?
>> Is it not amazing, her weakness and her strength?

Al-Hasan said, 'Umar ibn al-Khattab, may God be pleased with him, said, "Women are deficient [lit: deficiency], so hide them in their houses, and treat their weakness with silence."'

   Umar also said, 'Don't put your women up in upstairs rooms, and don't teach them the Book [i.e. the Qur'an]. Use their nakedness [as a weapon] against them, and use the word "no" a lot with them, because "yes" encourages them to ask [further] questions.' Al-Asma'i said, 'Aqil ibn Ullafa, who was very jealous, was asked, "Who did you appoint as your successor [as head of the family]?" He said, "The two protectors – nakedness and hunger", meaning that he would keep them hungry so that they would not have fun, and deny them clothing so that they would not be cheerful.'

Note

1. ضَلَعٌ = 'sturdiness'; pun on ضِلَعٌ 'rib'.

8. Aural Arabic texts 1

i Transcription of the first part of برنامج الأسرة.

عايز أيه يا أفراد الأسرة – التوفير سلوك مفيد وضروري في حياتنا، حيثُ توفير الشخص لأي شيء بسيط مما توفر له في يوم يشعر فيه بالراحة ليوم آخر يقال عنه بأنه يوم أسود، يُبعد عنه الضيق ويخفّف من ضغطه ويكفي عزيزتي ربة البيت لو أنك وزوجك حاولتما استقطاع مبلغ معين للمال شهريا ووضعته في مكان معين على أن تتّفقا معا على عدم لمس ذلك المبلغ إلا عند الحاجة، والحاجة الضرورية، ويكون ذلك المال كاحتياطي لكم من ظروف قد تأتي مما يجعلكم بحاجة للمال فمثلا لو تعرض أحد أفراد الأسرة لا قدر الله لمرض ما فهو سيحتاج بالطبع لمصاريف العلاج والطبيب، أو تعطل جهاز في المنزل كان يعمل، وأنتم بحاجة لأن يكون يعمل دائما، فبالتالي أنتم بحاجة للمال لإصلاحه فلا غنى لكم عنه.

ii Transcription of the remainder of برنامج الأسرة.

وما إلى ذلك من أمور قد تحدث لا تكون في الحسبان. أيضا عملية التوفير لها من الفوائد الأمور الكثيرة، حيثُ تُحقّق المتعة والرفاهية والسعادة للأسرة، فقد تكون الأسرة بحاجة لجهاز معين كتليفزيون أو مكينة خياطة أو غسالة، ويمكن لها أن تُحقّق ذلك عن طريق التوفير، حيث قد لا يتمكن الأب من شراء ذلك بالثمن المطلوب وفي الوقت المناسب، ولكن بالتوفير وبجمع المال يُمكن شراء ما تريده الأسرة وما يخدمها ويُدخل عليها المتعة والسعادة، أيضا يُمكنكما بالتوفير واستقطاع المال البسيط شهريا وجمعه في نهاية السنة وفي إجازة الأولاد من قضاء رحلة سعيدة ممتعة تُعيد للجميع الحيوية والنشاط وبالتالي استقبال العام الجديد بكل نشاط وحيوية، وتعودوا عايز أيه على التوفير وتعلموا وعلّموا من حولكم فوائد التوفير وعوائده الكثيرة.

9. Aural Arabic texts 2
Complete transcription of extract from BBC Arabic Service news broadcast from Mar. 5, 1990.

النبأ الأخير في هذه النشرة:

بدأت أعمال مؤتمر دولي حول التعليم يُقال إنه أكبر مؤتمر يُعقد في هذا الصدد ، بدأت في منتجع «غونج جونك» في تايلاند بهدف مكافحة الأمية. وقد أبلغ المشاركون في المؤتمر بأن مائة مليون طفل في جميع أنحاء العالم لا يتلقّون أي نوع من أنواع التعليم وأن هذا العدد يُتوقع أن يتضاعف خلال السنوات العشر القادمة كما يُنتظر أن يركز المؤتمر على نقص فرص التعليم المتوفرة للنساء اللاتي يشكلن ثلثي الأميين في العالم وعددهم ألف مليون شخص.

10. Written English texts

(a) Suggested translation of 'Egypt's first feminist organisation'.

ذكرياتُ رائدة نسائية

أُسّستْ أولُ منظمةٍ نسائيةٍ في مصرَ سنةً ألف وتسعمائة وثلاث وعشرينَ . وترأستْها هدى الشعراوي حتى وفاتها عامَ ألف وتسعمائة وسبع وأربعينَ . ولمدة جيلٍ كانتِ الشعراوي شخصيةً معروفةً محترمةً .

وخلالَ السنواتِ الأربعينَ الأولى لحياتِها عاشتِ الشعراوي ، كغيرها من نساء الطبقة العليا في مصرَ في ذلك الوقتِ ، في حالةٍ من العزلةِ . ولكنّها بخلافِ أغلبيةِ نساءِ هذه الطبقة سجّلتْ هذه « السنينَ المخفيةَ » في ذكرياتِها التي استكتبتْها سكريتيرتَها في أواخر حياتها .

وفي أوائلِ السبعيناتِ قد اكتشفتْ هذه الذكريات مرغو بدران وهي مؤرخةٌ أمريكيةٌ تبحثُ في تاريخِ النساءِ في مصرَ . وبالتعاونِ الوثيق مع حوّاء إدريس ابنة خال هدى الشعراوي قدْ حرّرتْ بدران هذه الذكرياتِ وترجمتْها إلى الانجليزيةِ .

(b) Suggested translation of 'She was born on the Nile delta'.

وُلدت في دلتا النيلِ في قريةٍ حيثُ أصبحَ والدُها أولَ شخصٍ يتلقى العلومَ. وبعدَ مرورِ جيلٍ واحد أصبـحتْ هي أولَ فتاةٍ تدخلُ الكليةَ. لقد كانتْ تودُ دراسةَ الأدب، ولكن بدرجاتِها العاليةِ أُقنعتْ بالذهابِ إلى المدرسةِ الطبيةِ. وفي النهايةِ نجحتْ في مجالي الطب والأدب. وبرغمِ أنّها كانت امرأةً ومن أسرةٍ فقيرةٍ وغيرِ مؤثرةٍ ارتقتْ إلى أن تصبحَ مديرةَ التربيةِ والتعليمِ في وزارةِ الصحةِ المصريةِ وبقيتْ في هذا المنصبِ من سنةِ ألفٍ وتسـعمائةٍ وستٍ وستينَ حتـى سنةِ ألفٍ وتسعمائةٍ واثنتين وسبعينَ. فقد اعترفتْ، ومنذُ أيامِها في المستوصفِ بأنّه الفقرُ وليسَ المرضَ الذي عليها أنْ تحاربَه.

11. Précis

(a) Suggested guidance questions for the précis in Arabic of القمة النسائية.

١ – أين عُقدت القمة النسائية؟

٢ – من شارك فيها؟

٣ – ما هو موضوع بحث القمة؟

٤ – ما هي أهمية هذه القمة؟

٥ – كيف تختلف تربية الأطفال في الدول النامية عن تربيتهم في الدول المتطورة؟

٦ – حسب الكاتب، لماذا تشكل الأوضاع التي تعيشها المرأة الريفية في الدول النامية «عائقا أمام خطط التنمية»؟

٧ – ماذا يعمل أزواج الكثير من النساء الريفيات في العالم الثالث؟

٨ – ماذا يعني هذا عمليا؟

٩ – لماذا يقول الكاتب إن «الصندوق الدولي للتنمية الزراعية .. أحسن صنعا حين اختار الدعوة إلى قمة نسائية»؟

١٠ – ماذا سيحدث نتيجة لهذه القمة؟

(b) Suggested guidance questions for the précis in Arabic of خيوط قصة.

١ – من هي الشخصيات الرئيسة في القصة؟

٢ – أين حدثت القصة؟

٣ – ما هي مهمة أعمار الشخصيات في القصة؟

٤ – ماذا تريد الزوجة؟

٥ – هل للحب في هذه القصة دور؟

٦ – في رأيك، ما هي رسالة القصة؟

11
Popular culture

4. Written Arabic texts 1

(a) Additional translation exercise. Suggested translation of ‏ترجمة حياة جحا‎.

Juha's life story

Sheikh Nasreddin Juha Al-Rumi is of Anatolian Turkish origin. He studied the Islamic sciences and became such an expert that he was appointed preacher, *imam* and Qur'an teacher in a number of cities. As a preacher,[1] he used to deliver his sermons in the form of jokes and sayings. He was courageous in standing up to rulers and judges and others in positions of power. He was a pious and ascetic man who used to till his own land and collect his own firewood. His home was a refuge for strangers and poor peasants. It is recorded that in 674 AH his mediation saved one town from the tyrant Tamburlaine [/Tamerlane/ Timur (the Lame)]. He lived to be sixty years old.

Juha has a magnificent tomb in his home town of Akshehir, which is crowned by a dome set on four pillars. It is said that the door of his tomb has a huge lock, even though the other three sides of the tomb are open. It is possible that this is something which he stipulated in his will, as a joke. The people of Akshehir are firm believers in the miracles of Juha. They festoon the door of his tomb with rags, in an attempt to cure themselves of fevers and to gain blessings. When they visit his tomb they laugh a lot, since they believe that anyone who goes there and doesn't laugh will be afflicted with some misfortune from which he will never recover. When they get married it is also the custom for the bride and bridegroom to first visit Juha's tomb and to invite the sheikh to the marriage party, with the words, 'Honour us together with your disciples'. They believe that anyone who gets married without performing this task will not have a happy marriage.

Note

1. ‏رحمه الله‎ 'God have mercy on his soul' missed out in translation.

5. Written Arabic texts 2

(a) **i** Answers to comprehension questions relating to الأدب هو تعبير عن حقيقة
وواقع إنسانيـين.

1. The writer defines أدب as an expression of human truth and reality.
2. Gnomic poetry is the result of the poet contemplating existence and the morals of man.
3. Sayings become proverbs when people use them repeatedly to recall the times when they were first coined as sayings.
4. Proverbs and gnomic poetry developed from notions which appeared in one or two verses of a *qasida*.
5. The originator of the proverb intends the proverb to express an opinion or principle.

ii Suggested translation of first paragraph of الأدب هو تعبير عن حقيقة وواقع
إنسانيـين

> Literature is an expression of human truth and reality. This makes it a record of what we observe, experience and either think or feel. Most literary texts – whether they be poetry or prose – have been spoken on different occasions. This applies to all forms of literature, including gnomic poetry which results from the poet contemplating the nature of existence and the morals of men, and deriving from this thoughts, lessons and counsel.

(d) **ii** Suggested translation of ثم يذكر أنه كان يحب الخروج من الدار.

> Then he remembered that he used to like to go out of the house when the sun was setting and people were having supper. He would lean on this fence-post deep in thought until he was brought back to his surroundings by the voice of a poet who had sat down a little to his left. People gathered around him and he began to recite to them in a strange but pleasant tone the tales of Abu Zayd, Khalifa and Diyab. They were silent except for when they were carried away with delight or were stirred by something. Then they would start to argue and shout again and the poet would fall silent until they had stopped their racket after a little or a long while. Then he would start up again with his pleasant recital in a tone which hardly ever changed.

6. Written Arabic texts 3 (classical)

(a) Suggested translation of الحريري صاحب المقامات.

Al-Hariri: the most famous composer of *Maqamat*

Abu Muhammad al-Qasim ibn Ali ibn Muhammad ibn Uthman al-Hariri, al-Basri al-Harami, the writer of the *Maqamat* [*of al-Hariri*] was one of the leading figures of his era and was blessed with the highest esteem in composing *maqamat*. These *maqamat* involved a great deal of the Arabic language, its dialects, proverbs and allusions to the secrets of its idioms. Those who knew the *maqamat* well could use them to demonstrate the superiority of this man, his knowledge and the abundance of his material. His son, Abu al-Qasim Abdullah, explained the reason for him compiling the *maqamat*. He said, 'My father was sitting in his mosque in Bani Haram when a an old man dressed in [no more than] a couple of old rags came up to him. The old man had just returned from travelling; he was of shabby appearance, eloquent, and elegant in his expressions. The assembled group asked him where he was from. He said he was from Saruj, so they asked him for his *kunya* and he said, "Abu Zayd". Then my father produced the *maqama* known as al-Haramiyya, which was the forty-eighth *maqama*. He attributed it to the above-mentioned Abu Zayd and it became famous. The minister Sharaf al-Din Abu Nasr Anushirawan ibn Khalid ibn Muhammad al-Qasani, minister of the Imam al-Mustarshid Billah came to hear about it. When he acquainted himself with it he liked it and urged my father to produce more, and in the end he completed fifty *maqamas*.'

(b) Suggested translation of السمكات الثلاث.

The three fishes

Once upon a time[1] there was a pool with three fishes. One who was cunning, one who was even more cunning, and one who hadn't got a clue.[2] The pool was in a far away place, so people scarcely ever approached it. Near to the pool was a flowing river. It happened[3] that two fishermen crossed the river. They saw the pool and arranged to come back with their nets and catch the fish in it. The three fishes heard what they said. When it hear what they said, the most cunning one [of them] grew suspicious and was afraid of them. It did not stop until it had made its escape from the place where the water entered the pool from the river. The one who was [less] cunning remained where it was until the two fishermen came. When it saw them and realised what they wanted, it made to escape at the point where the water entered the pool, but[4] they had blocked that place. Then it said, 'I have been careless, and this is the result of being careless. How can I find a way out of this situation? Those who do things in haste and under pressure are rarely successful, but those who are intelligent do not lose faith in the value of judgement, or despair, or abandon rational thought and activity.' Then it pretended to be dead. It floated on the surface of the water, rolling first over onto its back and then onto its front. The two fishermen took it out and put it on the ground between the river and the pool. It sprang into the river and escaped. The one who hadn't got a clue, though,[5] kept [swimming] up and down until it was caught.

Notes

1. زعموا lit: 'They claim …' is a traditional beginning to a tale.
2. Indefinite singular adjectives cannot be translated as such into English.
3. اتفق أن 'it happened'. اتفاقي 'accidental', 'fortuitous'.
4. إذا ب generally introduces a new subject which suddenly comes into view or is involved in a surprising event. It does not, in this case, mean 'suddenly they blocked the place', but rather, that the fish suddenly (and surprisingly) found that the place had been blocked by the men.
5. Translation of أما … ف introducing a different contrastive subject (cf. ch. 2, 7aii; ch. 17, 7a).

8. Aural Arabic texts 1

ii Answers to comprehension questions relating to حصاد الشهر, no. 33, side 2, item 2, هل جحا شخصية حقيقية أو أسطورية؟.

1. Muhammad Radwan Daya is the person who asks about Juha, and he is from the Faculty of Arts in the University of Damascus.
2. According to the writer, Juha is also called Nuh, Dujayn, Abdullah and Nuh al-Fazari.
3. Juha's kunya is Abu al-Ghusn.
4. Juha was born in 60 AH.
5. He died in 160 AH.
6. Mahdi is the son of Ja'far Mansur.
7. In his anecdotes Juha sometimes comes across as clever and sometimes as stupid.
8. Al-Khawja Nasr al-Din is said to be the Turkish Juha.
9. Some researchers do not believe that al-Khawja Nasr al-Din was a real person.
10. Nasr al-Din worked as an Imam, a teacher, a judge and a preacher.
11. He was known for his life of asceticism and piety.
12. His tomb is renowned for its miracles.

iii Complete transcription of ؟هل جحا شخصية حقيقية أو أسطورية
.

لقد ورد إلى برنامجنا «لكل سؤال جواب» سؤال عن حقيقة جحا.
فكلف البرنامج الدكتور محمد رضوان داية الأستاذ في كلية الآداب
بجامعة دمشق بإعداد الإجابة وقد قرئت الإجابة بالنيابة.

جحا شخصية حقيقية وليست أسطورة. وجحا هو اسمه وقيل بل
إنّ له اسم آخر فقيل هو نوح أو دجين أو عبد الله وروي عن الجاحظ أنه
نوح وهو جحا أو نوح الفزاري نسبة إلى قبيلة فزارة ويكنى أبو
الغصن. ولد جحا نحو سنة ٦٠ هجرية وأدرك عمر بن أبي ربيع الذي
قال «دلّهت عقلي وتلاعبت بي حتى كأني من جنون جحا». وتوفى سنة
١٦٠ بعد أن عمّر نحو قرن من الزمان وأدرك مدة أبي جعفر منصور
وابنه مهدي. ويظهر جحا من خلال أخباره ونوادره رجلا ذكيا فصيحا
قادرا على التكيف السريع مع الظرف والمناسبة، وهو يعالج الموقف
بالذكاء حينا وبالتحامق حينا آخر. وقد غلب عليه التحامق حتى أدخله
المؤلفون في إعداد الحمقى والمغفلين. ويرتبط الحديث عن أبي الغصن
جحا بالحديث عن نصر الدين خوجا الذي يقال فيه إنه جحا التركي. فإن
الشائع بين أيدي الناس من كتب مطبوعة عن نوادر جحا هو في
الحقيقة خليط بين نوادر جحا العربي والخوجا نصر الدين التركي.
والخوجا أي المعلم نصر الدين شخصية حقيقية أيضا وإن وجد في
الباحثين من ينكر وجوده. وقد تلقى نصر الدين علومه في بلدتي آق
شهر وقونية وتولى مناصب رفيعة كالإمامة والتدريس والقضاء
والخطابة في المساجد. وكان فقيها وواعظا مرشدا يأتي بالمواعظ في
معرض النادرة، وكانت له جرأة على الحكام والقائمين على الأمور وعُرف
بحياة الزهد والتقوى والنزاهة في كسب المعاش إلى كرم وجود
مشهورين. وفي تحديد زمان الخوجا نصر الدين خلاف ولعله كان في
القرن الهجري السابع/الثالث عشر الميلادي وتوفى عن ستين عاما، فهو
إذن أدرك أواخر دولة السلاجقة وبداية الدولة العثمانية، وكانت له
تنقلات واسعة في بلاد أناضول وله ضريح مشهور في آق شهر وهو عند
الناس معروف بكراماته وكرامات ضريحه. ونوادر جحا المدونة
والمتداولة على ألسنة الناس تجمع خليطا من أخبار جحا الحقيقية
ونوادره وأخبار نصر الدين ونوادره.

9. Aural Arabic texts 2

i Answers to comprehension questions relating to حصاد الشهر, no. 17, side 2, item 3, موسم التـين.

1. Man is said to be suffering from a cultural crisis today because there is a loss of balance between huge technical advancement and the relatively slow advancement in the human sciences.
2. The plants which play a role in Palestinian folklore are: olives, dates, grapes, figs and wild thyme.
3. The fig season in Palestine is in August.
4. Farmers call this seasons موسم القيـظ because of the intense heat.
5. During the fig season young men hope to be able to catch a glance of the girls of their dreams as they return to the village carrying baskets of figs and grapes on their heads.
6. The سوادي fig is said to be also called سلطان التـين because of its sweet flavour.
7. The بياضي fig is white in colour.
8. The سماوي fig is the most common fig in the country because it can withstand natural conditions better than any other type of fig.
9. The عسالي fig is so called because of its honey colour and its sweet taste.
10. The خضاري fig is greenish and similar in taste to the سماوي.
11. According to the speaker, the القيـسي fig probably got its name at the time of tribal conflict between the Qays and the Yemen.
12. The عديسي fig is said to have a colour similar to red lentils and to be similarly round.
13. The موازي fig is said to be as yellow as a banana.

ii Complete transcription of موسم التـين.

لن نخرج بموضوعنا التالي عن العلم ولو أننا سوف نتناوله من جانب
آخر هو الجانب التراثي الشعبي وهو يعكس حياة مجتمع معين وفق
المقومات الحياتية المتوفرة فيه وفي ظروف اقتصادية واجتماعية مميزة،
وبناءا على ذلك نشهد اليوم وثبة هائلة في ميدان البحوث الفكلورية
العربية . فعلم الفلكلور يسعى مع غيره من العلوم الاجتماعية إلى جعل
حياة الإنسان أكثر استمرارا ، وخصوصا في مثل هذا العصر الذي
يعيش إنسانه أزمة حضارية تتبين ظواهرها في فقدان التوازن بين
التقدم التقني الهائل والتقدم البطيء نسبيا في العلوم الإنسانية ،
ويرى الدكتور عيسى المصو أن البشرية اليوم أحوج ما تكون إلى
استعادة ثقتها بالقيم الأخلاقية والمثل العليا التي تمثّل مرتكزا قويا من

المرتكزات التي يقوم عليها الفلكلور. لقد زخر الفلكلور العربي الفلسطيني بثروة عظيمة تتعلق بالنبات على اختلاف أنواعه كالزيتون والبلح والعنب والتين والزعتر، ومنذ القدم اهتم الإنسان الفلسطيني بشجرة التين بحيث أصبح تراثها الشعبي ومأثوراتها القولية جزءا لا يتجزأ من واقعها، وكان لموسم التين في الفلكلور الفلسطيني حديث أسهب الدكتور عيسى المصو في الحديث عنه لبرنامجنا «ركن الثقافة» واعتبارا من هذا العدد سنبدأ بتقديم الجزء الأول منه:

يُعتبر شهر آب (أغسطس) بداية موسم التين ، ويطلق عليه الفلاحون اصطلاح موسم القيظ لشدة حرّه، ومعناه عند بعضهم التموين إذ يستكفي بعض الفلاحين بالإفطار صباحا على ثمار التين، ومن هنا جاء المثل «في موسم التين فيش عجين» كما كان القُطّين يبادل ببعض السلع التموينية، وكان هذا الموسم من أجمل المواسم الزراعية يترقبه الجميع كبارا وصغارا بفارغ الصبر والشباب يتمشورون في هذا الموسم في زرافات قبل الغروب نحو كروم التين أملاً في اقتناص نظرة نحو فتيات أحلامهم عند عودتهن إلى القرية حاملات سلال التين والعنب على رؤوسهن ، ويعبّر الأدب الشعبي بصدق عن أحاسيس الشباب في هذا الموسم: «سقى الله أيام العنب والتين يوم من الحلوى تصير تلاقيني غرب البلد لزراعة القطين يوم تمرقي بتذكرينا». وللتين أسماء محلية عديدة منتزعة من صميم بيئة الفلاح وقد نجد أسماء مختلفة للنوع الواحد في المناطق المختلفة، وهي على وجه العموم أسماء اصطلح الفلاحون عليها ومن أشهرها السوادي ويُسمّى بسلطان التين لحُلو ثمره، البياضي سمّي كذلك لبياض لونه الذي يميل إلى الخضرة، السماوي وهو الأكثر شيوعا في البلاد نظرا لتحمله ظروفا طبيعية تفوق قسوة ما يتحمله غيره من أنواع التين ، العسالي وسُمّي بهذه التسمية لأنه عسلي اللون ولأنه أكثر أنواع التين حلاوة ومن خصائصه ظهور نقطة من السائل الحلو على رأس الثمرة الناضجة ، الشحيمي وتتميز قشرته بسمكها وكأن طبقة من الشحم تعلوها، الخضاري ولونه يميل إلى الخضرة وطعمه شبيه بطعم السماوي، القيسي وهو حامض المذاق وربما أطلق اليمنيون هذه التسمية زمن الصراع القبلي بين القيسية واليمنية، المُلَيَّسي وتنزلق الثمرة من اليد عند محاولة قطفها لرقة قشرتها، العديسي ويشبه لونه لون حبة العدس الأحمر كما

يشبهها باستدارته، الموازي وثمرته طويلة ولونه أصفر كالموز. ومن أنواعه أيضا الشنّيري والأصبيعي والقراعي والمواني وغيرها، وهذا الأخير مخصص لأكل العائلة لكونه من أجود أنواع القطين. أما الأنواع الأخرى فقد لا تزال تُزرَع في الكرم الواحد ولكن لا يُزرع إلا القليل منها لكي يُؤكل ثمرها طازجا فقط. فتُسَمَّى «أطعَام» نسبة للطعام.

10. Written English texts

(a) Suggested translation of 'The Moroccans claim Si' Djeha as an inhabitant of Fez'.

يزعمُ المغاربةُ أنّ سي جحا من سكان مدينة فاس فيسمّونه سي جحا الفاسي كما أنهم سمّوا شارعًا باسمه في المدينة نفسها. أما تاريخُ جحا في المشرق فأعقدُ من ذلك بكثيرٍ. فيُذكر في كتاباتٍ عربيةٍ ترجعُ إلى العصور الوسطى أنّ رجلا اسمُه جحا عاش من العمر مائةٍ في مدينةِ كوفةَ في العراقِ في القرنِ الثامنِ الميلادي. وفي عام أَلفٍ وثمانيمائةٍ وثمانينَ م. صدر في القاهرةِ أولُ مجموعةٍ حديثةٍ لرواياتِ جحا تحتَ عنوان «نوادر الخوجةِ نصرالدينِ المسمَّى جحا الرومي». وهناك قبرٌ يُدَّعَى أنه قبرُ الخوجةِ نصرالدينِ التاريخي في مدينةِ «آق شهير» في تركيا لا يزالُ يقومُ بزيارتِه المعجبون بجحا. ويُقال إنّ جحا هذا عاش فترةً مع حاشيةِ قائدِ الموغول «تيمورلنك»، الذي غزى الأناضولَ وبغدادَ في القرنِ الرابعِ عشرَ الميلادي.

(b) Suggested translation of 'Si' Djeha and the Qadi's coat'.

سي جحا وبرنس القاضي

ذاتَ يومٍ كان سي جحا يتنزهُ على أطراف المدينة فصادف القاضيَ يشخرُ تحتَ شجرةٍ وهو يصحو من سكرتِه الأخيرة. كان القاضي قد استغرق في النوم استغراقاً لدرجة أنّ سي جحا استطاع أنْ يخلعَ منه برنسَه الصوفيَ الجديدَ الجميلَ دونَ أنْ يوقظَهُ.

وعندما استيقظ القاضي وأدرك أنّ برنسَهُ الثمينَ قـد سُرق منه بعث برجاله للبحث عنه . وبعد وقتٍ قصيرٍ تعرّفوه على ظهرِ سي جحا وجرّوه إلَى المحكمة . وطلب منه القاضي « كيف أصبحتَ تملكُ مثلَ هذا البرنس الجميل ؟ » فأجاب جحا « رأيتُ كافرًا قد سكرَ سكرةً شديدةً يَرقدُ تحتَ شجرةٍ وتنبعثُ منه ريحـةُ الخمـرِ ، فـبصـقتُ على لحيـة الكافـرِ وأَخَذتُ منه البرنسَ ، ولكن إذا طالب حضرتُكم بالبرنسِ فمـن حـقِّكم أَنْ تستـرجـعـوهُ » وأجاب القـاضي فـاحـاً « لم أرَ هذا البـرنسَ في حياتي ، إليك عني وخذْ معك البرنسَ ! »

11. Précis
Suggested guidance questions for the précis in Arabic of علي بن زايد.

١ – ماذا نعرف عن علي بن زايد؟

٢ – هل علي بن زايد شخصية حقيقية أو أسطورية؟

٣ – لماذا يقول الكاتب « أما من حيث العصر الذي عاش فيه علي بن زايد، فلا نستطيع الوقوف علي تاريخ محدد لذلك »؟

٤ – ماذا يقول الكاتب عن أقوال علي بن زايد؟

12
Muslim Spain

5. Written Arabic texts 2

(b) **ii** Suggested translation of كان المجتمع الأندلسي فريدا من نوعه.

The social structure of Islamic Spain was unique, comprising not only Arabs and Berbers, but also the indigenous inhabitants of the country. Of the latter, some embraced Islam and were known initially as *masalima* ('new converts') while their descendants who were born and brought up in an Islamic environment were called *muwalladun* ('Muslims by adoption'). Others remained Christian and these people were known as *'ajam* (i.e. 'non-Arabs'), or *musta'ribun* ('would-be Arabs'), or in Spanish Mozarab. The *muwalladun* included both freemen and slaves. Some of the *muwalladun* retained their old Spanish names. Over time close links grew up between the original Muslims and the new converts as a result of contact and intermarriage. This intermixing had a marked effect on the ethnic composition of Islamic Spanish society. In the tenth century, a new client-group appeared known as the *saqaliba* ('Slavs'[1]). This group originally consisted of prisoners taken from the north of the country. Islamic Spain also contained a large number of non-Muslims, both Christians and Jews, who provided the Muslims with valuable services during their conquest of the peninsula.

Note

1. cf. Bernard Lewis, *The Arabs in History*, p. 136.

6. Written Arabic texts 3 (classical)

(a) **i** Suggested translation of ذكر سلفنا رضي الله عنهم.

Our ancestors, may God be pleased with them, mentioned that there is a certain island in India, which is south of the equator, and that on this island people come into being without a mother or a father ...

... There are those who reject this account, and have given a different account of what happened to him, which we shall tell to you. According to this account, there was opposite that island, another huge island with large cultivated areas. It was bountiful, and densely populated, and was owned by a man who was extremely proud and jealous. This man had a daughter, whom he held back and prevented from marrying, because he had found no-one equal to her. He had a relative called Yaqdhan, who married this girl secretly in a way which was lawful according to the religious customs which they followed at that time. The girl subsequently became pregnant by Yaqdhan and gave birth to a child. She became fearful that she would be discovered, and that her secret would become known, so she took the baby out at nightfall, with a group of her servants and confidantes to the edge of the sea. Her heart was burning with love and fear for the baby. Then she bade it goodbye, and said, 'My God, you created this baby, and it was not anything to be mentioned; you nurtured it in the darkness of the womb, and looked after it until it became complete. Now I entrust the baby to Your care and beseech Your grace for him, out of fear of this unjust, tyrannical and willful king. So, give him Your support, and do not deliver him to the king, oh Most Merciful of the Merciful.' Then she threw the baby into the water, and a powerful current of water carried him off that very night to the shore of the island which has previously been mentioned. At that time the tide reached up to a point which it would only reach again in a year's time. The water carried the baby into a thicket of reeds, which closed in around, and was sweetly shaded, which was protected from the winds and rain, and sheltered from the sun, which was deflected from it when it rose, and inclined away when it set. Then the water began to go out again. The box remained where it was, and the sands subsequently built up, until they blocked the water from entering the reed thicket, so that the high tide couldn't reach that far. The nails of the box had been weakened and its boards had been shaken loose by the action of the water against them in the reed thicket. When the child began to feel hungry, he cried and called out for help, and tried to move. His cries were heard by a gazelle which had lost her fawn, and she followed the sounds, thinking that they came from the fawn. She eventually reached the box, and tested it with her claws, while the baby was crying inside. Suddenly, one of the boards came away from the top of the box. The gazelle bent down, soothed him and gave him her teats to suck. She suckled him with her freely flowing milk, and continued thereafter to take care of him, rear him, and protect him from danger.

ii Additional exercise: identification of *pronoun>noun* shifts in English translation of ‪.ذكر سلفنا رضي الله عنهم‬

The English translation of this Arabic text illustrates very well the tendency for English to make greater use of nouns, and for Arabic (and particularly classical Arabic) to rely more on pronouns. As a supplementary exercise, students who have done the translation exercise (and have possibly been given a copy of this suggested translation) could be asked to identify *pronoun>noun* shifts from the Arabic original to the English translation.

(b) Suggested translation of ‪.سلام على تلك الديار‬

A greeting to those abodes

(composed while the poet was in prison;
he recalls Cordoba and the days which he spent there as a young man)

Noble Cordoba, is there any hope of return to you?
And can a heart be quenched which has become parched through
    separation from you?
Is there any way back to your nights of high renoun?
For beauty is made visible in you, and pleasure audible,
And the far expanses of the earth are made easily accessible.

Is it not extraordinary that I should be so far away from you?
I live as though I have never forgotten your fragrance.
As if I had never met up with old friends in your paths,
As if my creation did not originate with your dust,
As if I had not been first embraced by your quarters.

Your day is bright, and your night is clear.
Your ground receives the morning shower and your branches become
    intoxicated.
Your earth is clothed when your air is naked.
Your fragrance is refreshment for the soul – as aromatic as basil.
Sufficient for all desires is your shadow when its shade is sought.

My imprisonment gives no pleasure to my enemies,
For I have seen the sun deal harshly with the dark clouds.
I have been but a stern and angry sword in a sheath,
A lion in a forest, or a hawk in a nest,
Or a precious stone lying hidden in a musk-box.

8. Aural Arabic texts 1

ii Complete transcription of أول ترجمة للاتينية.

المذيع … من برنامج «معرض الرأي» موضوعًا يتعلق بتأثير عرب الأندلس في أوروبا. ويناقش هذا الموضوع الأستاذ الدكتور حسين مؤنس الأستاذ بجامعة القاهرة ومدير معهد الدراسات الإسلامية في مادريد والأستاذ الدكتور وليد عرفات الأستاذ في جامعة لندن. والموضوع هو كما يلي: حكم العرب في إسبانيا قريباً من ثماني مائة سنة. فما الذي خلفه العرب هناك وما الذي أحدثوه من آثار في المدنية الغربية؟ يا دكتور مؤنس تفضل ..

د. مؤنس أولاً نحن لا نقول اليوم إن العرب حكموا إسبانيا، إن إسبانيا كانت عربية.

المذيع لطيف.

د. مؤنس لم يكن هناك عرب يحكمون الأندلس لأن العرب في أي بلد دخلوه تمثّلوا البلد وتمثّلهم البلد وأصبح أهل البلد عرباً.

المذيع لطيف.

د. مؤنس وفي الأندلس نقول إن إسبانيا نفسها كانت في دور من أدوار حياتها … تاريخها … عربية. وفي هذا الدور لم تكن كل الأندلس عربية طوال الثماني مائة سنة. إنما كان هناك مدّ وجزر وزيادة ونقصان حتى انتهى الأمر في شهر يناير ١٤٩٢ بنهاية القصة.

المذيع نعم.

د. مؤنس خلال هذه المدة بنى العرب وأعْلَوْا، وفي كل فن من الفنون وفي كل علم من العلوم، تركوا آثاراً جليلة يُستحسن أن نتناولها واحدة واحدة وسيتفضل أخي الدكتور عرفات بذكر العلوم واحدةً – أو واحداً واحداً وننظر ماذا بنى

العرب فيه وماذا تركوا.

المذيع   تفضل يا دكتور.

د. عرفات   شكراً. الواقع أن التراث غني فلا يدري الإنسان من أين يبدأ. لعلّ أبسط الأمور التي ترد على الذهن حالاً أن التلامذة من الغرب كانوا يأتون إلى الجامعات العربية في إسبانيا يدرسون كما يأتي الطلاب العرب الآن من أنحاء العالم أو الطلاب من جميع أنحاء العالم ... عرب ... وغير عرب إلى الجامعات في الغرب. ففي القرن الثالث عشر مثلاً بدأت أول مدرسة للدراسات الشرقية في طليطلة وفي ذلك الوقت جاء من إنجلترا Adelard of Bath، Robert of Chester، Roger Bacon، Michael Scot ثم Gerard of Cremona. جاء هؤلاء فأخذوا عن العلماء العرب العلوم بأنواعها من الطب وعلم الهيئة، الجغرافية، ثم النبات ... كُتُب قيمة جدًا في مواضيع الطب والجراحة ... كفرعين منفصلين دُرسا كما يُدرسان اليوم في مدارس الطب. مثلاً جاء Adelard of Bath فتَرجم إلى اللاتينية «زيج» الخَوارزمي (أو الخُوارزمي) ثم ترجم Gerard of Cremona «كتاب الهيئة» لجابر ابن الأفلح، وترجم أيضاً «كتاب التعريف» للزهراوي، «المنصوري» للرازي، و«القانون» لابن سينا. هناك استعملوا أول ما استعملوا كلمة «الجيب» في الرياضيات ...

د. مؤنس   المثلثات ...

د. عرفات   ابن سبعين الغافقي ...

د. مؤنس   أظن توفّي سنة ألف ومائة وخمسة وستين ميلادية.

د. عرفات   جمع أسماء النبات وأضاف أسماءها بالعربية واللاتينية والبربرية. يعني هذا العمل في حد ذاته هو ما يطمح إلى مثله عالم النبات اليوم أو في أي وقت آخر ... في أي زمن آخر ...

المذيع   لطيف.

د. عرفات   ابن البيطار في النبات والصيدلة. تَصَوَّرْ كتب ابن رشد في الطب. ثم ابن ميمون وهنا يمكن للإنسان أن يُضيف أن

هذا الرجل الإسرائيلي اشترك في تقديم شيء للتراث العربي تحت السماح الذي عُرف به التقليد [الإسلامي]. ثم اُضطرّ إلى الخروج من إسبانيا فذهب إلى مصر.

د. مؤنس   نعم.

د. عرفات   وهكذا في الفلسفة نقلوا ما كتبه الأغريق. وكثير من تراث الإغريق حفظه للغرب – للأجيال التالية – العرب في نصوص عربية وأضافوا إليه ما أضافوا. الموسيقى. حتى ابن العربي الصوفي المعروف تأثر بها وأثّر. ثم طليطلة، كانت مركزاً للترجمة وRobert of Chester ترجم القرآن أول ترجمة للاتينية.

9. Aural Arabic texts 2

i Answers to comprehension questions relating to حصاد الشهر, no. 7, side 2, item 3, دين الغرب للعرب في الموسيقى.

1. Eleven instruments introduced by the Arabs into Spain are listed in the text.
2. Seville was the centre of production of Arab musical instruments.
3. Cordoba was the centre of Arab sciences.
4. Mansur Ben Abd al-Mu'min presided over the debate mentioned in the text.
5. According to Averroes, if a scholar died in Seville then his books would be taken to Cordoba to be sold.
6. According to Averroes, if a musician died in Cordoba then his possessions would be taken to Seville to be sold.
7. According to the text, the Arabs conquered Spain in the eighth century AD.
8. Music books and manuscripts were translated into Latin in Toledo.
9. 'Villancico' singing became widespread in Spain in the fifteenth century AD.
10. The Arabs in Granada were the first to use letters of the alphabet to indicate the position of the hand on the guitar.
11. The emotional characteristics of Fado music are sadness and longing.
12. Dr Husayn Mu'nis describes Fado music as Bedouin chanting which has reached us across the seas and epochs in a Bedouin guise.

ii Complete transcription of دين الغرب للعرب في الموسيقى.

أدخل الفاتحون العرب إلى شبه جزيرة إيبيريا عددا كبيرا من الآلات الموسيقية الجديدة. فبالإضافة إلى الآلات الموسيقية الخمس والعشرين التي وردت أسماؤها اللاتينية في معجم المشتقات من تصنيف اسيدور

فإن العرب أضافوا الآلات الموسيقية التالية والتي أصبحت تُعْرَف باللغة الإسبانية بالأسماء الآتية: «الدوف» وهي من الدف، «الجبابة» وهي من الشبابة، «البوغند» البوق، «النفيل» النفير، «التبل» الطبل، «كنون» القانون، «اندرت» البندير أو الطنبور، «سوناخس دي السوفار» سنوج الصفر أو النحاس، «نكير» نقارة، «لوت» العود، «ريبك» الرباب. وكانت إشبيليا مركز صناعة الآلات الموسيقية العربية كما كانت قرطبة مركز العلوم العربية. قال ابن سعيد: «وجرت مناظرة بين يدي منصور بن عبد المؤمن بين الفقيه العالم أبي الوليد ابن رشد والرئيس أبي بكر ابن زهر»، فقال ابن رشد لابن زهر في كلامه «ما أدري ما تقول، غير أنه إذا مات عالم بإشبيليا فأُريدَ بيعُ كتبه حُملت إلى قرطبة حتى تباع فيها وإذا مات مطرب بقرطبة فأُريدَ بيع تركته حُملت إلى إشبيليا». إن فاتحي الأندلس المسلمين في القرن الثامن الميلادي لم يُدخلوا معهم آلات موسيقية عديدة ما زالت تحمل في اللغة الإسبانية أسماءها العربية الأصلية فحسب بل إنهم جلبوا معهم كذلك رسائل وكتبا في الموسيقى العربية تُرجمت إلى اللغة اللاتينية في مدينة طليطلة ثم ذاعت منها في شمال إسبانيا. وثمة أوجه شبه كبيرة بين الأزجال الأندلسية والغناء الإسباني الذي ذاع في القرن الخامس عشر الميلادي والمعروف باسم «فيلانجيكو» مما جعل بعض الباحثين يعتقدون بوجود صلة قوية بين النوعين من الأشعار الغنائية، كما أن ثمة من الدلائل الأدبية الباقية ما يوحي بأن العرب في مملكة غرناطة قبل سقوطها في أيدي النصارى عام ألف وأربع مائة واثنين وتسعين للميلاد كانوا أول من استعمل الحروف الهجائية للدلالة على موضع الإصبع من القيثار. إن الزائر إلى بلاد البرتغال في أيامنا هذه يحرص على الاستماع إلى وصلات من الغناء الشعبي البرتغالي يرافقه عازف على القيثارة وهو غناء يشوبه الحنين والحزن ويُعرف بالبرتغالية باسم «فادو» وهذه الكلمة تحريف للفظ العربي الحدو أو الحداء. إن هذا اللون من الغناء الشعبي البرتغالي هو كما يقول الدكتور حسين مؤنس حداء بدونا عبر البحار والعصور وصل إلينا في غلاف برتغالي.

10. Written English texts

i Rough translation of 'The Arabs left their mark on Spain' with alternatives.

فـقد تـرك الـعرب أثرهم فـي إسبـانيـا [an it is also possible to use –] ليـس فـي ... فـقط/فـحـسب .... بل أيضًا فـي خـبـرة [/مـهـارة/بـراعـة] الـفـلاح [الإسبـاني] والـصنائـعي [/الصانـع] [الإسبـاني][/فـلاحيها وصانعيـه] وفي الكلمات التي يسـتـعمـلها أبـنـاء الشـعب لـيصفـوا هذه الخبرة وفي فـن شبـه الجزيرة [/شبـه الجزيرة الإيبيرية] ومبـانيـها [/فنها المعماري] ومـوسيقاها وفي علوم الغرب في العصور الوسطى وفلسفتها [/وفيـما تطور فـي العـصور الوسطى فـي الـغـرب مـن علوم وفلسفـة] والتي [كـان قـد] أَثْـرَاها الـعـرب بـنقل تـراث العـالـم العـتيق [/الثـقافات القديمة] مـحـفـوظةً [بإخـلاص] مطورةً [/مزيّنةً].

وقد استمـر أيضًا ذكرى الأندلس [/إسبانيا العـربيـة] عند المغـتـربين [/المهـجـرين/الجـاليـة الأندلـسيـة] في المغرب [العربي/الكبير/شمـال أفريقيا] والذين لا يزال الكثير منهم يحـملون الأسمـاء الأندلسيـة ويحـتـفظون بمفاتيح بيـوتهم [الكائنة/الموجودة] في قرطبة وإشبيلية معلقةً على حيطانهم [/الحيطان] في مـراكش والدار البيـضـاء، كـمـا أن الزوار المشارقة إلى إسبانيا في الأوقات [/السنوات] الأخيـرة مثل الشاعر المصري أحمد شوقي والعالم السوري محـمد كرد علي قـد ذكّروا عـرب الشرق بإنجازات إخوانهم الأندلسيـين فـأعادوا ذكر الإسلام الإسبـاني إلى مكانته المناسبة [/إسبانيا الإسلامية إلى مكانها المناسب] [/المكانة التي يستـحـقـها] في الوعي القومي العربي [/الوعي العربي القومي].

ii Suggested final translation of 'The Arabs left their mark on Spain'.

قد ترك العرب بصماتهم في إسبانيا ليس فقط في خبرة فلاحيها وصانعيها وفي الكلمات التي يستعملونها ليصفوا معلوماتهم بل وأيضاً في فنون شبه الجزيرة ومبانيها وموسيقاها وما تطور فيما بعد في الغرب خلال العصور الوسطى من علوم وفلسفة والتي أثْرَاها العرب بنقل تراث الثقافات القديمة التي قاموا بالمحافظة عليها بل وتطويرها.

ولم يخبُ بين المهاجرين الأندلسيين في شمال أفريقيا ذكرى وطنهم الأول حيث لا يزال الكثير منهم يحملون الأسماء الأندلسية ويحتفظون بمفاتيح البيوت التي تركوها في قرطبة وإشبيلية معلقةً على جدرانهم في مراكش والدار البيضاء، كما أن الزوار المشارقة القادمين إلى إسبانيا في السنوات الأخيرة مثل الشاعر المصري أحمد شوقي والعالم السوري محمد كرد علي قد ذكّروا عرب الشرق بإنجازات إخوانهم الأندلسيين فأعادوا بذلك مكانة إسبانيا إلى عهدها السابق في الوعي العربي القومي.

iii Additional exercise: comparison of translations of 'The Arabs left their mark on Spain'.

Ask students to compare their own translation with the various alternatives offered in the two translations above.

11. Précis
Suggested guidance questions for the précis in Arabic of إذا كانت تلك المنطقة.

١ - كيف اقتاد الممالك المسيحية في شمال اسبانيا بملوك الاندلس الاسبانية؟

٢ - من هي مانويلا كورتيس؟

٣ - ما هو دور عبد الرحمن الاول في نشر الموسيقى العربية في الاندلس؟

٤ - ما هو دور عبد الرحمن الثاني في هذا الصدد؟

٥ - من هو زرياب، وماذا عمل؟

٦ – في اي مدينة تركزت المدارس الموسيقية؟

٧ – كيف نُظمت الحفلات الموسيقية في عهد ملوك الطوائف؟

٨ – ماذا حدث بالموسيقى الاندلسية في العالم العربي بعد سقوط غرناطة؟

٩ – ما هما الشقان اللذان يتكون منهما البحث عن الموسيقى الاندلسية في رأي مانويلا كورتيس؟

١٠ – ماذا بقي من الموسيقى العربية في الممالك المسيحية الاسبانية بعد سقوط غرناطة؟

١١ – ما هو دور المورسكيين في ابقاء الموسيقى العربية بعد سقوط غرناطة؟

١٢ – ما هي اهم آثار الثقافة العربية التي ما زالت موجودة في الثقافة الاسبانية الشعبية حتى يومنا هذا؟

13
Arab nationalism

4. Written Arabic texts 1

(c) Suggested translation of يقوم الوعي القومي.

National consciousness is based primarily on a true interpretation of the community's past, an understanding of the natural and historical factors which have gone towards making it what it is today, and a discovery of the sources of its particular spiritual strengths which distinguish this community from others. The nationally conscious Arab knows where he has come from, the historical path taken by his community, and the roots of his present life. He can pinpoint the origin of the Arab race; he can follow it as it spread from the Arabian Peninsula to surrounding countries, and came to dominate and mingle with other races, developing into a community which although of mixed blood and race, is – far more importantly – united by the bonds of nationhood, i.e. by language, tradition, past struggle, and present and future commitment. Despite all this, the nationally conscious Arab also knows what modern scholars have to say about the meaning of the word 'race', and the importance for the formation of a race of genetic factors, on the one hand, and of the environment, on the other. He also understands the nature of the relationship of race to nationalism, and the political, social and intellectual movements which have emerged in response to problems of ethnicity in both East and West.

5. Written Arabic texts 2

(a) **ii** Suggested translation of اتفاق اليمنين.

The agreement between the two Yemens: a stronger Arab world

The agreement reached between the two parts of Yemen to solve the outstanding border disputes and to engage in joint exploitation of oil is an important step on the road to unity for the two halves of the country. It is a victory for [the will of] rationality over ignorance, and for [the will to] goodwill over hatred. The people of Aden and the people of Sana'a need joint action towards unity; even more they need oil money in order to build up their country which has suffered enormously during the long years of poverty and deprivation.

The Arab world does not need further bloodshed on top of the continuing inter-Arab bloodletting. This was why the agreement between the two parts of Yemen was greeted with such joy and optimism in the Arab world both by politicians and by a general public which has suffered and continues to suffer, just as Yemen has suffered, from division and internecine slaughter.

Yemeni oil means a stronger Arab world, and will bring great benefit to the people of Yemen. Something which brings benefit should not be a cause of division and internecine strife within one country. On the contrary, joint investment in oil in the disputed regions will strengthen the sense of unity amongst Yemenis, and will confirm their feelings that the continuing division of their country is a national calamity.

(b) **ii** Suggested translation of كم كتب عن حريق القاهرة.

How much has been written about the Fire of Cairo, and how much more remains to be written. Everyone was accused of starting it, including myself. I have no objection. I do not absolve myself of guilt for what happened; however my involvement is quite unlike that claimed in the police interpretation of the 'conspiracy', as they called it. If 'involvement' in the Fire of Cairo of 26th January, 1952 is taken to mean participation in and encouragement of demonstrations, possession of explosives, or destruction of cinemas and other places of entertainment, these are matters of which I am entirely innocent, and with which I have no connection. However, if what is meant is the involvement of the entire people in bringing down a[n entire] regime, then of course I am one of the people.

However, there is a very fine line between criminality and revolution. In the case of the Fire of Cairo the two were so intertwined that historians, academics and lawyers have found it impossible to reach a definitive conclusion regarding the person or persons responsible for the Fire of Cairo.

According to the Nationalists, it was the Palace and the British who burnt the Egyptian capital. To this list the Communists add the Muslim Brothers and sometimes Young Egypt. Others have claimed that the Wafd were implicated; others again the Free Officers. Once again I find myself saying, 'I have no objection'. More important than all of this is to draw the line between criminality and revolution. The Fire of Cairo was not ignited by a single spark; rather, there were many contributory factors.

By the end of 1949 my associates and myself had begun to move beyond the phase of chance encounters, spontaneous outbursts and cliquish gatherings. We took the first steps towards setting up the main cell of the Organisation of Free Officers, of which I was chosen as leader, as I have previously mentioned. We took a keen interest in the 'sparks' which had begun to fly since the end of the war in Palestine. We followed the revolution of Husni al-Zaim in Syria, which had proved successful in March of that year, for example. We also followed the repeated failure of Farouq to establish any minority constitutional government, as well as the wave of assassinations of individuals, one of which I personally took part in.

(c) Answers to comprehension questions relating to أفلام للمناسبة ويوم عطلة.

1. The date of the Egyptian revolution was 23rd July 1952.
2. The title of the Egyptian president's speech in commemoration of the revolution was 'The importance of the revolution in writing a new political history of Egypt'.
3. The Third Channel can only be received in and around Cairo.
4. Yusuf al-Siba'i was the officer who held the post of Minister of Culture during the revolutionary era.
5. Opposition groups commemorated the event by holding seminars.
6. Over the past twenty years the event has been traditionally celebrated by a speech from the President, a film and a holiday.
7. The 'Open Door' economic policy was introduced by President Anwar Sadat.
8. Egypt is now describable as a 'quasi multi-party' society because a number of old forces have entered the political arena including the Wafd and the Muslim Brothers.
9. The three opposition groups and parties which are mentioned are: the Wafd, the Muslim Brothers and Young Egypt.
10. The odd thing about the Muslim Brothers is that they have entered the political arena despite the fact that they have still not been officially recognised [as a party].

11. The major current trend which is opposed to the principles of the Egyptian revolution is the peace process with Israel.

6. Written Arabic texts 3 (classical)
ii Suggested translation of وأمّا أحياءُ البدو.

The Bedouin tribes are restrained from violence against one another by their sheikhs and elders through the dignity and esteem with which they are standardly regarded by everyone. Their encampments are defended by the protectors of the tribe [namely] their courageous warriors and young men who are known amongst them for their bravery. They can only be properly defended and protected if they are are a group possessing social solidarity and [a group having] a single lineage, because through this their sense of vigour is increased and they are more greatly feared. The clamour which each one of them makes in battle on account of his lineage and tribal solidarity is of the utmost importance. The compassion and the furore in battle for those who are of the same parentage and family which God has placed in the hearts of His servants is one of the aspects of human nature. This gives rise to mutual aid and assistance and increases the fear of them in the enemy. Consider this in respect to the Qur'anic tale of the brothers of Joseph, peace be upon him, when they said to his father, 'If the wolf has eaten him, we, being a single band, are thereby the losers.' The meaning of this is that an attack on a person is unthinkable when he has the support of a group.

8. Aural Arabic texts 1
Complete transcription of جمال عبد الناصر, no. 7, side 1, item 3, حصاد الشهر
يؤمم قناة السويس.

قرار من رئيس الجمهورية بتأميم الشركة العالمية لقناة السويس .
باسم الامة ، باسم الامة ، رئيس الجمهورية ... مادّة واحد: تُؤَمم الشركة
العالمية لقناة السويس البحرية شركة مساهمة مصرية. وينتقل الى
الدولة جميع ما لها من اموال وحقوق وما عليها من التزامات. وتحَلّ
جميع الهيئات واللجان القائمة حاليا على إدارتها. ويُعوّض المساهمون
وحملة حصص التأسيس عما يملكونه من اسهم وحصص بقيمتها مقدّرة
بحسب سعر الإقفال السابق على تاريخ العمل بهذا القانون في بورصة
الاوراق المالية بباريس ويتمّ دفع هذا التعويض بعد إتمام استلام الدولة
لجميع اموال وممتلكات الشركة المؤممة.

9. Aural Arabic texts 2

i Suggested additional exercise: transcription of aural text.
Complete transcription from 'Extracts from speeches by Gamal Abdul Nasser',
side 1, item 1, ‏أيها المواطنون‏.

‏أيها المواطنون اننا لن نمكن من المستعمرين او المستبدين، اننا لن نقبل
ان يعيد التاريخ نفسه مرة أخرى، اننا قد اتجهنا قدما الى الامام لنبني
مصر بناءا قويا متينا نتجه الى الامام نحو استقلال سياسي واستقلال
اقتصادي، نتجه الى الامام نحو اقتصاد قومي من اجل مجموع هذا
الشعب، نتجه الى الامام لنعمل. ولكنا حينما نلتفت الى الخلف انما
نلتفت الى الخلف لنهدم آثار الماضي آثار الاستبداد آثار الاستعباد آثار
الاستغلال آثار السيطرة، انما نتجه الى الماضي لنقضي على جميع
آثاره. واليوم ايها المواطنون وقد عادت الحقوق الى اصحابها. حقوقنا
في قناة السويس عادت الينا بعد مئة سنة. اليوم انما نحقق الصرح
الحقيقي من صروح السيادة ونحقق البناء الحقيقي من ابنية العزة
والكرامة. لقد كانت قنال السويس دولة في داخل الدولة شركة مساهمة
مصرية ولكنها تعتمد على المؤامرات الاجنبية وتعتمد على الاستعمار
وأعوان الاستعمار. بُنيت قنال السويس من اجل مصر ومن اجل منفعة
مصر ولكن كانت قنال السويس منبعا للاستغلال واستنزاف المال. وكما
قلت لكم منذ قليل ليس عيبا ان اكون فقيرا او ان اعمل على بناء بلدي
ولكن العيب امتصاص الدماء. كانوا يمتصون الدماء يمتصون حقوقنا
ويسلبونها. واليوم حينما نستعيد هذه الحقوق اقول باسم شعب مصر
اننا سنحافظ على هذه الحقوق ونعض عليها بالنواجد، سنحافظ على
هذه الحقوق ودونها ارواحنا ودمائنا، اننا سنحافظ على هذه الحقوق
لاننا نعوّض ما فات، اننا حينما نبني اليوم صرح العزة والحرية
والكرامة نشعر ان هذا الصرح لا يمكن ان يُبنى او يكتمل اكتمالا الا اذا
قضينا على صروح الاستبداد والذلة والمسكنة وقد كانت قنال السويس
صرحا من صروح الاستبداد وصرحا من صروح الاقتصاد وصرحا من
صروح الظلم.‏

ii Suggested translation of أيها المواطنون.

Fellow citizens! We will not concede power to the despots and colonialists. We will not allow history to repeat itself. We have taken the first step towards building a strong and stable Egypt. We are moving forwards towards political and economic independence. We are moving forwards towards a national economy for the benefit of the entire Egyptian people. We are moving forwards to create something new. And when we look back, we only look back in order to destroy what remains of the despotism, servitude, exploitation, and domination of the past. We only turn to the past in order to destroy all that remains of it. Today, fellow citizens, our rights have been returned to their rightful owners. Our rights to the Suez Canal have been returned to us after one hundred years. Today, we are building the edifice of true sovereignty, honour and glory. The Suez Canal was a state within a state, an Egyptian limited company, but one which depended on foreign conspiracies, and on the combined forces of colonialism. The Suez Canal was built for the sake of Egypt and for the benefit of the Egyptians. But it became a source of exploitation and of financial expropriation. As I said to you earlier, there is nothing shameful in being poor, or in working to build one's country. What is shameful is to be a parasite. These people were parasites; they stole from us and expropriated our rights. Today, as we regain these rights, I say in the name of the Egyptian people: We will retain these rights; we will hold fast to them; we will sacrifice our lives for them if necessary. We will hold fast to these rights because we are recompensing ourselves for everything that has passed. Today, as we build the edifice of glory, freedom and honour, we believe that this new edifice can only be properly built if we destroy the edifice of despotism, servility and misery. The Suez Canal was part of the edifice of despotism, economic power, and oppression.

10. Written English texts
Suggested translation of 'Gamal Abdul Nasser'.

جمال عبد الناصر (١٩١٨-١٩٧٠)

وُلد جمال عبد الناصر في خمسة عشر يناير/كانون الثاني عام ألف وتسع مائة وثمانية عشر م. في مدينة الإسكندرية حيث عمل أبوه كاتباً في مكتب البريد، وكان أكبر طفل في أسرة متكونة من أحد عشرة طفل وتربى أثناء نضال مصر لتحقيق

استقلالها الوطني من بريطانيا. فساهم ناصر في الكفاح الوطني وهو لا يزال طالبًا في المدرسة ثم شرع في دراسة القانون في جامعة القاهرة لكنه انضم إلى الجيش المصري عام ألف وتسع مائة وسبعة وثلاثين م. وسرعان ما تفوّق كعسكري وشارك في حرب فلسطين عام ألف وتسع مائة وثمانية وأربعين.

وأما في عام ألف وتسع مائة وتسعة وأربعين فأسس ناصر منظمة الضباط الأحرار وكانت منظمة سرية داخل صفوف الجيش المصري هدفها القيام بثورة في مصر وهو هدف حققوه خلال انقلابهم المنشود يوم اثنين وعشرين يوليو/تموز عام الف وتسع مائة واثنين وخمسين فأرسلوا الملك فاروق إلى منفاه. وكان من الواضح أن ناصر هو اليد الحديدية في الفئة الحاكمة الجديدة فأصبح في نوفمبر/تشرين الأول عام الف وتسع مائة وأربعة وخمسين رئيسًا لجمهورية مصر.

11. Précis
(a) Suggested guidance questions for the précis in Arabic of ثورية الوحدة العربية.

١ – ماذا يقول الكاتب في اهداف «البعث العربي»؟

٢ – متى أُسّس «البعث العربي»؟

٣ – لماذا تسمى بـ«البعث العربي»؟

٤ – على قول الكاتب ما هو الفرق بين البعث العربي وغيره من الاحزاب الناشئة في الاقطار العربية؟

٥ – في رأي الكاتب ما هو الفرق بين الحرية والاشتراكية؟

٦ – ماذا يمنع اتحاد الاحزاب القطرية ذات الاهداف الواحدة؟

(b) Suggested guidance questions for the précis in Arabic of حفنة تراب.

١ – لماذا جاء الناس إلى بور سعيد؟

٢ – ماذا حدث لتمثال الجندي المجهول؟

٣ – كم عمر الجنود الكنديين بصفة عامة؟

٤ – بأي مدن أوروبية يقارن الكاتب مدينة بور سعيد؟

٥ – من أين سيأتي السواح في رأي الكاتب؟

٦ – ما معنى عبارة «سيكون هناك بحر»؟

٧ – أين توارى البوليس الدولي بالليل؟

٨ – ما اسم المطربة اليونانية؟

٩ – ما هي مناسبة دعوة زوجة صديق الكاتب؟

١٠ – لماذا استدرجت هذه الزوجة الكاتب إلى البلكونة؟

١١ – ماذا قال الزوج عن الصور؟

١٢ – كيف تغير سلوك الزوج؟

14
Islamic fundamentalism

4. Written Arabic texts 1

(a) Suggested brief paraphrase of الأصوليـون هاجمـوا مكتبـة.

> The day before yesterday Islamic fundamentalists attacked the office of
> a Coptic Christian organisation in Asyut. They destroyed tapes of
> church music and broke a number of chairs before the police arrived.
> The police arrested the fundamentalists and are looking for seven others
> who were involved in the attack.

(b) Suggested structure translations based on مقتل متظاهر.

١ – عَيَّنَتـه الحكومـةُ رئيسًا للجنة.

Note forms such as رئيسٌ وزيرٌ للداخليـة 'Minister of the Interior'.
It is also possible to say وزيرُ الجمهورية 'President of the Republic'.
رئيس الجمهورية , الداخليـة, etc.

٢ – أمرهـم الجيش بعدم التظاهر.

The structure with أمَرَ is أمـر شـخصًا بشيء 'order s.o. to do s.t.'
This parallels a number of verbs of saying or informing; e.g. شـخصًا
أنذر شـخصًا بـشيء 'inform s.o. of s.t.', or as in this text أفاد بـشيء
'warn s.o. of s.t.' 'Not to' can be expressed by عدم + noun 'lack of
....'. عدم + noun (especially verbal noun) often gives the sense of
'non+noun' in English, e.g. عـدم الانحيـاز 'non-alignment', عدم
التدخل 'non-interference'.

٣ – كان هناك ركودٌ مما أسفر عن المزيد من المشاكل الاقتصادية.

Note that in the phrase كان هنـاك/سيكون هنـاك 'there was/will be',
the noun (in this case ركود) is the subject. This is also true in structures
using the other common verb meaning 'there is/was', etc. وُجـدَ, e.g.
سـيُوجَد ركودٌ (cf. ch. 1, 7d). The phrase مما is used to mean
'that/which' when the relative clause relates to the entire main clause, and

not simply to a particular noun (or noun phrase) within it (cf. ch. 8, 7d).
Thus, in this example it is **the fact** *that there was an economic recession*
which led to further economic problems, and not simply the economic
recession (although this second interpretation would also be possible, in
which case the sentence would be translated as كان هناك ركودٌ أسفر
الأمرُ is مما (عن المزيد من المشاكل الاقتصادية). An alternative usage to
الذي (literally 'the matter which') (cf. ch. 12 7d), and this sentence
could also be translated as كان هناك ركودُ الأمرُ الذي أسفر عن المزيد
من المشاكل الاقتصادية. The most idiomatic way of translating
'further/additional/more' + noun is المزيد من. So 'more/further
information' المزيد من المعلومات. This is more common than the use of
an adjective such as إضافي.

٤ – عملت مهندسةً.

The normal way of saying 'work as' is to use the verb عمل or, less
formally اشتغل followed by the relevant noun in the accusative.

٥ – اعتقلوا الوزير السابق المُتَّهَم بالفساد.

اعتقل is perhaps the most common Standard Arabic word meaning
'arrest'. Alternatives are قَبَضَ علـى and وقّف, the latter having a
slightly wider range of meanings (cf. Wehr). 'To accuse s.o. of s.t.' is
اتّهم شـخـصـاً بشيء (و هـ م) (form VIII from root). Participle forms
frequently translate as English 'who/which/that'. Participles, like other
adjectives, are always directly preceded by الـ as the marker of
definiteness, and never by الذي, etc. It is possible to substitute a
participle with a verb in an example like this. Thus اعتقلوا الوزير
السـابـق الذي أتُّهم بالفساد. In this case الـ is substituted by الذي etc.
as the marker of definiteness.

٦ – تحدّثت الجريدة عن قتل الجيش عددًا من المتظاهرين

There are two possible structures involving verbal nouns which
correspond to the simple sentence قَتَلَ الجيشُ عددًا من المتظاهرين 'the
army killed a number of demonstrators', i.e. a simple sentence involving
subject, *verb* and *object*. The first is تحدّثت الجريدة عن قتـل الجيش
عددًا من المتظاهرين i.e. *idafa* construction consisting of *verbal noun*
(corresponding to verb in simple sentence) + *noun* (corresponding to
subject in simple sentence) followed by *object* (noun in accusative,
corresponding to object in simple sentence). The second possible
construction is تحدّثت الجريدة عن قتل الجيش لعدد من المتظاهرين:
i.e. *idafa* construction consisting of *verbal noun* (corresponding to verb
in simple sentence) + *noun* (corresponding to subject in simple sentence)
followed by *noun*+لـ (corresponding to object in simple sentence). The
second of these two structures is the more common.

٧ – الديمقراطية هي التي يطالب بها الشعب.

The sentence can be broken up into two parts in Arabic (i) الديمقراطية (known in traditional Arabic grammar as المُبْتَدَأ, i.e. *the initial element*), and (ii) هي التي يطالب بها الشعب (known in traditional Arabic grammar as الخبر, i.e. *the new element/information*). The second part هي التي يطالب بها الشعب can be again divided into two parts, (i) هي and (ii) التي يطالب بها الشعب. This kind of structure *noun* X + *pronoun* Y + *noun* Z (or phrase functioning as a noun, such as التي يطالب بها الشعب) is typically translated either as 'X is what etc. Z ...', or 'It's X what etc. Z ...' . Thus المدير هو الذي أريد أن أُقابله, 'The director is who/the one who I want to meet' or 'It's the director I want to meet' (cf. ch. 14, 7b).

٨ – ستُجَنِّبُ هذه الإصلاحاتُ الحكومةَ ثورةً.

Form V verbs are often intransitive, where form II verbs are transitive. So كَلَّمْتُه 'I spoke to him', but تَكَلَّمْنا 'we spoke (to one another)'. In this case the form II verb expresses the idea that the action was done to someone else, while the form V verb expresses the basic event. In cases where the form V verb is transitive, as in تَجَنَّبَ 'to avoid', the form II verb may be doubly transitive (take two objects), as in جَنَّبَ. In this case, it will sometimes be necessary to translate the form II verb into English by a phrase, rather than a single word, e.g. 'allow to/cause to/make avoid'. Note that it is possible to have the word order *verb–subject–object1–object2*. However, this is a little inelegant, and writers might well put the subject first, e.g. هذه الإصلاحاتُ ستُجَنِّبُ, أمّا هذه الإصلاحاتُ فَستُجَنِّبُ الحكومةَ ثورةً or الحكومةَ ثورةً, assuming these are appropriate to the context (cf. ch. 13, 7aii).

5. Written Arabic texts 2

(a) **iii** Suggested translation of ليس إسلامًا

This is not Islam, and these are not Muslims

As an Arab and an Egyptian, I would claim to know as much about Islam as any enlightened Muslim. I would also claim that together with Islamic civilisation Islam forms the very basis of our culture, embracing all the positive aspects of the non-Islamic cultures which have contributed towards our national consciousness.

I can therefore claim with a clear conscience that none of the incidents which have recently taken place in Al-Minya, Abu Qarqas, Beni Mizar or elsewhere have anything to do with Islam, or have even been perpetrated by Muslims.

None of the noble Quranic verses or the genuine or fabricated

Hadiths which are used by these evil groups to influence the simple masses can change this incontrovertible truth.

Is there any true Muslim who would burn down his Christian neighbour's house or shop, or would attempt to kill him, because there is a rumour – or a 'fact' – to the effect that one particular Christian has engaged in immoral behaviour?

Two or more years ago a rumour started going around in my own home town of Tama in Upper Egypt about a Coptic 'scientist' from the area who invented a gadget containing a coloured liquid, which, when it is fired at the clothes of young Muslim women, imprints them with the sign of the cross!

Not even Soviet or American scientists have been able to come up with such an astonishing invention. What miracles take place in Egypt!

The resulting communal discord has, unfortunately, been encouraged by some elements of the Cairo press, which, under the pretext of defending Islam, have talked in all seriousness about the possibility that certain Copts might actually have carried out such imbecilic acts, and have even set about trying to locate the gadget which regularly sprays crosses, but has never once sprayed a crescent moon!

(b) Suggested translation of لقد تطورت ظاهرة التطرف الديني.

Religious fundamentalism has grown very rapidly over the past ten years, spreading from one Arab country to another, and broadening its base – especially among the young – in most Arab countries. In a number of Arab states, fundamentalism has been transformed from a marginal element, with little influence on mainstream life, to an active and rapidly expanding phenomenon; and in many Arab and Islamic societies, supporters of fundamentalist movements exercise an ever-increasing influence on political and social affairs. The last five years have also witnessed the failure of simple security measures, as have been employed by many governments, to combat the plethora of Islamist groups which engage in various forms of social and political violence. Rather than leading to the disappearance of these groups, however, or a change in their tactics, or the intimidation of the masses who provide the popular base for their support, such measures, which have been excessive in certain Arab countries, have led to a spiralling cycle of tit-for-tat violence, resulting in the death and injury of hundreds of people, the further deterioration of the security situation, and increasing social and political destabilisation. Even more seriously, the intellectual and political attitudes of many of these groups have begun to make increasing headway amongst the young, and there has been a marked increase in general social tension. As a result, it has begun to seem as if religious extremism is the only problem facing Arab and Islamic governments and peoples, and that, at the same time, it is a problem without any foreseeable solution.

6. Written Arabic texts 3 (classical)
(a) Suggested translation of أهمية الولاية.

The importance of authority

It should be known that the exercise of authority over people's affairs is one of the most important religious duties. Indeed, it is impossible for religion to function without it. For human beings can only achieve what is in their common interest through collective action, because of the need they have for one another; and when they act collectively, they must necessarilyhave a leader. As the Prophet, God bless him and grant him salvation, said, 'If three people set off on a journey, they should invest one of them with authority.' This was related by Abu Da'ud, on the authority of Abu Sa'id and Abu Hurayra.

Imam Ahmad said in the *Musnad*[1] on the authority of Abdullah Ibn 'Amr that the Prophet, God bless him and grant him salvation, said, 'It is only permissable for three people to be in trackless country, when they have invested one of them with authority.' So the Prophet enjoined the granting of authority to one person even in the case of minor and transient collective action on a journey, thereby drawing attention to other kinds of collective activity, because God has enjoined man to command what is customary [good] and to forbid what is not customary [evil]. This can only be achieved through power and authority. The same is true with regard to other things which God has enjoined such as *jihad*, upholding justice, performing the pilgrimage, the Friday prayer, prayer on feast days, aiding those who have been wronged, and executing lawful punishments. These can only be achieved through power and authority.

For this reason, it has been related, 'The ruler is the shadow of God on earth.' It is also said, 'Sixty years with an unjust ruler is better than a single night without any ruler.' Experience shows this to be true. Therefore the early followers of the Prophet, such as Al-Fudayl ibn 'Iyad and Ahmad ibn Hanbal and others used to say, 'If we were to have one prayer which was to be answered, we would pray on behalf of the ruler.' The Prophet, God bless him and grant him salvation, said, 'God wants you to abide by three things: to worship Him and not associate anything with Him, to hold fast together to the rope of God and not to scatter, and to give good counsel to those whom God has placed in command of your affairs.' This was related by Muslim. He also said, 'There are three things which the heart of a Muslim will never betray: devotion to the work of God, giving good counsel to those in authority, and abiding by what has been agreed by the Muslims.' This prayer would be answered on their behalf. This is recounted by the *Compilers of the Sunan.*[2] In the *Sahih,*[3] it is recounted that the Prophet said, 'Religion is to ask advice. Religion is to ask advice. Religion is to ask advice.' They said, 'Of whom, Messenger of God?' He replied, 'Of God, of His book, of His Messenger, and of the leaders of the Muslims and of the common people.'

It is necessary to consider leadership a part of religion and a good deed through which one draws closer to God. For drawing close to Him in doing such a good deed, in obeying Him and obeying His Messenger is one of the best good deeds one can do, although most people become corrupted by it because of their desire for leadership or wealth through it [authority].

The goal of the man who wants leadership is to be like Pharaoh, and the goal of the man who amasses wealth is to be like Korah. God Almighty has revealed in His book the situation of Pharaoh and Korah. The Almighty has said, 'Did they not walk on earth, and did they not see the end of those who came before them? They were more powerful than them, and had greater influence on earth, but God took them for their sins and there was no-one to protect them from God.' The Almighty has also said, 'That is the Other Abode, which we shall make for those who do not desire superiority on earth or corruption, and it is the end for the God-fearing.' People are of four kinds:

One group who want to be exalted over other people and want corruption on earth. This is a sin against God. Those corrupt kings and leaders such as Pharaoh and his associates, these are the worst of creatures. God Almighty has said, 'Pharaoh exalted himself on earth and made the people of earth into different factions, weakening one group of them, slaughtering their sons and letting their women live. He was one of the corrupt.'

The second group are those who desire corruption without exaltation, such as thieves and other criminals and ignoble people.

The third group desire to be exalted without corruption, such as those who have a religion through which they desire to exalt themselves over other people.

The fourth group are the people of heaven, who desire neither exaltation nor corruption on earth, although they may be exalted over other people. As the Almighty has said, 'Do not lose courage or become downhearted for you will be the exalted ones if you are Believers', and He has said, 'Do not lose courage, but call for peace, and you are the exalted ones. God is with you and will not bring your deeds to nought.'

He has also said, 'Greatness belongs to God, to His Messenger and to the Believers.'

Notes
1. The *Musnad* (المسند) is a collection of 30,000 hadiths produced by the jurist أحمد ابن حنبل, who was the founder of the Hanbali school of law (مَذْهَب).
2. The أهل السنن are the compilers of the nine authoritative collections of *hadith*, the most important of which are the collections of البُخَاري and مُسْلِم, both of which, but particularly the former, are known as الصَحيح.
3. The *Sahih*: i.e. الصحيح of البخاري.

(b) Suggested translation of ينكر تعالى.

God Almighty rejects [all] those who deviate from His judgement – which is firmly established, embraces all that is good, and rejects all that is evil – and turn away to other opinons, whims and practices which have been established by men without basis in the Law of God. This was how the people of the pre-Islamic era used to make their judgements on the basis of erroneous and ignorant notions. It is also how the Tatars rule on the basis of royal ordinances [lit: policies] taken from their King Genghis Khan, who drew up the *yasaq* for them. This is a book put together from judgements adopted from various codes of law: Jewish, Christian, Islamic [lit: [that of] the Islamic nation], and others. It also contains numerous judgements which are simply based on Genghis Khan's own views and whims. Amongst his descendents, it has become a code of law which is adhered to, and to which precedence is given [lit: to which they give precedence] over the judgements of the Book of God and the practice of the Apostle of God (God bless him and grant him salvation).

8. Aural Arabic texts 1
Complete transcription of the recording by الشيخ كشك from a tape entitled زلزال القاهرة.

أيها الاخوة الاعزاء، يؤسفني كثيراً ان اقرأ يوم الاثنين الماضي في إحدى الصحف ان عضوين من اعضاء مجلس الشعب تقدّما بسؤال الى وزير الثقافة والاعلام، وقلتُ سبحان الله، هل يسألانه «لماذا لم تطبّقوا شرع الله؟» هل سألاه «لماذا لم تغلقوا شارع الهرم ليفيض عليكم الله بالكرم؟» هل سألاه «لماذا لم تغلقوا الخمّارات؟» هل سألاه «لماذا لا

تمنعون السيارات الملاكي التي تحمل ذئبا ونعجة فيها يزنيان؟ لماذا لم تمنعوا موائد القمار في جبل المقطَّم بالعملة الصعبة؟ لماذا يا وزير الاعلام لم تنظر الى اولادنا بعين الرحمة فتحجب إعلامك الفاسدَ عن بيوتنا؟» الامتحانات على الابواب. لم يبقَ على الامتحان إلا ثلاثة أشهر ... لماذا لم تمنع افلامك؟ ومسرحياتك؟ ومبارياتك؟ على أولادنا الذين هبط مستواهم إلى الدَرَك الاسفل من المعرفة؟ لماذا؟ ألأنك تملك ستين مدرِّساً يدرِّسُ لاولادك دروساً خصوصية وغالبية الشعب لا تجد الغذاء ولا الكساء ولا الغطاء ولا الدواء؟ لماذا؟ امنع اعلامك، امنع مسرحياتك عن بيوتنا، امنع افلامك، امنع مبارياتك، امنع هذا الإعلام الذي حطّم البيوت وحرَّض النساء على الرجال. لكن شعرت بالأسى وكأني اردد قول القائل «تمخَّض الجبل فولد فأرًا» . أتدرون ماذا كان السؤال الذي توجّب .. توجّه .. به اثنان من مجلس الشعب الى وزير الثقافة؟ ان هذا السؤال سؤال مرّ ومؤسف، مؤسف جدا. هل سألاه عن مصير المسجد الاقصى؟ هل سألاه عن تحرير فلسطين؟ هل سألاه عن هؤلاء الذين يُضرَبون بالنابالم ويحاربون بالحرب الجراثيمية في افغانستان؟ لا انما سألاه وقالا له «لماذا منعتم اذاعة برنامج على الناصية؟ » يا خيبة الله غذّي السيرَ مُسرعةً، برنامج على الناصية. اي ناصية؟ ناصية كاذبة خاطئة. اي ناصية. اي ناصية يا عضوي مجلس الشعب؟ يا من وضع الشعب أيديَه في يديكما وعاهدتما الشعب على المطالبة بتطبيق الكتاب والسُنّة ولكن فاقد الشيء لا يعطيه. أيقطعون يد السارق؟ اذا قطعوا يد السارق فمن الذي يصفق. إنَّ التصفيق بيد واحدة لا يقع ولا يكون. أيحرِّمون الخمر؟ هل هم على استعداد أن يفقدوا أمزجتهم؟ هل يحرِّمون أكل الحرام وما مُلِئَت البطون إلا بالحرام؟ برنامج على الناصية. كم خاب ظنّي فيكما كم خاب ظنّي فيكما، ولكنني اشكوكما الى من يعلم خائنة الأعين وما تُخفي الصدور. كفى تهريجاً. كفى ضحكاً على ذقون الشعب. برنامج على الناصية، وهل برنامج على الناصية سيُطْعِم البطون الجوعى؟ هل برنامج على الناصية سيوجد مسكناً لكل شابّ يريد الزواج؟ هل برنامج على الناصية سيُكبِّرُ رغيف العيش بحيث يُشبع الطفل؟ والله إنها خيبة، إنها خيبةُ ما بعدها خيبة.

9. Aural Arabic texts 2
Complete transcription of حصاد الشهر, no. 7, side 1, item 4, هـل تـسـتـطـيـع الثقافة العربية أن تواكب العصر؟.

اما عن الثقافة العربية فمضى الاستاذ الشاذي القليبي يقول:

ان منزلتها اليوم لا تختلف اختلافا جوهريا عن منزلة المجتمعات العربية نفسها في التبعية وعدم الاقتدار على التصرف الذاتي، ذلك ان الحركة الثقافية عندنا تتجاذبها نزعتان كبيرتان: نزعة الحفاظ على الماضي وما يكتنفه من تراث وتقاليد، ونزعة التقليد لكل ما يظهر عند الامم المتقدمة من مذاهب ادبية وفنية وفكرية، لذلك لم تزل ثقافتنا هي ايضا في منزلة من التبعية المزدوجة تجاه التراث القديم وتجاه الثقافات الاجنبية الغازية، وان ظاهرة التبعية هذه هي التي تعلل ما نجده في العالم من قلة الاهتمام بثقافتنا المعاصرة، ومن اعراض عن ترجمة نماذج من انتاجنا الادبي والفكري الى مختلف اللغات الحية، ذلك ان انتاجنا لم يرتق بعدُ الى منزلة من الشمول الانساني تجعله ينفذ الى كبرى الاغراض من خلال التأصل في البيئات المحلية، والقضية لا تخص محتوى الانتاج وحده بل هي تهمّ ايضا اللغة التي تُستعمل في الاداء والتبليغ، فالفصحى لغة كانت قد انقطعت مدة طويلة عن حركة الانشاء والابتكار في كل ما يرجع الى الحياة اليومية والفكرية فلم يكن من الهين ان تسترجع قدرتها على الاداء والتبليغ، نحن ننتمي لحضارة قـد دخلت منذ قـرون في طور الانغلاق والانكمـاش في كافـة المـيـادين الفكرية والعلمية والصناعية والاقتصادية، فتعطل الحوار فيها تدريجا بين الفكر والواقع وبين المجتمعات العربية وسائر المجتمعات التي انطلقت نحو الرقي والازدهار، فتباطأت حركة الخلق الحضاري عندنا حتى تجمدت وتحجرت واصبحت مجتمعاتنا آلة عن الماضي لا تمارس عملية الابداع والابتكار الا قليلا في مختلف شؤون الاجتماع والفكر فكان من المحتوم ان تتقلص طاقاتها الانشائية في كافة مجالات الحضارة المادية منها والادبية. واليوم نعود تحريك اوصالها ودفع الحيوية في احشائها لانا ثقافيها من روح العصر وهو من اعظم العمور، ولكنا اقدمنا على هذا العمل وفي انفسنا كتلة من المركبات تجعلنا لا نقوى على الانطلاع بالتـجـديد على الوجـه الصـحـيـح، ذلك انه غلب علينا الشعور، الشعور بالنقص تجاه الحضارة الجديدة واتهمنا انفسنا ولعنّا

الماضي وتقاليده مما لم يضع لنا طاقة على الايمان والخلق، فبقدر ما نؤمن ان احياء الثقافة العربية لا معنى له اذا عزمناه عن العملية الحضارية الرامية الى احياء المجتمعات العربية، نعتقد ان لا طائلة من وراء هذه العملية او تلك اذا لم تكن في سياق روحي صحيح اي اذا لم تكن متجهة معا الى الحفاظ على الاصالة الروحية والقضاء ايضا على العراقيل التي تمنع التطور والنمو والتفتح وتحول دون الخلق والابداع.

10. Written English texts
Suggested translation of 'Islamic fundamentalism'.

<h1 dir="rtl" style="text-align:center">الأصولية   الإسلامية</h1>

A. Paragraph 1, lines 1–4 – in context of presentation of new line of argument (cf. ch. 16, 7bii.iii).

لقد اجتذبت مدن الدول الإسلامية نتيجةً للنمو الاقتصادي المتسارع في أعقاب صحوة الاستقلال السياسي لهذه الدول أعدادًا هائلة من المهاجرين القادمين من الأرياف والذين ينتابهم الشعور بالضياع وعدم الإنتماء إلى محيطهم الجديد.

B. Paragraph 1, lines 1–4 – in context of continuation of previous argument (cf. ch. 13, 7ai.iv).

ونتيجةً لتسارع النمو الاقتصادي الذي أعقب صحوة الاستقلال السياسي في الدول الإسلامية اجتذبت المدن أعدادًا هائلة من المهاجرين القادمين من الأرياف والذين ينتابهم الشعور بالضياع وعدم الإنتماء إلى محيطهم الجديد.

Remainder of passage

وتكتظّ هذه الجماهير اللامنتمية في الأزقّة الفقيرة من المدن الكبرى وتشكل أرضية خصبة للجماعات المتطرفة والثورية الدينية منها والعلمانية.
ويحاول الأصوليون المسلمون أن يحشدوا هؤلاء

اللامنـتمـين والمستضـعفين بـاسم الإسـلام والذي يُبـرزونـه كدين
يتصف بـالعدالة والإنصاف بينما يُعيّرون الطبـقة الحاكمة بأنها
ظالمة ومنـاهضـة للإسـلام ويعمّها الفساد قـائلين بأنـه يجب على
المؤمنـين الصادقين إسـقـاطها إمـا عن طريق القيـام بـالثـورة
عليها أو على الأقلّ عن طريق استبدالها بالوسائل السلمية.

وتتـراوح التكتيكات المستعملة لتحقيق هذا الهدف مـا بين
إقامة الخلايا السرية ومخاطبـة المجموعات الكبيـرة من المصلّين
في داخل الجوامع أو في خـارجها، وخوض المعارك الدامـيـة مع
قوات الأمن والاشتراك في الانتخابات، كما أنها تتراوح ما بين
تنفيـذ الأعمـال الإرهابيـة، والقيـام بالتظاهرات السلمـيـة،
والتـسلل إلى المؤسـسـات الرسمـيـة من أجل استـمـالتـها
والاعتـزال التـام عن المجتمع، ومحـاربـة الدولة الكافرة محـاربـةً
علنيةً ومجادلة الخصوم العلمانيين مجادلةً عقلانية.

Note
The modern political nature of this text requires the use of general modern
political vocabulary, e.g. تكتيكات, لامُنْتَم, أصولية. At the same time, the
Islamic subject matter also makes it sensible to use terms with an Islamic
connotation where appropriate, e.g. فساد, ظالم, مستضعف.

11. Précis

(a) i Suggested guidance questions for the précis in Arabic of وكانت البشرية.

١ – حسب قـول سيد قطب مـا هي الآلهة الجديـدة التي اتخذتها امـريكا
وروسيا؟

٢ – الى اي اشياء تقود هذه الآلهة الجديدة؟

٣ – لماذا لا يصدق الكاتب الدعاية السوفياتية؟

٤ – كيف يصف الحياة في امريكا؟

ii Suggested guidance questions for the précis in Arabic of العقيدة في الله.

١ – كيف تتميز دعوة الاسلام في رأي الكاتب؟

٢ – ماذا يقصد الكاتب بقوله إن «شجرة الحضارة البشرية تهتز وتترنح اليوم»؟

٣ – ماذا يكفل النظام الاجتماعي الاسلامي في رأي الكاتب؟

٤ – من يرتكبون الجريمة في حق البشرية قبل ان يرتكبوها في حق الاسلام؟

٥ – كيف يصف الكاتب مهمة الحركة الاسلامية؟

(b) Suggested guidance questions for the précis in Arabic of والتقط الإخوان المسلمون.

١ – كيف كانت الجماهيرُ تقيِّم حركةَ الإخوان المسلمين؟

٢ – ما هو رأي الإخوان المسلمين في التطورات الاقتصادية والاجتماعية والسياسية والفكرية؟

٣ – لأي أشياء اعلنت حركة الإخوان المسلمين رفضها، ولماذا؟

٤ – ما هي نقطة انطلاق دعوة الإخوان المسلمين؟

٥ – كيف فسَّر الإخوان المسلمون الصراعات الدائرة محلياً وعالمياً؟

٦ – صف/صفي نمو الإخوان المسلمين في السنوات العشرين الأولى تقريباً من تأسيسها.

٧ – بأي شيء كانت تبدأ عضوية حركة الإخوان المسلمين؟

٨ – ما هو «الوجه الآخر لهذه العملة» في رأي الكاتب؟

٩ – ما هي الأمور الأخرى التي ساعدت في نمو حركة الإخوان المسلمين؟

15
Democracy

4. Written Arabic texts 1

(b) **i** Answers to comprehension questions relating to ٤٧٨١ مرشحا يتنافسون

على ٣٠١ مقعد.

1. Yesterday the beginning of the elections campaign and permission to candidates and parties to use the official media to canvass support were announced.
2. On 27th April the electorate will go to the polls.
3. There are 3429 independent candidates taking part in this election.
4. There are nineteen parties taking part in the elections.
5. President Ali Abdullah Salih heads the General People's Congress.
6. The Ba'thist Party is supported by Iraq.
7. The three main parties are: the General People's Congress, the Yemeni Socialist Party, and the Islah ('Reform') Party.
8. The party with the strongest chance of election in Sa'dah is the al-Haqq Party.
9. The party with the strongest chance of election in Shabwa and Hadramawt is the League of the Sons of Yemen.
10. The report rates the chances of the Ba'th Party as very low.
11. The National Socialist Party is not permitted to put forward any electoral propaganda because they do not have enough candidates (less than fifteen).
12. Other parties in the same position include the Democratic September Organisation, the People's Organisation for Liberation, the Revolutionary Democratic Party, the National Union, the Democratic Movement and the United Democratic Movement.
13. Abd al-Rahman Ahmad Muhammad Nu'man is the Secretary General of the Constitutional Liberal Party.
14. He has decided to enter the election as an independent candidate in constituency sixty-three in the province of Ta'izz.
15. Sources close to Nu'man say that he will gain the support of the Yemeni Socialist Party.
16. Sheikh Abdullah Ibn Husayn al-Ahmar hopes to become Head of Parliament (Speaker).

17. خمر is in the province of Sana'a.
18. The report says that women have a prominent presence in this election. There are forty-nine women candidates of whom thirteen are from official parties. The largest number of women candidates is in Aden with twenty, then Sana'a with seventeen and the rest of the women candidates are in Ta'izz, Ibb, al-Hodeida and al-Bayda.
19. Sources expect that when coordination or alliances are established between the parties in the next few days many candidates will withdraw.

ii Suggested translation of the first two paragraphs of ٤٧٨١ مرشـحا يتنافـسـون
.على ٣٠١ مقعد

> Preparations for the Yemeni elections entered a new stage yesterday with the official announcement of the beginning of the election campaign, allowing candidates and parties to make use of the offical media until 26th April, that is until a day before the electorate go to the polls.
>
> The day before yesterday the committee supervising the election process drew up the final lists of candidates which show that there are 4781 candidates contesting 301 seats. Of these, 3429 are independent candidates while 1352 are associated with one of the ineteen parties and organisations. These include the General People's Congress lead by President Ali Abdullah Salih with 290 candidates, the Yemeni Socialist Party lead by Deputy-President Ali Salim al-Bayd with 228 candidates, the Islah ('Reform') Party lead by Sheikh Abdullah al-Ahmar with 246 candidates, the Socialist Arab Ba'th Party which is supported by Iraq with 160 candidates, the Nasserite People's Union Organisation with ninety-six candidates, the League of the Sons of Yemen with ninety candidates, and the al-Haqq Party with sixty-two candidates.

5. Written Arabic texts 2
(b) **i** Answers to comprehension questions relating to جبهة الانقاذ تتـوقع الفـوز
.بـ٤٤٪ من مقاعد برلمان الجزائر

1. The temporary head of the Executuve Bureau of the Islamic Salvation Front (FIS) is Abd al-Qadir Hashani.
2. By the morning of 28th December the FIS had won 189 seats.
3. All the other parties had won forty-one seats.
4. Thirty-one seats still remained to be declared.
5. The next round of elections is to be held on 16th January.
6. Hashani predicted that the FIS would obtain 44% of the 430 seats in parliament.
7. This would give them an absolute majority and enable them to form the next government.

(d) **i** Answers to comprehension questions relating to قيادة جماعية تحكم الجزائر.

1. The day before Algeria instituted a new type of government President Chadli Benjedid resigned.
2. This government will be based on collective leadership.
3. The Supreme State Council will definitely include the President of the Constitutional Council, the Deputy President of State, the Prime Minister, the Minister of Defence, the Minister for the Interior and the Minister of Justice.
4. The Minister for Human Rights may also be in the Supreme State Council.
5. The Council will fill the political gap arising from the resignation of President Benjedid and the legislative gap arising from the absence of the National People's Council.
6. The National People's Council was officially dissolved shortly before the first round of elections.
7. As a result of this dissolution the State Council will be in charge of formulating and issuing laws.
8. It will be responsible for appointing senior officials such as governors.
9. The formation of this council is problematic because the Algerian constitution does not recognise the existence of such organisations.
10. Such a council could be formed under a state of emergency.
11. These special circumstances would then allow for the suspension of the constitution and the freezing of activities of all political parties, associations and trade unions.
12. The Ministry of Defence announced yesterday at dawn that the army would respond decisively to the Prime Minister's call to maintain public security and that it reconfirms its loyalty to the constitution and its confidence in the existing constitutional organisations.
13. A number of sources expected that the elections would be called off.
14. The Islamic Front broke its silence by making a statement.
15. The announcement was made by the Front's temporary executive office.
16. The Islamic Front accused 'dubious elements' of showing their determination to get the upper hand over the Algerian people and lead them against their will.
17. From the statement you can infer that the Islamic Front won the first part of the elections.
18. The Islamic Front's announcement accused proponents of recent [political] developments of 'aiming to plunge the country into a whirlpool of tension'.
19. The Islamic Front describes the legal process as the sole guarantor of stability and protection of state interests.
20. According to the announcement, political prisoners should be released.
21. These political prisoners include leaders of the Islamic Front.
22. The army establishment and security organisations are called to uphold the choice of the people and not give in to the whims of the reckless and their despotic desires.

23. The 'reckless' are accused of not hesitating to plunge the country into a whirlpool of struggle.
24. The people who are said to benefit from this situation are the enemies of Islam and Algeria.
25. It is asked how far the leadership of the Salvation Front can restrain their political bases and control the 'radical tendency'.
26. This radical tendency initially opposed participation in the elections.
27. The National Liberation Front held a meeting yesterday.
28. This meeting was held to discuss the position of the Liberation Front in the new administration.

ii Suggested translation of first three paragraphs of قيادة جماعية تحكم الجزائر.

> Algeria is today moving towards a new form of government based on collective leadership through a Supreme State Council – an idea which was effectively imposed on the government the day after the resignation of President Chadli Benjedid. The Council is to include the President of the Constitutional Assembly (the Deputy President of the Republic), the Prime Minister, the Minister of Defence, the Minister of the Interior, the Minister of Justice, and perhaps also the Minister of Human Rights.
>
> The Council is intended not only to fill the political vacuum resulting from the resignation of President Benjedid, but also to address the urgent problem of the legislative void left by the dissolution of the National People's Assembly, which was officially dissolved shortly before the first round of elections. Accordingly the State Council will be authorised to draft and enact legislation as well as possibly being entrusted with the appointment of senior officials such as governors. The legal status of the State Council, however, remains problematic, as the Algerian constitution does not provide for such a body. The establishment of the State Council, or any similar body under another name, is in fact dependent on the announcement of a state of emergency, for which the constitution does provide, since this allows for the suspension of the constitution itself and the freezing of all party political and trade union activities.
>
> In a statement issued early yesterday morning, the Ministry of Defence said that the army 'would respond decisively to the Prime Minister's call to maintain public security.'
>
> The statement continued, 'The National People's Army reaffirms its loyalty to the constitution and its confidence in the established constitutional institutions.' The army also reaffirmed that it would maintain public order. A number of sources predicted that the elections would be annulled.

6. Written Arabic texts 3 (classical)

(a) Suggested translation of الشورى.

Consultation

Those in authority cannot dispense with consultation, for God Almightly ordered the Prophet to consult: He said, 'Forgive them and ask forgiveness for them and seek their counsel.' Abu Hurayra, may God be pleased with him, said, 'No one was more ready to consult than the Messenger of God, may God bless him and give him salvation.' It is also said, 'God ordered His Prophet to do this so that the hearts of his followers should be reconciled, and that those who followed him should be guided by his example, and that he should ask their opinion when he had not received divine inspiration on matters of war and other secondary matters. People other than the Prophet, may God bless him and give him salvation, are thus in the greatest need of consulting others.' God has praised the believers on this account when He said, 'What God has is better and more enduring for those who have believed and placed their trust in their Lord and those who avoid grievous and abominable sins, and if they get angry they forgive, and those who responded to their Lord and performed the prayers, and whose affairs are decided by consultation among themselves. They spend out of what We have granted them.'

There are two types of people who have authority: rulers and religious scholars; and if they are righteous then the people will be righteous. It is the duty of each one to make their words and deeds [strive to] obey God, and His Messenger, and conform to the Book of God. Whenever it is possible in problematic cases to ascertain the guidance given by the Book and the Way of the Prophet this guidance is obligatory. If this is not possible because of the lack of time, or the incapacity of the person seeking guidance to judge, or a balance between the various pieces of evidence which he has available, or for some other reason, he must adopt that which conforms to his knowledge and his religious insights. This is the most acceptable point of view.

(b) Suggested translation of المشاورة والرأي.

Consultation and opinion

Al-Ziyadi said that Hamad ibn Zayd said on the authority of Hisham on the authority of al-Hasan, 'The Prophet, may God bless him and give him salvation, used even to seek the advice of women. They would advise him about something and he would take their advice.'

I read in the *Taj*[1] that one of the kings of Persia sought the advice of his ministers. One of them said, 'The King should not seek advice from any of us unless he is alone with him, for this behaviour is more likely to ensure that the secret is kept, and to maintain the inviolability of opinions, and is more conducive to well-being and more likely to lead to one of us being forgiven for the calamity brought on by the other. It is safer to reveal a secret to one man than to reveal it to two and to reveal a secret to three people is equivalent to revealing it to everybody. This is because the first person is the [sole] guarantor for what has been revealed to him, but the second person removes from him that status as guarantor, and the third even more so. If a man's secret has been revealed to one person, he should not show fear of him or favour to him. If the secret has been revealed to two people the king becomes beset by doubts, the two people are led to excuses, and their punishment is the punishment of two men for the sins of one. If the king accuses them he accuses an innocent man of the crimes of the guilty one, and if he forgives them his forgiveness is given to one who has committed no crime as well as the other about whom there is no proof.'

I read in a book from India that a king once asked the advice of his ministers. One of them said, 'The resolute king is strengthened by the advice of resolute ministers just as the contents of the sea are strengthened by rivers. He gains through his resoluteness that which he cannot gain through the use of force and armies. There are different types of secret. There are those secrets which are shared with a small group, those for which the help of a larger group is asked, and those for which one confidant is sufficient. In guarding one's secret there is triumph over need and release from shortcoming. He who asks for advice, even if he has a better opinion than the person he asks, has his opinion strengthened by another opinion, just as the light of a fire is strenghthened by oil. If a king keeps his secret, avoids saying what is in his heart, chooses his advisors carefully, inspires fear in the hearts of the common people, is sufficiently virtuous, is not feared by the innocent, does not give sanctuary to the suspect, works out carefully the benefits of his actions and what he spends, he is worthy to remain ruler. This secret of ours is only good for two tongues and four ears. Then he should keep it to himself.'

Note
1. Reference to the classical book تاج العـروس لجـواهر القـامـوس, which is a commentary by المرتضى الزبيـدي on the dictionary entitled القاموس المحيط by فيروزبادي.

8. Aural Arabic texts 1

Complete transcription of حصاد الشهر, no. 14, side 1, item 7, هل من خطر على
البلاد العربية من الشيوعية؟.

من ارشيف مكتبتنا الاذاعية يسرنا ان نُسمعكم جانبا من ما قاله
الرئيس التونسي الحبيب بورقيبة. وكان آنذاك رئيس الحزب
الدستوري في تونس، وكلامه التالي جاء من رد على سؤال طُرح على
الوجه التالي: هل من خطر على البلاد العربية من الشيوعية؟ وإذا كان
الامر كذلك فكيف السبيل الى مكافحتها؟

تجولت كثيرا في البلاد العربية شرقا وغربا فوجدت [و]¹ان هناك
خطرا عظيما من الشيوعية يهدد البلاد العربية والسبب في ذلك ان
البلاد العربية كثيرة التذمر ولها اسباب قوية للتذمر والحقد والنقمة
على النظام، فيتوهم الكثير [و]¹ان النظام الشيوعي هو العلاج لما هم
فيه من شر، والشر الذي يتخبط فيه البلاد العربية هو نوعان [نوعين]،
النوع الاول هو الحكم الاجنبي والاحتلال الاجنبي، والنوع الثاني النظام
الاجتماعي في الكثير من البلاد نظام اقطاعي يجعل من الاكثرية
الساحقة من الشعب لا تملك شيئًا في خساسة في ضيق الفقر والمرض
والجوع، فيتبادل لذهن البسطاء وهم يجهلون كل شيء عن الشيوعية
وعن النظام الشيوعي بما ان روسيا عدوة النظام الحالي عدوة
الرأسمالية وعدوة دمقراطية الدول الاستعمارية فإن خلاصهم في
الشيوعية ، فمن هذا التمنمن وهذا التذمر الذي ظهر² بوادره في موجة
الاغتيالات الموجودة الآن والتي نتأسف منها في البلاد العربية نرى ان
هناك خطرا يجب النظر اليه نظرة واقعية لاستئصال اسبابه حتى
نكون اعظم .. نكوِّن حصناً ضد تفشى الشيوعية في البلاد العربية.

Notes

1. و appears in the text, but is not required according to the grammar.
2. ظهر appears in the text. Grammatically, this should be ظهرت.

9. Aural Arabic texts 2

(a) Complete transcription of BBC Arabic Service news broadcast from Sept. 1995
on sending of observers to the Algerian presidential elections.

قرّرت جامعة الدول العربية ايفاد مراقبين الى الجزائر لرصد انتخابات
الرئاسة التي ستجرى هناك في اواخر هذا العام وقالت اذاعة الجزائر
ان القرار اُتخذ تلبية لطلب الرئيس الجزائري امين زروال إبان الزيارة
التي قام بها الدكتور عصمت عبد المجيد الامين العام للجامعة العربية
للجزائر في الآونة الاخيرة، وقال الامين العام للجامعة ان هذه هي المرة
الاولى التي يُطلَب فيها من الجامعة الاشراف على الانتخابات في دولة
عربية، يذكر ان احزاب المعارضة الرئيسية في الجزائر انتقدت
الانتخابات التي ستجري في نوفمبر/ تشرين الثاني ووصفتها بانها
محاولة من نظام الحكم العسكري لاضفاء الشرعية على الحكم وقالت
احزاب المعارضة انها ستقاطع الانتخابات.

(b) Complete transcription of BBC Arabic Service news broadcast from Sept. 1995
on release of pro-democracy demonstrators in Bahrain.

تفيد الانباء الواردة من البحرين ان سلطات الامن ستطلق سراح بضع
مــئـات من الـسـجـناء الذين اعـتـقـلوا اثناء المظاهرات المطالبــة
بالديمقراطية التي شهدتها البحرين العام الماضي وقال محامون في
المنامة ان مئة وخمسين سجينا سيطلق سراحهم في اواخر هذا الاسبوع
بموجب اتفاق تم التـوصل اليـه بين سلطات الامن وقادة المعارضـة
الشيعية المسجونين. واذا ما استمر هدوء الوضع واستقراره فإن من
تبقى من السجناء سيطلق سراحهم في اواخر هذا الشهر. يذكر ان
المظاهرات نظمت عقب اعتقال الشيخ علي سلمان احد كبار قادة الشيعة
الذي كان يطالب باستعادة برلمان البحرين الذي حُلّ عام خمسة وسبعين،
ويذكر ان الشيخ علي سلمان وعدد آخر من قادة الشيعة كانوا قد رُحّلوا
عن البحرين في وقت سابق من هذا العام.

10. Written English texts
(a) Suggested translation of 'Rumblings from a distant outbreak of democracy'.

عندما يتوجّه اليمنيون إلى صناديق الاقتراع هذه السنة في أول انتخابات في ظلّ التعددية الحزبية فإنهم سيقومون بأكثر من مجرّد اختيار حكومة جديدة. فمن المرجّح أن تكون لهذه الانتخابات التي ستمثّل المرحلة الأخيرة في تحوّل اليمن إلى دولة ديمقراطية بمعنى الكلمة انعكاساتها في جميع أنحاء الجزيرة العربية، حيث أن المجالس النيابية في هذه المنطقة – وإن وُجدت – لاتتمتّع سوى بنفوذ محدود للغاية وتُفضّل عليها في معظم تلك الدول «مجالس الشورى» التي يتمّ اختيار أعضائها بطريقة التعيين والتي تكون اجتماعاتها الوزارية أقرب إلى تجمّعات أسرية تضمّ الإخوة والأعمام والأخوال.

(b) Suggested translation of 'Algeria cancels polls'.

الجزائر تُلغي الانتخابات

مساء الأمس ألغى المجلس الأعلى الجزائري الانتخابات العامة فيما يدعي الأصوليون الإسلاميون أنه انقلاب دستوري بدعم الجيش قصده أخذ الفوز من الجبهة الإسلامية.

وفي تقرير أصدره المجلس في جلسة استثنائية بعد استقالة الرئيس الشاذلي بن جديد ليلة السبت أعلن المجلس «استحالة مواصلة المسار الانتخابي حتى الحصول على الضمانات الضرورية لقيام مؤسسات الدولة بوظائفها».

وحرس الجيش بمساعدة الدبابات المباني الحكومية الرئيسة وأقامت قوات الأمن حواجز لإيقاف السيارات كما اجتمع المجلس والذي يضم أعضاءه رئيس الجمهورية بالوكالة عبد الملك بن حبليس الذي حلّ محلّ السيد الشاذلي، وأهم رجال الجيش وقوات الأمن، ورئيس الوزراء، ووزراء الدفاع والداخلية والعدل حتى وقت متأخر من الليل.

11. Précis

Suggested guidance questions for the précis in Arabic of: كلمـة الثـورة الديموقراطيـة فـي اليمـن.

١ – على أي شيء يقوم النظام السياسي الجديد في اليمن؟

٢ – كيف يؤكد الرئيس علي عبد الله صالح على الاختيار الديمقراطي؟

٣ – ما هي مسؤولية الاحزاب والتنظيمات الديمقراطية الأخرى إزاء المبادئ الديمقراطية التي يقول بها الرئيس علي عبد الله صالح؟

٤ – بأي أشياء ترتبط ضرورة الديمقراطية؟

٥ – في رأي الكاتب أن الديمقراطية لم تأت تلبية لرغبة أو احتياج تكتيكي. فَعَن أي شيء تعبِّر الديمقراطية إذن؟

٦ – مـا هو هدف الزيارات التـي يقـوم بهـا الرئيس علي عبـد الله صالح للمواقع العسكرية؟

٧ – كيـف يحمي الرئيسُ القوات المسلحة من استعداء الشعب عليها؟

٨ – ما الذي يُكْمل تقديرَ الكاتب لقيمة الديمقراطية؟

16
Death and succession

4. Written Arabic texts 1

(b) Answers to comprehension questions relating to موت السادات.

1. The writer describes Sadat's death as 'his sudden disappearance from the political stage'.
2. He describes Sadat as America's central pivot in the region.
3. It is clear that Husni Mubarak will succeed Sadat.
4. The principal question being asked about Sadat's successor is what position he will take vis-à-vis Israel.
5. This question is being asked in particular because Mubarak has never visited Israel.
6. The Arabic terms used to describe Sadat's death are:

موت السادات المفاجيء، اختفاؤه، الاختفاء المفاجيء ... من ساحة السياسة الدولية، موت السادات، هذه الوفاة المباغتة، كارثةٌ ما بعدها كارثة

7. The policy of Mubarak may differ from that of Sadat vis-à-vis Israel in that he may not show the same degree of 'understanding'.
8. The writer believes that Mubarak may behave differently from Sadat if Israel were to carry out operations such as the bombing of the Iraqi factory and the bombing of Beirut.
9. According to observers, the final stage of Israeli withdrawal from Sinai may herald a change in Egyptian policy.
10. This change would probably still have taken place had Sadat not been killed.
11. This is because of the big gulf between the Egyptians and the Israelis over the issue of Palestinian self-determination.
12. Sadat is described as the man of Camp David and the central pivot in American Middle-Eastern policy.
13. The writer sums up the effect Sadat's death will have on the Middle East and on the world as a whole as causing deep, fundamental changes in the region and in the balance of power in the world as a whole.

(c) Answers to comprehension questions relating to شهيد مصر.

1. According to the writer, Sadat was killed because the enemies of Egypt plotted against it in a series of conspiratorial acts.
2. Sadat is described in this text as the leader of Egypt's destiny, the head of its family, and the maker of its growth.
3. The tone of this text is far more regretful, emotional and involved and far less objective than the tone of text (b).
4. The writer says that Sadat represented the mind of the people, the spirit of the community, the greatness of the past, the glory of the present and the prosperity of the future.
5. The writer describes Sadat as being a ruler, a president and a leader only because the Egyptian people wanted him to be so.
6. Sadat is being addressed in the final paragraph.

(d) Suggested translation of اغتيال معوض فاجعة عادية.

Mouawad's assassination: an ordinary disaster

Possibly the most important lesson to be drawn from the assassination of the Lebanese President Rene Mouawad is that the political situation resulting from the Taif agreement is now sufficiently stable that virtually the only way in which it can be threatened is by threatening the security situation. And the fact that national security can only be threatened through a treacherous act of assassination demonstrates that the security situation resulting from the most recent ceasefire is no less stable than the political situation.

Under these circumstances it is no exaggeration to say that, in terms of its implications for the survival of Lebanon as an entity, and the maintenance of the political status quo, the assassination of the Lebanese President is no different from the assassination of any president or leader of a stable state.

When the Democrat, Kennedy, was assassinated, he was succeeded by his vice-president, Johnson, and the Democratic Party continued to rule the country.

When Indira Ghandi was assassinated, she was succeeded by her son, Rajiv, and the Congress Party continued to rule the country.

Now that Rene Mouawad has been assassinated, he must be succeeded by his designated 'son' or deputy, i.e. by someone who represents the same political stance which brought the Lebanese Deputies to Taif and the army base of Al-Qileat in order to begin the process of consolidating the Charter of Agreement by addressing the shortcomings in the constitution.

In other words, if the Arabs are earnest in their desire to make use of the international support for the successes which have been achieved so far by the tripartite committee, the assassination of President Mouawad need not constitute anything more than the kind of disaster which may take place at any time in any country.

5. Written Arabic texts 2

(a) ii Answers to comprehension questions relating to إيران تودع الخميني.

1. Khomeini was almost eighty-seven at the time of his death.
2. Two weeks before his death he had an operation to stop bleeding in his digestive tract.
3. Following Khomeini's death a five-day public holiday and national mourning for forty days were announced.
4. The Council of Experts was called into emergency session to listen to the will of the late Imam.
5. Khomeini's funeral will take place today.
6. The funeral will be reported by foreign news reporters, and live television and radio.
7. In their statement, the Iranian Army and Revolutionary Guards declared their support for Hashimi Rafsanjani.
8. Muntaziri was recently removed from his position as successor designate to the deceased Iranian leader.
9. He called on the Iranians to remain peaceful and continue with the revolution.
10. The Mojahideen-e Khalq organisation congratulated the Iranian people and said that the death of Khomeini was the final end of a bloody regime.
11. Iranian opposition leaders predict strikes in the post-Khomeini period.
12. Aboulhasan Bani Sadr is the former President of Iran.
13. His expressed hope is that the death of Khomeini will open the door to democracy.

iv Suggested structure translations relating to إيران تودع الخميني.

١ - سوف يُعلن عن انتخاب الحكومة الجديدة قريبا.

٢ - توفى بعد حوالى شهر من الهجوم الارهابي.

٣ - للطلاب عطلة صيفية لمدة ثلاثة اشهر.

٤ - من اللازم دعوة جلسة عاجلة للمجلس.

٥ - لا يسمح لك بالتدخين في هذه الغرفة.

٦ - أُنتخب رئيسا للجمهورية اللبنانية.

٧ - تتوقع تغييرات جذرية في فترة ما بعد جرباكوف في أروبا الشرقية.

٨ - آمل في أن يصلوا قريبا.

(b) **i** Suggested translation of وفاة الخميني.

Revolutionary guards deployed in Tehran. Calls for calm and unity to safeguard regime.

Khomeini dies. Khamanei elected as successor.

Yesterday saw the beginning of a new phase in the history of Iran and the region with the death of the Iranian leader Ayatollah Khomeini at the age of eighty-eight. Iranian television reported that the Council of Experts, which comprises eighty-three members, elected the fifty-year old President Ali Khamanei as successor to the 'Guide of the Revolution' by a majority of over two thirds.

However, according to a number of experts on Iranian affairs, real power is for the time being in the hands of a troika consisting of Khomeini's son Ahmad, the President of the Consultative Council (the Parliament), Ali Akbar Hashimi Rafsanjani, and Khamanei himself.

These experts also believe that Khomeini's son is in a position to take control within the country through his allies, the Minister of the Interior, Mohtashemi, and Intelligence Minister, Rishari.

Before lines of communication were cut between Iran and the outside world, Tehran residents reported that hundreds of Revolutionary Guards had taken to the streets as a precaution against any possible coup, and that the army had been placed on a state of alert. It was officially announced that Khomeini's funeral would take place today. It was also apparent that the various factions vying for power were taking care to present a facade of unity, having announced that their first priority was to safeguard the regime.

The Iranian leader's testament was read out yesterday to a session of the Council of Deputies. The testament consists of twenty-nine pages plus a single-page appendix. Khomeini's son Ahmad announced that the testament would be made public in the near future.

ii Suggested structure translations relating to وفاة الخميني.

١ – سوف يُعلن عن وفاة الرئيس قريبا.

٢ – توفى عن عمر يناهز الثالثة والثنانين.

٣ – وصل الجيش بعد ساعة من الهجوم.

٤ – سوف يكون هناك اضطراب عام لمدة ثلاثة ايام.

٥ – لا يسمح للاجانب بالدخول في هذه المنطقة.

٦ – من هو القائد العام بالوكالة للقوات المسلحة؟

٧ – انتخب رئيسا باغلبية تفوق الثلثين.

٨ – أُذيع رسميا ان الحكومة قد استقالت.

٩ – حرص حافظ الاسد على الظهور كانه ديمقراطي.

١٠ – بدأ امس الوزير الخارجي يزور مصر.

(c) Suggested translations of the first two paragraphs of إيران ما بعد الخميني.

i Literal translation of إيران ما بعد الخميني.

Iran after Khomeini

The death of Imam Khomeini has opened a new chapter in the struggle for succession between the various factions vying for power in Iran. The outcome of this struggle will determine the new political identity of Iran, and the nature of its relations with its neighbours and the rest of the world. Whatever the outcome may be, it is certain that the policy of exporting the revolution, which was bound up with the era and personality of the late imam, led Iran into a series of problems and crises, the most important of which was the war with Iraq, which cost the country more than two million dead and hundreds of thousands of wounded and disabled. It also resulted in a total collapse of the economy, depleted the country's resources and led to debts and a financial deficit which amounts to more than one thousand billion dollars according to the most impartial estimates.

At this time when it is paying its last respects to its leader, Iran needs to pause, and to reassess its calculations, its relationships and the legacy of the last ten years of its history. Events have proved the futility of its previous orientations which have damaged the reputation of the country and have debilitated it internally in a way which never previously occurred even in its darkest periods.

ii Idiomatic translation of إيران ما بعد الخميني.

Iran after Khomeini

With the death of Ayatollah Khomeini the power struggle in Iran has entered a new phase, the outcome of which will determine the future political identity of the country and the nature of its relations with its neighbours and the rest of the world. Whatever the ultimate result of this struggle, one thing is certain: the policy of exporting the revolution, which was intimately bound up with the rule and personality of the late Ayatollah, has merely served to embroil Iran in a series of grave crises. Most important of these was the war with Iraq, which not only cost the country more than two million dead and hundreds of thousands of seriously wounded, but also resulted in the total collapse of the economy, depleting the country's resources and leading to huge debts and a financial deficit, which according to impartial estimates now stands at over one hundred billion dollars.

At a time when it is paying its last respects to its leader, Iran needs to reflect, and to reassess its calculations and relationships and the legacy of the past ten years. For events have shown the futility of its current political orientation, which has proved more devastating to the country and its reputation than anything which has occurred even in the darkest periods of its history.

iii Additional exercise: comparison of translations of إيران ما بعد الخميني.

Ask students to compare their own translations with the two sample translations given here, and to assess the merits and demerits of the various alternatives offered.

6. Written Arabic texts 3 (classical)
6. (a) Suggested translation of وفاة رسول الله.

The death of the Messenger of God

Ibn Ishaq and al-Zuhri said, 'Anas ibn Malik told me that on Monday when God took his Messenger (may God bless him and grant him salvation), he went out to the people while they were performing the morning prayer. The curtain was lifted and the door opened. Then the Messenger of God (may God bless him and grant him salvation), went out and came to A'isha's door. The Muslims were distracted from their prayer by [their thoughts of] the Messenger of God (may God bless him and grant him salvation) when they saw him with joy and they looked [at him], [but] he told them, "Carry on with your prayers!" The Messenger of God (may God bless him and grant him salvation) smiled with happiness at the way in which he saw they were carrying out their prayers. I had never seen the Messenger of God (may God bless him and grant him salvation) looking better than he did at that time. Then he returned and the people went away thinking that he had overcome his pain. Abu Bakr returned to his family in Sunh [an outlying district of Medina].' Ibn Ishaq said, 'Muhammad ibn Ibrahim ibn Harith told me on the authority of al-Qasim ibn Muhammad that the Messenger of God (may God bless him and grant him salvation) had said when he heard Umar say الله أكبر during the prayer, "Where is Abu Bakr? God and the Muslims forbid this." If it were not for something Umar said on his death, the Muslims would not have doubted that the Messenger of God (may God bless him and grant him salvation) had appointed Abu Bakr as his successor. But Umar said as he died, "If I appoint a successor one better than me has also appointed a successor; and if I leave them [without appointing a successor] someone who is better than me has also left them [without appointing a successor]." So the people knew that the Messenger of God (may God bless him and grant him salvation) had not appointed anyone as his successor. Umar was not suspected of hostility towards the Messenger of God (may God bless him and grant him salvation).'

(b) Suggested translation of حدثنا زكرياء بن يحيى الضرير.

Zakariyya' ibn Yahya al-Darir said, on the authority of Abu Awanah on the authority of Dawud ibn Abdullah al-Awdi on the authority of Humayd ibn Abd al-Rahman al-Himyari, 'When the Messenger of God, may God bless him and grant him salvation, died, Abu Bakr was in a part of Medina. He came, uncovered the Prophet's face, and kissed him, saying, "May my father and mother be your ransom! How good you are both living and dead! By the Lord of the Ka'bah, Muhammad is dead." Then he went out to the pulpit and found Umar ibn al-Khattab standing [there], threatening the people and saying, "The Messenger of God, may God bless him and grant him salvation, is alive and not dead. He will go out after those who spread lies about him, cut off their hands and strike their necks and crucify them."' Abu Bakr told him to listen, but he refused to listen, so Abu Bakr spoke, saying that God had said to His Prophet, may God bless him and grant him salvation, "You will die, and so will they. Then on the Day of Resurrection you will dispute before your Lord." He continued, "Muhammad is only a messenger, and other Messengers have gone before him. If he dies or is killed, will you turn back on your heels?", until he finished the verse. "He who worshipped Muhammad, his deity is dead; but he who worships God, who has no associate, his God is alive and immortal."

Some people from among the companions of Muhammad, who were alive at the same time as ourselves, swore that they did not know that those two verses were revealed until Abu Bakr recited them that day.'

(c) Suggested translation of فتكلم أبو بكر.

Abu Bakr spoke, and left nothing out that was revealed [in the Qur'an] about the Ansar or was said by the Messenger of God, may God bless him and grant him salvation, with regard to their fine qualities. He said, 'You know that the Messenger of God said, "If most people took one way and the Ansar another, I would take the Ansar's path." Sa'd, you

know that while you were sitting the Messenger of God said, that
Quraysh were in charge of this matter. The righteous follow their kind,
the wicked follow theirs.' Sa'd replied, 'You have spoken the truth. We
are the viziers and you are the rulers.' Umar said, 'Stretch out your
hand, Abu Bakr, so that I may pay allegiance to you.' Abu Bakr said,
'No, rather you, Umar. You have a stronger claim than me.' Umar was
indeed the stronger of the two [i.e. he had more men whose support he
could call on]. Each of them wanted the other to stretch his hand so that
he could strike the bargain with him. Umar stretched out Abu Bakr's
hand, saying, 'You have my strength together with your stregth,' and
the people gave their oath of allegiance. They demanded confirmation of
the oath, but Ali and al-Zubayr stayed away. Al-Zubayr drew his
sword, saying, 'I will not put it back until the oath of allegiance is given
to Ali.' When Abu Bakr and Umar heard about this, Umar said, 'Seize
al-Zubayr's sword and hit it with a stone.' Umar went out to them and
brought them along forcibly. 'Either you pay allegiance willingly', he
said, 'or you pay it unwillingly.' So they payed allegiance.

8. Aural Arabic texts 1

Complete transcription of حصاد الشهر no. 19, side 1, item 1, أضواء على الملك
الراحل سعود.

وُلد الملك سعود ابن عبد العزيز آل سعود عام اثنـين وتسعمائة وألف في
الكويت حيث لجأت أسـرته بـعد هزيمتها على يد آل الرشيـد في حائـل.
وكان الابن الثاني للملك عبد العزيز المشهور حيث تُوفي أخوه الكبير
وهـو شاب يافع، وفي عام اثنين وثلاثين وتسعمائة وألف عُين والدهما
عبـد العزيز سـعود وليا للعهد ونائبـا له في ولاية نجد، لكن الملك عبـد
العزيز استمر في الحكم بشخصيته القوية ونفوذه الكبيـر بحيث لم تتح
الفرصة لولده سعود كي يشارك في الحكم رغم ذلك التعيين. وكان سـعود
رجلا دمثا وذا شـخـصـيـة قـويـة، وفي غـزو اليـمـن عـام أربعـة وثلاثين
وتسعمائة وألف قاد جيشا سعوديا زحف على اليمن عن طريق الجبال
الـوعـرة فتأخر وصولـه وسبقـه جيش أخيـه فيصل الذي زحف عن طريق
تهـامـة بسـرعـة وفـاز بـالفـخـر دون سـعـود. وفي عـام خـمـسـة وثلاثين
وتسعمائة وألف بينمـا كان الملك عبد العزيز وابناؤه يؤدون مناسك الحج
قام جماعة من اليمنيين بمحاولة جريئة لاغتيال عبد العزيز، فاحتضن
سـعود أبـاه وتلقى بـجسمه الضـخم طعنات الخناجر ونجا عبد العزيز من
القتل، فزادت محبة عبد العزيز لولده سـعود. وفي شهر نوفمبـر عـام
ثلاثة وخمسين وتسعمائة وألف بعد وفاة الملك عبد العزيز بُويع سعود

ملكا خلفا لأبيه في الوقت الذي تضاعف فيه إنتاج النفط السعودي خلال اربع سنوات، وبدأت عائدات النفط بالملايين ترد على البلاد وتحولت المملكة الفقيرة نسبيا إلى دولة عظيمة الثراء، ومن مآثر الملك سعود أنه أسّس جامعة الرياض وأمر ببناء المدارس العديدة والمستشفيات وبفتح الطرق الطويلة، ولكن الملك سعود الذي اشتهر بالكرم العظيم لم يقتصر إنفاقه على الجامعات والمدارس والمستشفيات والطرق بل بنى العديد من القصور الفخمة وفي عهده ثارت مشكلة واحة البريمي فأغدق الأموال على المتمردين الوطنيين في سلطنة عمان وفي عدن ضد البريطانيين، وكان الملك سعود قد ورث شقاقا مع الهاشميين ونتيجة لذلك زادت صلته وثوقا مع سوريا ومع مصر، وقامت صداقة حميمة بينه وبين الرئيس السابق جمال عبد الناصر وأيده تأييدا قويا في النزاع على قناة السويس عام ستة وخمسين حيث كان المبادر إلى استخدام سلاح النفط ومنع النفط عن بريطانيا وعن فرنسا. ولكن الملك سعود سرعان ما خشي أن يطغى حب الناس لجمال عبد الناصر على حبهم له وعاد فصالح الهاشميين وقدم الدعم المالي إلى الملك حسين، وفي شهر يناير(كانون الثاني) عام ثمانية وخمسين اتهم الرئيس جمال عبد الناصر الملك سعود بأنه يحاول تدبير اغتياله وراجت الدعايات ضد الملك سعود وصارت المملكة العربية السعودية عندئذ قريبة من الإفلاس، ولهذا تم إقناعه بأن يترك تصريف أمور الدولة في يد أخيه الأمير فيصل. ولكن الإجراءات التقشفية التي أتبعها الأمير فيصل أغضبت الملك سعود فأقصاه في شهر ديسمبر عام ستين، وفي نهاية عام اثنين وستين عاد الملك سعود فاستدعى أخاه الأمير فيصل ومع معاودة المرض على الملك سعود وكثرة تغيبه خارج المملكة صار الأمير فيصل يتصرف بشؤون البلاد تصرفا كاملا مع توظيف رجاله في الوظائف الرئيسية في الحكومة. وفي أوائل عام أربعة وستين ذهب الملك سعود إلى القاهرة ليحاول حل مشكلة اليمن بالدبلوماسية الشخصية مع الرئيس جمال عبد الناصر، وعاد في شهر مارس (آذار) وحاول أن يسترجع كامل السلطات من الأمير فيصل لكنه اكتشف أن كافة أفراد الأسرة السعودية قد وقفوا ضده وقفة واحدة، بل وجد نفسه محروما من قيادة الحرس الوطني ومرغما على قبول راتب محدود لأن مجلس العلماء قرر ضرورة هذه الإجراءات لمنع المشاكل، ووقع على قرارهم ثمانية وستون أميرا وحاول الملك سعود أن يخرج

مِن هذا الموقف المسيء إليه حسب رأيه وأن يكسب التأييد، ولكنه
فشل. وقرر مجلس العلماء خلعه في شهر نوفمبر عام أربعة وستين
وتسعمائة وألف واختار أن يقيم في أثينا حيث توفي رحمه الله في
شهر فبراير عام تسعة وستين وتسعمائة وألف وحاولت الملكة نسيان
عهده سنوات طويلة ولكن تم مؤخرا الاعتراف بما كان له من مكانة
وظهرت صورته إلى جانب صور والده وأخوته وأعيد اسمه إلى الجامعة
في الرياض فصارت تُعرف باسم جامعة الملك سعود.

9. Aural Arabic texts 2

i Answers to comprehension questions relating to BBC Arabic Service news
   broadcast from Mar. 9, 1992.

1. Begin died today [on the day of the news broadcast – 9th March 1992].
2. Thousands of people gathered in Jerusalem for his funeral.
3. Begin was buried on the Mount of Olives next to his wife.
4. He was seventy-eight years old.
5. He was awarded the Nobel Peace prize along with President Anwar Sadat.
6. The Egyptian Foreign Minister said that Begin's wish to exchange peace for land
   had strengthened peace efforts in the Middle East.
7. Jihan Sadat said that Begin was a hard negotiator but that he was honest and a
   great leader.
8. The opposition Labour Party said that Begin was a great politician and a prime
   minister who had given the chance for peace to be achieved in the Middle East.
9. Begin was born in Poland.
10. At the beginning of World War II he was arrested by the Soviet authorities and
    exiled to Siberia.
11. He went to Palestine in 1941.
12. He led a secret Zionist movement against the British mandate.
13. He planned the bombing of the British military headquarters which led to the
    killing of nearly 100 people.
14. In 1948 his organisation was responsible for killing 250 Arabs in the village of
    Deir Yassin.

ii Complete transcription of BBC news broadcast from Mar. 9, 1992.

شارك آلاف الأشخاص في تشييع جنازة مناحم بيغين رئيس الوزراء
الإسرائيلي الأسبق في القدس اليوم، وقد ووري جثمان مناحم بيغين
الذي تُوفي اليوم في جبل الزيتون إلى جوار زوجته، وكان بيغين يبلغ
الثامنة والسبعين من العمر وقد حصل على جائزة نوبيل للسلام عام

تسعة وسبعين مع الرئيس المصري أنور السادات بعد أن وقعت مصر وإسرائيل اتفاقية السلام التي تعد الوحيدة بين إسرائيل وأي من الدول العربية. وقال وزير الخارجية المصري عمرو موسى مثنيا على مناحم بيغين إن رغبته في مبادلة السلام بالأرض قد عززت من جهود إحلال السلام في الشرق الأوسط، وقالت جيهان السادات أرملة الرئيس المصري الراحل أنور السادات إن مناحم بيغين كان مفاوض صعبا إلا أنه كان أمينا وقائدا عظيما. وقال حزب العمل الإسرائيلي المعارض إنه كان على خلاف واضح مع سياسة مناحم بيغين إلا أن مناحم بيغين كان سياسيا عظيما ورئيسا للوزراء أتاح الفرصة لإحلال السلام في المنطقة.

وُلد مناحم بيغين في بولندا عام ألف وتسعمائة وثلاثة عشر وانضم قبل أن يبلغ العشرين إلى منظمة أرغون الصهيونية المتشددة ثم أصبح رئيسا لها، وفي بداية الحرب العالمية الثانية اعتقلته السلطات السوفياتية ونفته إلى سيبيريا ومن ثم سافر إلى فلسطين عندما أُفرج عنه في عام واحد وأربعين. وهناك قاد حركة صهيونية سرية ضد الانتداب البريطاني وخطط لتفجير قنبلة في مقر القيادة العسكرية البريطانية في القدس، مما أسفر عن مقتل مائة شخص تقريبا. وكانت منظمته مسؤولة أيضا عن ذبح مائتين وخمسين عربيا في قرية دير ياسين عام ثمانية وأربعين.

10. Written English texts
(a) Suggested translation of 'The death of Mohammed'.

وفاة الرسول (ص)

رفض عمر أن يقبل الخبر المذهل فقام في ساحة بيت النبي (ص) يدعو الحشود من الناس القادمين من كل جهة ومن بينهم رجال أسامة، ويقول لهم إن محمدا صلى الله عليه وسلم لم يمت، وإنه قد ذهب إلى الله لفترة كما ذهب موسى في جبل سيناء، فسوف يرجع ويقطع أيدي وأرجل الذين قد نشروا إشاعة وفاته. كان قد بُعث لأبي بكر والذي جاء بسرعة من السنح وذهب إلى كوخ عائشة مباشرة، ثم رفع البردة التي غطت الجثة فقبّل وجه سيده وصاحبه الميت. ثم خرج وحاول

سدى إطمئنان عمر . وبعد ذلك تكلم إلى الناس كذي سلطة،
فقال: أيها الناس، فمن كان يعبد محمدا فقد مات ، ومن كان
يعبد الله فإن الله حي لا يموت.[1] وبعد ذلك تلا آية من القرآن
برهـانـا لـه، «وَ مَا مُحَمَّدٌ إلا رَسُولٌ قَدْ خَلَتْ مِنْ قَبْلِه الرُّسُلُ
أَفَإِنْ مَاتَ أَوْ قُتِلَ انْقَبَلْتُمْ عَلَى أَعْقَابِكُمْ؟ » والغـريب فـي هذا –
ولعله أمر مثيـر للريب – أن الناس لم يستعيدوا هذه الآية، بل
تأثروا بها وأخذوها عن أبي بكر. لا يبقى مجال للشك. كان
الأمر صحيحا. فقد مات الرسول محمد (ص).

Note
1. Cf. text beginning حدثني زكريا بن يحيى الضرير (ch. 16, 5b).

(b) Suggested translation of 'Ayatollah Ruhollah Khomeini'.

آية الله روح الله الخميني

تُوفي آية الله السيـد روح الله مصطفـوي المعـروف بموسـوي
الخميني في الثامنة والثمانين من العمر يوم الثالث من يونيو
عـام ألف وتسعمـائة وتسعة وثمـانين، وذلك بعـد اثني عشـر
يومـا من عمليـة جراحيـة، وكان الخمـينـي مؤسس جمهوريـة
إيران الإسلامية وقائدها.

كان آية الله الخميني ابن عالم، ولد عـام ألف وتسعمـائة
وثلاثة في مدينة الخمين الصغيرة في محافظة إصفهان. وأكمل
دراسـاته الابتدائيـة في الخامسة عشرة من العمر وبدأ دراسـاتـه
الدينية على أيدي أخيـه آية الله باسنديده (٩٧ عامـا/الذي يبلغ
عمره سبعة وتسعين عامـا الآن) والذي لا يزال يعيش في مدينة
قم. وغادر الخميني قم إلى مدينة أراك في عام ألف وتسعمـائة
وعشرين ليواصل تعليمـه ومنهـا انتقـل إلى قم عـام ألف
وتسعمـائة وواحد وعشرين حيث قضى خمس سنوات في اتمام

دراساته الدينية المتقدمة، ثم بدأ يعمل كفقيه ومدرس ديني؟.

وفي أوائل الستينات قاد آية الله الخميني الحركة المناهضة لـ«الثورة البيضاء» التي أدخلها شاه إيران، ونُفي نتيجة لذلك عام ألف وتسعمائة وثلاثة وستين أولا إلى تركيا ثم إلى مدينة النجف الإسلامية المقدسة في العراق. وطرد من النجف بعد اتفاق بين العراق وإيران واضطر في أواخر السبعينات إلى السكن قريبا من باريس، ثم رجع إلى طهران في الثاني من فبراير عام ألف وتسعمائة وسبعة وسبعين بعد فترة قصيرة قضاها في باريس حتى بعد نشوب الثورة الإسلامية في الحادي عشر من فبراير من العام نفسه. ثم انتقل بعد ذلك إلى قم، وهي تعتبر عاصمة إيران الدينية، حتى أجبرته المشاكل القلبية على العودة إلى طهران حيث كان يعيش في الضواحي الشمالية منها حتى وفاته.

11. Précis
Suggested guidance questions for the précis in Arabic of نجاة عرفات.

١ – ماذا أدى إلى هبوط طائرة عرفات؟

٢ – من كان على متن الطائرة؟

٣ – من منهم لقي مصرعه؟

٤ – كيف جرت عملية الإنقاذ؟

٥ – ماذا حدث بعد عملية الإنقاذ هذه؟

17
Arabic literature

4. Written Arabic texts 1

(b) Answers to comprehension questions relating to في ذكرى قاهر الظلام.

1. Taha Hussein is rated as one of the greatest literary critics.
2. Taha Hussein memorised the Qur'an in the Qur'anic school of his village in Upper Egypt.
3. He lost his sight as a result of ophthalmia.
4. He studied in the al-Azhar University and the former Egyptian University.
5. The subject of his doctorate in France was the philosophy of Ibn Khaldun.
6. In 1963 he was appointed head of the Linguistic Academy.
7. Taha Hussein wrote books of short stories, criticism, belles-lettres, poetry, history and philosophy.
8. In the mid-thirties he published articles in Kawkab al-Sharq.
9. In the late-fifties he became editor of the newspaper al-Jumhuriyya.
10. The writer of this text suggests that Taha Hussein sets the highest example in the triumph of the human will.
11. He played a significant role in the Arabisation of scientific terms.
12. According to the writer of this text, the first obstacle Taha Hussein had to overcome was his loss of sight.

5. Written Arabic texts 2

(a) Suggested translation of أقيمت بيوت الوقف.

> The *waqf* houses were set out in two parallel lines which made up our quarter. The two lines began in front of the big house and stretched out towards al-Jamaliyya. The big house itself had been left unsurrounded on all sides at the top of the quarter where it reaches the desert. Our quarter, the quarter of Gebelawi, was the longest quarter in the area. Most of the houses were built around courtyards like those of the Al Hamdan quarter, but there were a large number of huts from the centre

up to al-Jamaliyya. The picture would not be complete without mentioning the *waqf* administrator's house at the top of the right-hand row of houses, and opposite to this the house of the young men's brotherhood at the top of the left-hand row.

The big house had closed its doors on its owner and his immediate entourage. The sons of Gebelawi had died a long time previously, and of the descendants of those who had lived and died in the big house no-one remained except the Effendi, who was the *waqf* administrator at that time. As regards the ordinary inhabitants of the quarter, some worked as hawkers and others as shopkeepers or cafe owners, while not a few were beggars. There was also one profession which everyone who was able engaged in; this was drug pushing – and particularly hashish, opium and aphrodisiac potions.[1] Then, just as now, our quarter was full of bustle and noise. Half-naked, barefoot children filled the air with their screams and the earth with their filth. Women crowded in the doorways of the houses, one chopping *moulukhiyya*, another peeling onions, a third lighting the fire. The women exchanged gossip and jokes, and when necessary, insults and abuse. There was singing and crying from morning till night, and the beat of the *zar* [drum] aroused particular interest. Handcarts were forever moving about, and here and there fights – both verbal and physical – broke out. Cats mewed, dogs growled, and sometimes the two species would quarrel over the rubbish heaps. Rats would dart across the open spaces and up onto the walls, and not infrequently a small crowd would gather to kill a snake or a scorpion. And the only things more numerous than the lice were the flies; they shared the people's plates when they ate and their cups when they drank, they danced in their eyes and sang in their mouths as if they were the friends of all.

Note

1. According to Hinds and Badawi (1986) مَدْفَع in Egyptian Arabic is a 'folk preparation eaten by men to enhance sexual powers'.

(b) Suggested translation of شيء يجـنن.

An infuriating thing

I cannot mention the name of the town where the general prison is located. The story has not yet become common gossip; it is still no more than a bit of news circulated by the inmates, prison employees and their respective relatives. Anyway, there are not many general prisons, thank God! There is hardly one such prison in the capital of every province for those who have been sentenced to imprisonment from the provinces itself and from surrounding *markazes* [مركز = sub-division of امديرية] and governorates.

To begin: there is a French proverb which goes 'cherchez la femme'. However, we won't find a single woman in that public prison because it is strictly for men. The only female allowed to wander around the prison is not a woman at all, but rather a female dog, or to be precise, the governor's dog. In every general prison the governor has a house inside the prison which is indistinguishable from the other buildings from the outside, but looks quite superb from the inside. It is usually near the entrance and has its own door, but it is surrounded by the same terrible wall which surrounds the prison on all sides.

6. Written Arabic texts 3 (classical)
Suggested translation of أبو علي الحسن بن هانئ.

Abu Ali al-Hasan ibn Hani'

Abu Ali al-Hasan ibn Hani', known as Abu Nuwas, was born in Ahwaz and grew up in Basra. It is said that he was a *Client* of al-Jarrah ibn Abdullah al-Hukmi, the governor of Khurasan. He often spent time with Abu Zayd al-Ansari. Even strangers wrote about him He memorised 'the Days of the People' under Abu Ubayda Mu'ammar ibn al-Muthanna and he studied Sibawayhi's grammatical theory. Amr ibn Bahr al-Jahiz said, 'I have never seen anyone who is more knowledgeable about language or more eloquent in his speech than Abu Nuwas and more inclined to use the beautiful and avoid the inelegant. He recited other people's poetry and used to quote his own.' Abu Ubayda Mu'ammar ibn al-Muthanna said, 'Abu Nuwas was to the Moderns what Imru' al-Qays was to the Ancients.' Ishaq ibn Isma'il said, 'Abu Nuwas said, "I only started composing poetry myself when I had memorised the poetry of sixty Arab women, including al-Khansa and Layla. So how many men do you think I memorised the poetry of?"' Maymun said, 'I asked Abu Yusuf Ya'qub ibn al-Sakit which poetry he would choose to recite to me and he said, "If I recited poetry from the Jahili [poets] then Imru' al-Qays and al-A'sha, from the Islamic [poets] then Jarir and al-Farazdaq, and from the modern [poets] then only Abu Nuwas."' Abu al-Abbas al-Mubarrad said on the authority of al-Jahiz, 'After he had recited Abu Nuwas's wine poetry I heard Ibrahim al-Nazzam say, "He is the one who knows a great deal about words, and he has chosen the best of them."' Sufyan ibn Ayyina said, 'He is the most poetic of people,' Al-Jahiz said, 'I know no poetry which is more refined than that of Abu Nuwas.

How many a fire has been lit by a fire-lighter[1]
And how serious the joker has become.'   [*sari'* metre]

And he recited the verses. Imam Muhammad ibn Idris al-Shafi'i, may
God have mercy upon him, said, 'I went to Abu Nuwas when he was
on his death-bed, and I said to him, "What have you prepared for this
day?" He said,

"My sins were great indeed but when I compared them
With thy forgiveness, my Lord, that was greater still."'

[*tawil* metre]

Note
1. Or: 'How many a 'fire' has been lit by an inflammatory remark' (lit:
   'an inflammatory person'). This line involves a pun on قادح/قدح,
   which also means 'defame/defamer'.

8. Aural Arabic texts 1

ii Transcription of the first part of the BBC Arabic Service news broadcast from
Oct. 13, 1988.

منحت جائزة نوبيل للآداب لهذا العام للكاتب والاديب المصري المعروف
نجيب محفوظ الذي ولد في عام الف وتسع مائة وأحد عشر. وقالت
اللجنة المشرفة على الجائزة ان اعماله تشكل جزءا من ذلك النوع من فن
الرواية العربية الذي ينطبق على البشرية بأسرها. ويُعدّ الاستاذ نجيب
محفوظ رائد الرواية العربية في العصر الحديث واحدا من كتّاب المقالة
والقصة على مدى نصف قرن. وقد اثرى المكتبة العربية بإنتاج غزير
يزيد على خمسين كتابا استعرض خلالها مراحل حياة الشعب المصري
ورسم صورة صادقة لمشاكله وآماله.

iii Transcription of the remainder of the BBC Arabic Service news broadcast from
Oct. 13, 1988.

الزميل سامي حداد اتصل قبل قليل بالشاعر والاديب العراقي المعروف
بلند الحيدري وسأله اولا عن اهمية الاستاذ نجيب محفوظ التي ادت
الى حصوله على جائزة نوبيل للآداب فرد بقوله:
ليس في نظري ثمة قصاص عربي مد بقامته على مثل ما مد بها
نجيب محفوظ. لقد اسّس خصوصيته نجيب محفوظ على تلك المقدرة

الرائعة في رصد الانسان المصري وفي ادق مشاكله الحياتية واليومية
وان يمد بها في الآن ذاته الى اعمق العلاقات الانسانية التي تخرج بها
من الجو المحلي الى العالمية. هذه المقدرة على التواصل مع الانسان حيثما
يكون من العالم هي بلا شك التي رشحته لجائزة نوبيل. وأعجبت
بـ«زقاق المدق» بثلاثيته الرائعة التي كانت رصدا لحياة كاملة في
شارعه. أعجبت بقصته «السراب» وكيف استلهم الفرويدية في ابعاد
تخرج من الواقع ولو تذكرنا عام تسعة وخمسين لتذكرنا ايضا رواية
«اولاد حارتنا» والتي تذكرنا ان نشرها اولا مسلسلة في الصحافة
اليومية ومن ثم في عام ستة وستين صدرت في كتاب في بيروت. فهذه
القصة كانت تفجير للواقع السياسي والاجتماعي وبأبعاد رمزية عميقة.
كانت تستهدف ان تصور الواقع المصري السائد ولكن من خلال تحوير
ومن خلال تشويه ومن خلال تفجير الابعاد الممكنة لذلك الواقع.

   ما دامت الموضوعات التي طرحها كانت، يعني، تُعنى بالانسان
المصري او مشاكل الانسان في العالم الثالث واعطاها بعدا انسانيا
كبيرا. وان يعطى جائزة نوبيل للآداب، هل يعني ذلك ان قصصه
ومسرحياته قد تُرجمت على مستوى عالمي؟

بلا شك. انا كما روى لي احد الذين قاموا بترجمته هو الاستاذ «دنيس
جونسون دايفس» كان هذا الرجل منذ الاربعينات يتابع بهوس عظيم
نجيب محفوظ ولما سألته مرة «لماذا نجيب محفوظ دون غيره؟» قال لأن
نجيب محفوظ يعطي الادب الاوربّي ما يريده من عمق انساني من ناحية
وما فيه من محلية خاصة. هذا هو المدخل للعالمية كما كان قال به لي
الذي ترجم له غير كتاب من كتبه وهو دينس جونسون.

   الاديب العراقي بلند الحيدري يتحدث عن الاديب المصري نجيب
محفوظ الذي فاز اليوم بجائزة نوبيل للآداب.

9. Aural Arabic texts 2

Complete transcription of طه حسين يتحدث, حصاد الشهر, no. 27, side 2, item 1,
في حديث من إذاعة لندن.

   نرحب بكم الى بداية الجهة الثانية ونستهلها بالعودة الى عام الف
وتسع مائة وتسعة وخمسين. فخلاله أذاع القسم العربي حديثا للأديب
العربي الكبير الدكتور طه حسين. ففي ارشيف مكتبة التسجيلات

الخاصة بهيئة الاذاعة البريطانية تسجيل قارن فيه أدبينا الراحل بين وضع الادب العربي في العصر العباسي وبين وضعه في العصر الحديث. فايهما يا تُرَى الافضل. لنستمع اولا الى رأيه في العصر العباسي.

فقد استطاع الادب العربي في العصر العباسي ان يسيغ ثقافات اجنبية لم يكن للعرب عهد بها من قبل. فأساغ الثقافة اليونانية والفارسية والهندية واصبح ادبا عالميا باوسع معاني هذه الكلمة لا يُقارَن في هذا الا بالادبين العالميين القديمين الادب اليوناني واللاتيني. وكنا نظن وما زلنا نتحدث بأن العصر الذي نعيش فيه كالعصور التي سبقته انما هي عصور ضعف فيها الادب العربي ضعفا شديدا بالقياس الى حياته تلك في العصر العباسي القديم. ولكن شيئا من التفكير وشيئا من الموازنة يُظهرنا على اننا في نصف القرن الاخير قد خطونا خطوات واسعة بهذا الادب واتحنا له في حياته الجديدة اشياء لم تكن تتاح له في ما مضى ولم يكن من الممكن ان تخطر للماضين على بال. فقد كان ادبنا في العصور القديمة – العصور الذهبية القديمة – يمتاز باتصاله بالثقافات الاجنبية التي كانت معروفة في تلك الايام واساغة هذه الثقافات. ولكننا اذا وازنّا تلك الثقافات التي كانت معروفة في العصر العباسي بالثقافات التي تُعرَف الآن رأينا ان تلك الثقافات كانت شيئا قليلا ضئيلا جدا بالقياس الى الثقافات التي نتصل بها في هذه الايام. الثقافة اليونانية القديمة والفارسية القديمة واللاتينية القديمة لم تكن شيئا الى جانب ما تزخر به الحياة العالمية في هذه الايام من الثقافة الانجليزية والفرنسية والالمانية والايطالية والروسية ومن الثقافة الاسبانية ومن هذه الثقافات المتفرقة الكثيرة التي لا تكاد تُحصى والتي تتمايز فيما بينها ولها قيمها الرفيعة الخاصة وكل هذه الثقافات قد اتصلنا بها واستطاع ادبنا العربي الحديث ان يسيغ منها الكثير واستطعنا ان نترجم من هذه اللغات واستطعنا ان يترجَم ادبنا الى بعض هذه اللغات ايضا. وهذا شيء ما كان يمكن ان يخطر للقدماء على بال. ثم لم نكتفِ بهذا ولكننا اضفنا الى الانتاج الادبي العربي بعض الفنون التي لم يكن العرب القدماء يعرفونها. فالعرب القدماء مثلا لم يكونوا يعرفون القصص كما نعرفه نحن في هذه الايام ولم يكونوا يحفلون بالقصص كما نحفل نحن به في هذه الايام.

10. Written English texts
Suggested translation of 'The language of poetry'.

كانت القصائد تُوَلَّف للتلاوة الشفوية أمام الملأ يرويها إما
الشاعر نفسه وإما راوٍ متخصّص في ذلك، الأمر الذي تَرَتَّبت
عليه نتائج مُعَيَّنة منها ضرورة إفادة المعنى المقصود في البيت
الواحد وهو وحدة متكاملة من الكلام يستطيع المستمع أن
يُدْرِكه إدراكاً شاملاً كما أن كل أداء للقصيدة يتّسم بفردية
خاصة ويختلف عن الأداءات الأخرى. وتمتّع الشعراء والرُواة
بقدر لا بأس به من الحرية في الارتجال ضمن إطار من الأشكال
والنماذج اللفظية المتَّفق عليها كما أنه أُتيح لهم استعمال
كلمات معينة أو عبارات تتكون من هذه الكلمات أو من غيرها
من أجل التعبير عن أفكارهم ومشاعرهم. ولذلك فمن الصعب
إثبات أصلية هذه القصائد، وأما النسخ الواردة إلينا اليوم
فلفّقها اللغويون أو النقّاد في فترات متأخرة في ضوء القوانين
اللغوية أو الشعرية التي كانت سائدة آنذاك.

11. Précis
Suggested guidance questions for the précis in Arabic of Naguib Mahfouz's acceptance speech for the Nobel Prize. Students may like to look back to chapter 3, section 6 (a), particularly the discussion of Hurmus or Akhanukh in relation to Mahfouz's discussion of Akhenaten.

١ – من القى رسالة نجيب محفوظ ولماذا لم يلق الرسالة الكاتب نفسه؟

٢ – من حضر الاحتفال؟

٣ – من هما بنتي نجيب محفوظ؟

٤ – ما هما الموضوعان اللذان تناولهما نجيب محفوظ في رسالته؟

٥ – في رأي نجيب محفوظ ما هو الفائز الحقيقي لجائزة نوبل؟ ماذا يقصد
بهذا في رأيك؟

٦ – لماذا يقول نجيب محفوظ إنه ابن حضارتين؟

٧ – ما هي القصة التي يرويها نجيب محفوظ عن الحضارة الفرعونية؟

٨ – ما هي الرواية التي يرويها نجيب محفوظ عن الحضارة الاسلامية؟

18
Economics

(a) **ii** Suggested translation of الاوساط المالية.

Stock exchange
Financial circles warn of rumours and predict price rises as companies move to buy their own stocks

Sources close to al-Watan report that the fall in share prices on the stock exchange yesterday was a predictable consequence of the collapse of stock markets worldwide, in particular the Hong Kong stock market. Here the collapse was mishandled in a number of ways, and it would, in fact, have been possible to mitigate the psychological effect of the fall by extending trading hours on the stock exchange rather than closing it.

These same sources also predict that there is likely to be a [similarly] marked reaction in Hong Kong to any future developments on the New York stock exchange – whether positive or negative – and suggest that the reaction of the Kuwait money-market will be far more muted.

According to informed sources the intention of certain local companies to purchase a reported 10% of their own shares will have a positive effect on average share prices, since approximately 50% of shares in companies registered on the stock exchange are owned by the government, whilst 25% of currently traded stocks are either underwritten, or are owned by investors who are retaining them as stable investment portfolios and have no intention of selling them.

This leaves only 25% of total currently traded stocks. The purchase by companies of a reported 10% of their own stocks – i.e. 40% of available shares – will therefore push up prices and increase the value of assets.

Sources predict that any clearly negative developments on the international stock markets, as well as local political developments, will have repercussions on share movements on the Kuwaiti market.

They have also issued a warning to those engaged in spreading rumours, such as those which were responsible for the wave of fear which overwhelmed investors during the morning trading session.

(b) **i** Answers to comprehension questions relating to د. ب النشاط.

1. The current movement of share prices on the Saudi parallel market is described as brisk.
2. The recession lasted for a few years.
3. The Saudi budget was one of the principal factors which affected the current state of share prices.
4. The announcement of the budget had been delayed from last December.
5. The surprise element in the budget was allowance for higher levels of public spending than had been envisaged in 1989.
6. The effect of this surprise element was to restore confidence in commercial circles which regard the increase in Saudi government expenditure as beneficial to the national economy.
7. The two factors mentioned as encouraging to the Saudi economy are higher levels of public spending and the improvement in world oil prices.

ii Suggested translation of د. ب النشاط.

Saudi investors prepare for period of increased activity
Increased share activity following years of stagnation
Oil price improvement and announcement of budget boost interest in shares

Following a period of stagnation lasting several years, share prices on the Saudi parallel market have begun to rise sharply, and there is widespread agreement that recent government measures will have a significant effect on future market activity. Among the main factors behind the current price movement are the announcement of the national budget for 1990 (deferred since last December), and the improvement in world oil prices.

There is general agreement that the Saudi budget for the current year makes allowance for higher levels of public spending than had been envisaged in 1989. This has restored confidence in commercial circles which regard the increase in Saudi government expenditure, as well as the increase in expenditure by other oil producing and exporting countries, as beneficial to the national economy.

All these factors have helped restored confidence in the commercial sector, resulting in an increase in Saudi share prices. The average value of weekly traded shares rose from between three and four million Saudi riyals in November to 11.6 million riyals during the week ending 18th December last year. The following week the value of traded shares rose to 18.4 million Saudi riyals, although it subsequently fell back again to 6.5 million riyals during the week ending 1st January, 1987. In the week ending 8th January, 1987, however, share prices showed another big jump, and the value of traded shares rose to 37.3 million riyals.

5. Written Arabic texts 2

(a) **ii** Suggested translation of المنطق الثاني.

The second conclusion: the need to develop the local market

Since the early fifties the countries of the third world have passed through a phase of industrialization whose importance, in our opinion, lies not so much in the results achieved, which have been modest, as in the necessity of learning the lessons of the experience itself. This might appear self-evident. However, the facts show that the majority of third-world countries have so far failed to take suffiicent account of these lessons. Certainly, the policies upon which industrial development is based have not undergone any radical transformation of a type which would allow us to claim otherwise. One of the most important lessons to be learnt from the experience of third-world industrialization is that the arbitrary, or at least ad hoc, selection of industrial projects, whether as part of a policy of import substitution, or of export-orientated production, has resulted in the creation of uneconomic projects. This in turn has led to spiralling state expenditure to support these industries, and to the development of a general climate in which they are protected from both regional and global competition, on the pretext that they are nascent industries. The undeniable fact is that the state has found itself compelled to go on supporting these projects, despite the enormous burden they impose, because they have become a part of, or at least symbolic of, the liberationist political and economic regimes in these countries. The result is that these industries have remained nascent long after they have grown old and grey.

(b) **i** Rough translation of ملخص (لقد مر النشاط التجاري ...) with alternatives.

Synopsis/Summary/Abstract/Résumé

A: The modern era has witnessed/brought several phases of commercial activity/relations between the Indian sub-continent and the Gulf region.

B: During the modern era there have been several phases of commercial activity/relations between the Indian sub-continent and the Gulf region in/of/up to the modern era.

These include the rise and activity of the British East India Company, and its rivalry with the Dutch and Portuguese in both India and the Gulf, and period of British commercial hegemony and confrontation with/resistance to both old and new rivals/rival powers in the two areas/in these two regions. During this period there were important/ significant commercial relations between the Indian sub-continent and the Gulf, and goods were traded in both directions. Particularly following the occupation of India and Aden, however, such trade was carried on within a framework on terms imposed by the policies of Britain, which now controlled/dominated both regions, and its limits were determined by British commercial and political interests.

A: The level of commercial activity between India and the Gulf tended to vary as a result of/according to political and military events, particularly during the two World Wars,

B: Particularly during the two World Wars, the level of commercial activity between India and the Gulf tended to vary as a result of/according to political and military events,/.
and although/Although

A: there was a relative change/something of a change in the nature of commercial relations in the region

B: something of a change took place in the nature of commercial relations in the region

following the independence of the states of the Indian sub-continent in the post-independence era, in 1948, when these states entered a new era,/.
they/Despite this, however, they still retained their links with the past.

ii Idiomatic translation of (... ملخص (لقد مر النشاط التجاري.

Synopsis

During the modern era commercial relations between the Indian sub-continent and the Gulf region have passed through several phases. These include the rise to prominence of the British East India Company, its rivalry with the Dutch and Portuguese in India and the Gulf, and the period of British commercial hegemony and confrontation with both old and new rival powers in these two regions. Throughout this era there were significant commercial links between the Indian sub-continent and the Gulf, and goods were traded in both directions. Particularly following the occupation of India and Aden, however, such trade was carried on within a framework whose terms were imposed by the

policies of Britain, which now dominated both regions, and its limits
were determined by British commercial and political interests.

Especially during the two World Wars, the level of commercial
activity between India and the Gulf varied in accordance with political
and military events. Commercial relations in the region were also
somewhat affected by the independence of the states of the Indian sub-
continent in 1947, and their emergence into a new era, although they
even now retained their historical roots.

iii Additional translation exercise: comparison of translations of مـر (لقد مـر ملخص
.(... النـشاط التـجاري)

Take the rough translation given below with alternatives and, in class, discuss
ways of making it more idiomatic. At the end of the exercise compare the class
version with the idiomatic translation given below the rough translation.

(c) Answers to comprehension questions related to مـجـالا لا يـفسـح بما القـول يمكن
.لجدل أو شك

1. He claims they have now passed the stage of trial and error.
2. There are now around fifty Islamic banks and branches.
3. They hardly differ at all from other modern banks except inasmuch as they make
   no use of interest.
4. The western-style banks which come closest to Islamic banks are popular
   savings banks [trustee savings banks], and cooperative banks.
5. They are similar to Islamic banks in that they focus on participation and
   investment, and not solely on commercial security.
6. Co-operative socialists and some of the pioneers of the French socialist school
   called for the establishment of cooperative banks in the nineteenth century.
7. The Islamic banking experiment in the 1970s was one feature of the Islamic
   revival.
8. Islamic banks are not to be blamed for adopting modern techniques and
   machinery, because these are merely modern means which are used to achieve a
   goal.
9. The writer points out that the *haram* is equipped with modern lighting,
   loudspeakers, and electric sweepers.

6. Written Arabic texts 3 (classical)
(a) Translation of البـقرة سـورة ii. 275–6.

They who devour usury shall arise in the resurrection only as he arises
whom Satan has infected by his touch. This is because they say,
'Selling is like usury,' and yet God has allowed selling, and forbidden

usury. He then who when this warning shall come to him from his Lord, abstains, shall have pardon for the past, and his lot shall be with God. But they who go back [to usury], shall be given over to the fire; therein shall they abide for ever.

God will bring usury to nought, but will give increase for deeds of charity; God loves no ungrateful and sinful person.

(b) Suggested translation of حدّثنا يزيد بن عمرو.

Yazid ibn Amr said that Awn ibn Umara on the authority of Hisham ibn Hassan on the authority of al-Hasan that Umar ibn al-Khattab, may God be pleased with him, said, 'He who deals in something three times and does not gain from it should change from this [business] to something else.' He also said, 'Avoid the loss you might incur from one [slave or animal] dying. Buy two for the price of one and do not remain in a house where you are unable to earn a living.' He said, 'If you buy a camel buy, one with good conformation. Even if you are misled by something good don't let the market mislead you.' He said, 'Sell the animal – it is better than it being in your sight.' Al-Hasan said, 'Markets are the tables of God on earth; he who comes to one gets something from it.' Ibn Mubarak said on the authority of Ma'mar, on the authority of Zubayry, 'The Messenger of God – God bless him and give him peace – passed by a man who was selling something. He said, 'You should engage in selling when the market opens. For he who is generous always gains [lit: 'the gainer is with generosity']'.' It used to be said, 'Show generosity, and generosity will be shown to you.' According to a *hadith* which can be traced in an ascending order of authorities back to the Prophet, the Prophet, God bless him and give him peace, ordered the rich to take sheep and the poor to take chicken.' Al-Zubayr was asked, 'How have you gained the wealth which you enjoy?' He replied, 'I have never refused gain, nor hidden fault.' A group of people went to Mu'awiya, who asked them about their trades. They replied, 'Slave-trading.' He said, 'The most terrible form of trade is when one only looks after one's own interests [lit: 'guaranteeing for oneself and storing up food for one's own molar tooth'].'

8. Aural Arabic texts 1

i   Answers to comprehension questions relating to حصاد الشهر no. 30, side 1, item 1, البنوك الإسلامية.

1. Any loan which yields a profit is described as usury.
2. The Qur'an forbids the imposition of any profit on capital in the case of loans.
3. There is no difference between interest and usury.

4. We are told that Sheikh Ibrahim al-Tayyib al-Rayyih is head of the Islamic Investment Corporation in Sudan and that he is a member of the Islamic Finance House Administration Council.

5. He says that an Islamic Bank in Europe would show the world that it is possible to have a bank based on Islamic principles in the financial world centre.

ii Transcription of البنوك الإسلامية up to على وفق دينهم وشريعتهم.

سيداتي سادتي، يقول الله سبحانه وتعالى في كتابه الكريم:

«ذلك بأنهم قالوا إنما البيع مثل الرباواحلّ الله البيع وحرّم الربا»

صدق الله العظيم

والمقصود بالربا هنا حسب قول الفقهاء أن كل قرض جرّ نفعا فهو ربا. والاسلام يحرّم اشتراط أي زيادة على رأس المال عند القروض – أي أن يضمن البنك الممول رأس المال وأي زيادة متفق عليها. ويتساءل المرء هل الفائدة الحالية التي تتقاضاها البنوك على القروض تختلف عن الربا الذي حرّمه القرآن؟ والجواب الذي أجمع عليه كافة المجتهدين والفقهاء أن الفائدة الحالية التي تتقاضاها البنوك على القروض لا تختلف عن الربا الذي حرّمه الاسلام. فما البديل إذن؟ هذا السؤال مع أسئلة عديدة أخرى وجّهتها سهام الكرمي إلى الشيخ إبراهيم الطيب الريح رئيس مؤسسة الاستثمار الإسلامية في السودان وعضو مجلس إدارة دار المال الإسلامي في جنيف. وهاكم ما قاله لنا عن الغرض من وجود البنك الإسلامي في أوربا علما بأن وجوده كان في الأصل من أجل التعامل بين المسلمين.

وجوده في أوربا أوّلا يُتيح الفرصة للعالم بأن يسمع بأن هنالك بنك إسلامي قام في مركز المال العالمي وهو يعمل بأحكام الشريعة الإسلامية وبذلك أرَدْنا أن نُثبت للعالم بأن أحكام الشريعة الإسلامية تُمَكن المسلمين من قيام بنوك تعمل على وفق دينهم وشريعتهم.

9. Aural Arabic texts 2

i   Complete transcription of حصاد الشهر no. 23, side 2, item 1, ما هي اسباب
.وذيول ازمة سوق المناخ في الكويت؟

يوجد في الكويت منذ عام ١٩٥٢ سوق رسمية للاوراق المالية، غير ان
السوق المالية غير الرسمية المعروفة باسم سوق المناخ أُنشئت في عام
١٩٨١ نظرا لان الطلب عن الاسهم في السوق الرسمية كان يزيد على
المعروض. وكان الطلب قد انتعش نتيجة اتخاذ اجراءات في ذلك العام
ترمي الى تشجيع عودة رأس المال الخاص الذي خرج من الكويت اثر
اندلاع الحرب العراقية – الايرانية ، ونظرا لان الحكومة الكويتية قيدت
عدد الشركات المدرجة في سوق الاوراق المالية الرسمية فقد حوّل
المستثمرون الكويتيون انتباههم بدلا من ذلك صوب شركات جديدة
مسجلة في دول خليجية اخرى، وتم التعامل في اسهم هذه الشركات في
سوق المناخ غير الرسمية التي استمدت اسمها من المبنى الذي يضم
مكاتب تجار الاوراق المالية. ولم تخضع هذه السوق لاي نوع من
الضوابط على الاطلاق، كما ان بعض الشركات المسجلة فيها لم تكن اكثر
من اسم على ورق، ومع ذلك فقد كان الطلب شديدا على الاسهم لدرجة
انه عندما رفضت البنوك تقديم اعتمادات مالية بدأ المضاربون
المعتملون في شراء الاسهم بشيكات آجلة، وكانت هذه الشيكات تغطي
الاسعار الفورية للاسهم بالاضافة الى مبلغ مضاف يعكس زيادة متوقعة
في السعر. وقد ادت هذه الممارسة الى احداث زيادات اخرى في الطلب
على الاسهم، واخذت المبالغ المضافة ترتفع الى مستويات بلغت ثلاثمائة
واربعمائة بالمائة. وحدث الانهيار في شهر سبتمبر/ايلول عام ١٩٨٢
بعد ان بدأت اسعار الاسهم في التدهور عندما اصبح جليا ان الحكومة
لن تتدخل لانقاذ المضاربين، وبدأ حملة الشيكات الآجلة استنادا الى ان
القانون الكويتي يبيح تقديم مثل هذه الشيكات بغض النظر عن تواريخ
اصدارها بدأوا في التقدم الى صرفها قبل موعد الاستحقاق. ولم يكن
لدى مصدري الشيكات ارصدة كافية للوفاء بصرف قيمتها مما ادى الى
انهيار النظام بأسره. وقد اتسم حل المشكلة تعويض الاشخاص الذين
فقدوا اموالا في سوق المناخ بصعوبة لدرجة انه ادى حتى الى استقالات
من مجلس الوزراء الكويتي. وتكشف ان قيمة الشيكات الآجلة المعلقة
تصل الى مبلغ ضخم مقداره تسعون الف مليون دولار، وقد تم سداد

صغار المستثمرين الدائمين بمبالغ تصل الى سبعة ملايين دولار نقدا او بسندات اصدرها صندوق خاص للاغاثة. ثم تقرر في شهر اغسطس/آب عام ١٩٨٣ تحديد المبلغ المضاف على الشيكات الآجلة بنسبة خمسة وعشرين في المائة فقط او اقل بدلا من ثلاثمائة بالمائة او اكثر ، مما مكّن من تسوية مزيد من الديون. وبعد ذلك شُكلت لجنة تحكيم لاعادة تقييم ديون سبعة عشر شخصا ممن عجزوا عن سداد ديونهم وكانوا مسؤولين معا عن اكثر من ثمانين بالمائة من اجمالي المبالغ المعلقة والذين لا تكفي ممتلكاتهم لتقضية ديونهم. وشُكلت شركة لتحويل ممتلكات هؤلاء المدينين الى ممتلكات سائلة.

10. Written English texts

(a) Suggested translation of 'Natural gas reserves'.

احتياطات الغاز الطبيعي

تُبيِّن خريطةُ مصرَ النفطية أن معظم الآبار الحالية تتركَّز في حوض خليج السويس والذي يعود العمل فيه الى ما يزيد عن المائة عام. ولم تتمَّ أيُّ اكتشافاتٍ أخرى حتى أواسط الستينات حيث [/عندما] اُكتشف أول حقل للنفط في صحراء مصر الغربية وهو حقل العلمين والذي اُكتشف عام الف وتسع مائة وستة وستين. وتلا ذلك [/هذا] الاكتشافَ اكتشافاتُ أخرى، مثل حقل أبو ماضي في دلتا النيل الكبرى ثم حقل ابو قير الواقع في [/تحت] البحر الأبيض المتوسط. واستمر العمل الاستكشافي فأُضيفت الى هذه القائمة عددُ من حقول النفط الجديدة، إلا أن [/لكن} الحكومةَ المصريةَ لم تُعر اهتماماً كافياً للغاز المطلوق حيث [/فـ}أُحرِق معظم هذا الغاز. أما اسباب هذه السياسة فكثيرة منها وجود مصادر طاقة أخرى رخيصة نسبياً أوفت بمتطلّبات القطاع الصناعي [في مصر}.

(b) Suggested translation of 'One objection to interest'.

إن واحداً من اعتراضات [/ومن اعتراضات] المسلمين على الربا أنه يشكّل وببساطة نوعاً من المكافأة التي يتم الحصول عليها دون أي جهد إنتاجي. وأما الاقتصاديون الغربيون فيعتبرونه مكافأة على الانتظار أو على تأجيل الاستهلاك حيث أنّ البضائع التي سيتمّ استهلاكها في المستقبل هي أقل قيمةً في سعرها حالياً وأنه يتوجّب خصم قيمتها وهو أمر يُدخل عامل الربا. وأما المسلمون فلا يربطون بين المال والزمن على هذه المنوال فلا يمكن تطبيق المفهوم الغربي. وبالإضافة إلى ذلك فإنه يُنظر للربا باستنكار نظراً لتأثيره السلبي [/السيء] على [إعادة] توزيع الثروة حيث يجعل الفرد المنتج مُداناً لغير المنتج ويمكن أن يؤدّي إلى مديونية الفقير للغني. وعندما يُعسر المدين عن سداد ديونه يحثّ القرآن الكريم على التساهل بشأن إعادة جدولة تلك الديون في قوله تعالى:

(وإِنْ كَانَ ذُو عُسْرَةٍ فَنَظِرَةٌ إِلَى مَيْسَرَةٍ
وأَنْ تَصَدَّقُوا خَيْرٌ لَكُم إِنْ كُنْتُم تَعْلَمُون)
صَدَقَ الله العظيم

11. Précis
Suggested quidance questions for the précis in Arabic of مناخ الاستثمار في الجمهورية العربية السورية.

١ – اين تقع الجمهورية العربية السورية؟

٢ – ما هي اهمية موقع سوريا؟

٣ – بما يتمتع الساحل السوري الغربي؟

٤ – ما هي مساحة البلاد، وكم عدد سكانها؟

٥ – كيف تطورت السياسة الاقتصادية السورية منذ الخمسينات من هذا القرن؟

٦ – كيف تحاول الحكومة السورية ان تجذب الاستثمارات الوافدة؟

٧ – ما هو هدف المرسوم التشريعي رقم ٣٤٨؟

٨ – ما هو هدف المرسوم التشريعي رقم ١٠٣؟

٩ – ما هي المراسيم الهامة الاخرى التي تتعلق بالصناعة؟

١٠ – ما هي التدابير التي اتخذتها الحكومة السورية بالنسبة للاعفاء من الرسوم الجمركية؟

١١ – ما هي التدابير التي اتخذتها الحكومة السورية في مجال التسهيلات النقدية وغيرها من التسهيلات؟

19
Medicine

4. Written Arabic texts 1

(b) Answers to comprehension questions relating to لكل عشب فائدة.

1. Chamomile, rhubarb and colocynth are used to treat headaches.
2. Sarsaparilla is used to treat diabetes.
3. Chamomile, wild chicory and cumin are used to treat indigestion.
4. Pomegranate rind and cinnamon are used to treat diarrheoa.
5. Rhubarb is used to treat persistent coughs.
6. Coriander is used to treat ulcers.
7. Wild chicory is used to treat constipation.
8. Cinnamon is used to treat stomach cramps.
9. Rhubarb and caltrop are used to treat bladder disturbances.
10. Colocynth is used to treat earache.

(c) Suggested translation of أول كتاب صيدلة في العالم.

Law is not the only field in which the Sumerians excelled before other men. Excavations have uncovered a document which contains the first pharmaceutical statement [lit: law] in the world. This document mentions a diagnosis and a treatment which have no relation to magic, charms and incantations, but rather are purely scientific [diagnoses and treatments]. This type of medicine was common in Sumer during the third millenium before Christ.

The above-mentioned[1] document was [found] written in cuneiform on a tablet of dry clay. It mentions more than twelve types of treatment and is believed to be the first book on pharmacy known to mankind. The tablet was discovered during investigations carried out in Nafr. It is now to be found in the Philadelphia University Museum. [Information on] the tablet indicates that the Sumerian doctor who wrote the document used to make use of plants, animals and minerals as primary sources for [extracting/producing] medicines, just like his present-day counterpart.

Note

1. المذكورة أعلاه – a common way of referring to something mentioned previously.

5. Written Arabic texts 2

(b) Suggested translation of تمهيد: الطب الإسلامي.

In the name of God, Compassionate and Merciful

Praise be to God who guided us to this point; we would not have been guided had it not been for His directions. Blessings and peace upon the best of His messengers and the seal of His prophets, our lord Muhammad, and on his family and his companions, may He grant them salvation.

Preface

Islamic medicine first emerged following the death of the Prophet Muhammad and continued to flourish throughout the Islamic era. Although some people have termed this form of medicine 'Arabic', this is not strictly speaking correct. Rather, it is better regarded as Islamic, since it developed in the context of Islamic civilisation of which it was an integral part. With the subsequent decline of that civilisation Islamic medicine disappeared.

Before the rise of Islam, the Arabs did not possess any form of medicine which was specifically theirs. They lived in a state of ignorance which pervaded virtually all areas of life, and it was only after the rise of Islam that medicine began to flourish. Most of the famous pioneers of Islamic medicine such as Ar-Razi, Ibn Sina and Ali Ibn Abbas were in fact non-Arabs, who used Arabic in their writings because of their association with Islam but still retained their original ethnic identity. Similarly, a significant number of those involved in Islamic medicine, although subjects of the Islamic state, were non-Muslims. Such people made a significant contribution to Islamic medicine both through their translations and their own writings. This was only possible because they were fully incorporated into an Islamic civilisation which granted them the same rights as it granted to its Muslim subjects.

i Additional exercise: comparison of translations of الطب الإسلامي : تمهيد.

The suggested English translation of the above passage contains a number of changes in word order and sentence structure from the original Arabic. Students could be asked to compare the original, the suggested translation above, and their own English versions, and to consider the changes made in the suggested translation and in their own versions.

(c) **ii** Suggested structure translations relating to الفقر لا يعطي المحتاج حق ممارسة دور الطبيب.

١ – نأكل الخبز أكثر مما نأكل الجبنة.

٢ – هذا يمكن تسميته بـ«العلاج الذاتي».

٣ – يعتبرون العلوم سهلة لا تستحق التفكير العميق.

٤ – ما هي المشاكل الكثيرة الانتشار التي ذكرتها؟

٥ – عليك بعطلة قصيرة.

٦ – يصيبها نقص في الثقة بالنفس.

٧ – هذه الصناعات ذات الإنتاج العالي.

٨ – وصل الأمر إلى درجة أننا لا نستطيع أن نرجع.

٩ – سارعت إلى فتح الباب.

١٠. – كتب هذه الرسالةَ هو أو أحد أصدقائه؟

6. Written Arabic texts 3 (classical)
i Suggested translation of اعلم أيها الأخ.

> You should know, my friend – may God help both you and us with His spirit – that we have finished explaining the nature of the path to God Almighty and the means of attaining direct [i.e. gnostic] knowledge of Him, which is the ultimate goal. In this epistle we now want to talk about the belief of the Brethren of Purity and the Way of the Holy Ones, and to demonstrate in a manner which is comprehensively convincing rather than [merely] intellectually satisfying that the soul survives after leaving the body, a phenomenon usually expressed as the natural process of death.
> You should know that in times gone by it was said that there was a wise man who was well versed in medicine. This man once went into a town and saw that the mass of its people were afflicted by a hidden illness whose ill effects they could not feel. The wise man thought about them and considered how best to treat them in order to free them

from the sickness which had continued to ail them. He knew that if he told them what was wrong with them they would not listen to what he said or heed his advice; indeed they may even be openly hostile to him, reject his point of view, and dismiss his learning and his knowledge. He [decided to] go about his work surreptitiously out of his deep compassion and sympathy for his fellow human beings, and out of desire to cure them in accordance with what would be pleasing to God Almighty. So he sought out one of the most eminent men of the town who had the illness; he gave him one of the draughts which he had with him and which he had prepared in order to treat the people of the town, and made him sniff some vapours he had brought with him to treat them. Immediately the man sneezed, and found a lightness in his frame, repose in his senses, health in his body and strength in his soul. He thanked him and blessed him for what he had done, then said to him, 'Is there anything I could give you to recompense you for great goodness in curing me?' He said, 'Yes, you can help me to cure one of your brothers.' The man who had been cured replied, 'Of course I will.' So they agreed on this, and went to another man who in their opinion was very pious. They separated him from his companions, gave him the treatment and he recovered immediately. When he had got over his illness he blessed them and said to them, 'Is there anything I can do to recompense you for your kindness?' They said, 'You can help us to treat one of your brothers.' 'Of course!' he replied. So they agreed to do this. Then they found another man and treated him in the same way as they had treated the first man, so that he was cured. This man spoke just as the first man to be cured had done. And they gave the same reply as had been given by the first curer.

Then the various people who had been cured spread out across the town, treating people one after the other covertly until they had cured a large number of people, and they had many helpers, brothers and friends. Then they went up to the remaining people, and told them about the treatment and forced them to take the medicine. They sought out the townspeople one by one; one group of people would take the townsperson by the arms and another by the legs, and the others would force him to sniff and drink the medicine until they had cured everyone in the town.

ii Additional exercise: *pronoun>noun* shifts in translation of اعلم أيها الأخ.

The English translation of this Arabic text illustrates very well the tendency for English to make greater use of nouns, and for Arabic (and particularly classical Arabic) to rely more on pronouns. As a supplementary exercise, students who have done the translation exercise (and possibly been given a text of this suggested translation) could be asked to identify *pronoun>noun* shifts from the Arabic original to the English translation, and also consider cases in which the use of pronouns in the English translation is vaguer – i.e. where the reference is less immediately clear – than is typical in modern English writing. For a similar additional exercise, cf. chapter 12, section 6a.

8. Aural Arabic texts 1

(a) Answers to comprehension questions relating to حصاد الشهر, no. 5, side 2, item 5 الصيدلة والعقاقير عند العرب في القديم.

1. Dr Muhammad Zuhayr is professor of medicine and the history of pharmacy at the University of Damascus.
2. The Prophet Muhammad said that for every illness that people suffer from there is an appropriate cure.
3. The Prophet divided treatment into eating honey, cupping and cauterization.
4. Edward Browne presented the information in this way to show that the Arabs only knew a very few methods of treatment and medicinal drugs in early Islamic times.
5. The falsity of Browne's claim is demonstrated by considering the Arabic of pre-Islamic times where a large number of local and imported medicinal plants and medicines are mentioned by name.
6. Ibn Khaldoun says that medicine is essential in cities but not amongst the Bedouins because there is more illness in cities due to the fact that life is more opulent in the cities and city dwellers eat more and exercise less.
7. The three traditional divisions of medicine are surgery, nutrition and drugs.
8. The most important branch of medicine in the middle ages was drugs.
9. There are two types of medicinal drugs: simple drugs and complex drugs.
10. The Arabs were the first to apply chemistry to medicine and the first to consider the role of pharmacy as something separate from medicine.
11. The Arabs supplemented their knowledge of medicinal drugs gained from the Greeks and others by things they learnt from discovery and experimentation.

(b) Complete transcription of ما هو الفضل الشهر حصاد, no. 33, side 1, item 3, الذي أداه العرب للطب؟.

أما الآن فنبقى بمادتنا التالية مع الطب ولكن من زاوية تاريخية حتى
نعرف الفضل الذي أداه العرب للطب. وهذا موضوع أسهب قي الحديث
عنه خبراء برنامجنا الجديد «عبقرية الحضارة العربية». وقد اعتاد
الباحثون في العصور العربية المأثورة أن يقسموا عصر ازدهار الطب
في الدولة العربية الإسلامية إلى ثلاث مراحل : الأولى مرحلة الاكتساب
والثانية مرحلة الترجمة والثالثة مرحلة الإنتاج والابتكار.

ولكن المرحلة الثالثة شاهدت ظهور رجال بارزين في الطب كالرازي وابن سيناء والزهراوي الجراح الأندلسي المشهور وابن زهر وابن رشد وعشرات غيرهم . هؤلاء الرجال العظام تركوا وراءهم آثارا طبية خالدة أثبتوها في كتبهم البارعة التي ترجمت إلى اللاتينية في أوائل العصور الوسطى وعادت على أوروبا بفوائد عظيمة. وهناك حقيقة لا نكران لها وهي أن كتب الرازي وابن سيناء في الطب ظلت تدرس في الجامعات الأوروبية في برامجها الطبية حتى القرن السابع عشر، ومما لا شك فيه أن الغرب قد أقر في زمن من الأزمان وأفاد فائدة كبرى من علم رجال الطب الإسلامي.

هذا مما جاء في الحلقة الثانية من برنامج «عبقرية الحضارة العربية». أما الحلقة الثالثة منه فتناولت الجراحة عند العرب وتحدثت أولا عن ازدهار مدرسة الطب الاسكندرية خلال القرنين الرابع والثالث قبل الميلاد. ولعل أقدم المعلومات في علم التشريح التي وصلت إلى العرب هي مؤلفات «جالينوس» الذي عاش في القرن الثاني الميلادي ودرس علم التشريح في مدرسة الاسكندرية . ثم درس الأطباء العرب كل مؤلفاته التي ترجمها من اليونانية إلى العربية بكل دقة وأمانة حنين بن اسحاق العبادي المتوفى سنة ثمان مائة وثلاث وسبعين ميلادية. ومن هذه كتاب جالينوس المسمى «في عمل التشريح» والذي يقع في خمسة عشر كتابا حُفظت جميعها من الضياع في عدة مخطوطات عربية كاملة بينما فقدت الأصول اليونانية للكتب الستة الاخيرة مع الجزء الأخير من الكتاب التاسع. والسؤال الذي لا بد من طرحه الآن هو: ما سبب بذل جالينوس كل هذا الاجتهاد في علم التشريح؟ لنستمع إلى رأي الدكتور البير اسكندر الباحث والمؤلف في تاريخ الطب في معهد «ويلكوم» بإنكلترا.

يقول جالينوس إن اتقان علم التشريح لازم لكل طبيب حتى يتمكن من تشخيص أمراض الأعضاء الباطنة. ولازم للطبيب أيضا حينما يمارس فن الجراحة فتسلم أطراف الأعصاب الدقيقة من سلاح مبضعه الحد. فكم من طبيب جاهل لا يدري بوجود العصب الراجع إلى فوق فيبتره هفوا أثناء العمل بالحديد في جراحة الرقبة. فيشكو المريض بعد أيام من فقدان صوته أو انخفاضه إلى درجة الصرار والهمس.

ثم انتقل البرنامج فأعطى وصفا تشريحيا لأحد أطباء العرب

القدامى:

أيقن الأطباء العرب أن علم التشريح أساس لفن الجراحة. ونذكر على سبيل المثال عبد اللطيف بن يوسف البغدادي المتوفى سنة ستمائة وتسع وعشرين هجرية ألف ومائتين وإحدى وثلاثين ميلادية. والذي يذكر في كتابه المسمى «الإفادة والاعتبار» أنه فحص أكثر من ألفي جمجمة آدمية في مقابر بوسير وخرج بنتيجة عملية وهي أن الفك السفلي يتكون من عظم واحد فقط وبذلك فقد صحح الخطأ الكبير أن الفك السفلي يتكون من عظمين ملتحمين معا بدَرْز ماسك وثيق.

10. Written English texts
Suggested translation of 'Hospitals and medical education'.

Version A: لقد أصبح التصور السائد لدى العرب القدماء [/القدامى] للمستشفى النموذج الأوّل الذي مهّد الطريق إلى تطور المستشفى الحديث أي [/وهو/باعتباره} مؤسسة .....

Version B: إن المستشفايات التي أنشأها [/عرفها] العرب القدماء [/القدامى] قد أصبحت النموذج الأوّل للمستشفايات المتطورة في عهدنا الحديث وهي مؤسسات ....

يملكها إما القطاع الخاص أو العام وهدفها [/تتخصّص بـ] تحسين [/مراعاة] الصحة [العامة] وشفاء [/معالجة] الأدواء [/الأمراض] ونشر العلوم الطبية وتوسيعها. ومنذ بداية القرن التاسع الميلادي موّلت خزانةُ الدولة المستشفيات بسخاء في البلدان الإسلامية وقد قام بـإدارتها المديرون والموظفون المتخصصين في مجال الإدارة. وخدمت هذه المستشفيات الرجال والنساء في عنابر مختلفة. وفي القرن العاشر وبالتحديد في عهد الخليفة المقتدر الذي استمرّ حكمه من عام ٩.٠٨ م. إلى عام ٩٣٢ م. قـد وسّع سنان بن ثابت بن قُرَّة

الخدمات التي قدّمتها المستشفيات لتسدّ حاجات المناطق الريفية المجاورة والسجون والمناطق السكنية الواقعة في وسط المدينة وهو برنامج لم تتبنّه البلدان الغربية إلا في السنوات الأخيرة.

وأما الرازي وهو معاصر لسنان فقد اعتبر المستشفيات مؤسسات ذات أهمية كبرى [/بالغة الأهمية] من حيث توفير التدريب العملي في المهن الصحية وفي نشر المعلومات المتعلقة بالصحة. وفي أواخر القرن العاشر ذاع صيت مستشفى «العدودي» [الواقعة] في بغداد إلى جميع أنحاء المعمورة وهو مستشفى ذو أهمية بالغة يعمل فيه أربعة وعشرون طبيبًا ويشمل على قاعات للمحاضرات ومكتبة مولّتها السلطات بسخاء وكرم.

11. Précis
Suggested guidance questions for the précis in Arabic of «الجامع لمفردات الأدوية والأغذية» لابن بيطار.

١ – من هو ابن بيطار وماذا نعرف عن سنواته الاولى؟

٢ – ما هي مهمة كتابه «الجامع لمفردات الادوية والاغذية»؟ متى صدر الكتاب بالعربية؟ متى تُرجك الكتاب والى اي لغات؟

٣ – في الكتاب كم مصطلحا فنيا؟

٤ – ماذا ادخل ابن بيطار في كتابه لاول مرة في تاريخ الطب والصيدلة؟

٥ – من هم العرب المسلمون الذين اعتمد عليهم في الكتاب؟

٦ – اذكر بعض الادوية النباتات التي يذكرها ابن بيطار في كتابه.

20
Islamic heritage

4. Written Arabic texts 1

(c) Complete transcription of المسلمون هم الأوائل في تأسيس أقدم جامعة في العالم. (Words missing from the text in the textbook are put in curly brackets here.)

كثـيـرة {هي} الجامـعـات العربيـة الإسلاميـة العريقـة نذكر {منها} جامعة القرويين و{جامعة} الزيتونة و{جامعة} الأزهر و{جامعة} قرطبـة و{جامعة} نيسابور والنظاميـة والمستنصريـة {في} بـغداد، ويكاد الإجماع ينعقد {على} أن أقدم الجامعات العربيـة الإسلاميـة بل {أقدم} الجامـعـات {في} العالم طُرًّا {هي} جامعة القرويين في فاس بالمغرب {التي} تأسست {سنة} مـائتين وخمس وخمسين {هجرية} – ثمانـي مائة وثمان وستين ميلاديـة. فقد مضى {على} {تأسيسها} أكثـر من أحد عشر {قرنا} ونصف القرن، وظلت خلالها منارة إشعاع علمي إلى جانب شقيقتيها جامعة الزيتونة وجامعة الأزهر. و{مما} يُذكر {أن} هذه {الجامعات} العريقة كانت عند تأسيسها مساجد للعبادة تُعقد فيها حلقات لتدريس العلوم الدينية أساسًا. {ثم} اتسع نطاق {التدريس} وتطورت مناهجها التـعـليـمـيـة وانتظمت وتشعّبت {بحيث} أصبحت جامعات بالمعنى {المألوف}.

{عندمـا} تأسست مدينـة فاس المغربيـة {سنة} مـائة واثنتين وتسعين هجرية كان في عداد الذين هاجروا إليها {من} تونس محمد بن عبد الله الفهري القيـرواني {الذي} توفي بُعيد وصـوله {إلى} فاس تاركًا ثروة طائلة لكريمتيه فاطـمة ومريم. و{في} منتصف القرن الثالث الهجري بنت فاطمة أم البنين القيروانية {جامع} القرويين بعدوة القرويين في {الجانب} الغربي {من} نهر فاس. وسرعان ما أصبحت {مدينة} فاس قبلة

أنظار العلماء والأدباء فقد جعلت منها جامعتها الجديدة عاصمة ثقافية يحج إليها الطلاب لا {من} شمال إفريقيا {وحسب} بل ومن أطراف أوربا {أيضاً} ومن جملة من وفد إليها البابا سلفستر الثاني {الذي} درس في القرويين الأرقام {العربية}، ثم أدخلها {إلى} أوربا {بعد} ارتقائه سلطة البابوية.

ويلي القرويين {في} العراق {جامعة} الأزهر في {القاهرة} التي {تأسست} {سنة} تسع مائة واثنتين وسبعين ميلادية، فيكون {قد} مضى {على} تأسيسها أكثر {من} ألف {سنة}، وبعدها جامعة الزيتونة {في} تونس بنت جامعها عطف أرملة المستنصر الحصي {سنة} ألف ومائتين وثلاث وثمانين ميلادية، ونذكر في هذا {السياق} أنّ {أقدم} {جامعة} في أوربا {هي} جامعة أكسفرد التي {تأسست} {سنة} ألف ومائة وسبع وستين ميلادية، أي بعد جامعة القرويين بـ{حوالى} ثلاثة قرون، وتلتها جامعة كيمبريج {التي} {تأسست} بعد أكسفرد {بأكثر} من قرن {من} الزمان {سنة} ألف ومائتين وأربع وثمانين ميلادية.

5. Written Arabic texts 2
(a) Suggested translation of الكيمياء.

Chemistry

Chemistry[1] is one of the sciences which are related to medicine. The contribution of the Arabs to chemistry is so significant that European scholars regard them as centrally important to [lit: in their studies of] the history of chemistry. The first Arab to involve himself with chemistry was the Caliph Khalid ibn Yazid I (died 85 AH), who took into his employment a number of scholars of the Alexandria School. The Arabs were motivated to study chemistry by two things: (i) their great desire to convert base metals into gold, and (ii) their attempt to discover the supreme elixir – also known as the philosophers' stone – whose purpose was to restore youth and prolong life.

Jabir ibn Hayyan was the first person to produce sulphuric acid, also known as oil of vitriol. He also discovered nitric acid and sodium hydroxide. The Arabs invented procedures for distillation, filtration, vapourisation, dissolution and crystallisation. They also discovered the bases and silver nitrate. Their doctrines in chemistry were followed until the eighteenth century. The Arabs are regarded as the originators of chemistry as a practical discipline, while the Greeks were the originators of chemistry as a theoretical science.

Note

1. The Arabic كيمياء means both 'alchemy' and 'chemistry', and this texts covers activities under both fields, since alchemy, as an ultimately mystical activity, was not distinguished from chemistry as a scientific discipline in the medieval Islamic world. We have used the term 'chemistry' throughout in our translation.

6. Written Arabic texts 3 (classical)

Suggested translation of فيما يحتاج إليه المتطبب من علم طبائع البروج.

What the medical practioner needs to know about astronomy

You should know that the twelve signs of the zodiac give a general indication of the four humours, by which I mean fire, air, water and earth. The three signs Aries [the ram], Leo [the lion] and Sagittarius [the archer] make up a fiery, hot, dry triangle which indicates yellow bile and dry, bitter things as well as hot things and fire. Taurus [the bull], Virgo [the virgin] and Capricorn [the kid] make up an dry, cold, earthy triangle which indicates black bile and unpleasant, dry things and earthy cold things. Gemini [the twins], Libra [the scales] and Aquarius [the bucket] make up a humid, hot, earthy triangle which indicates blood, moderate, sweet things, hot things and ethereal things. Cancer [the crab], Scorpio [the scorpion] and Pisces [the fish] make up a moist, cold, watery triangle which indicates phlegm and liquid, sweet things, moist things and watery things.

You should know that Aries, Cancer, Libra and Capricorn are changeable and indicate sudden alteration and reversal in circumstances. Taurus, Leo, Aquarius and Scorpio are fixed and indicate slowness and difficulty in movement and change from one situation to another. Gemini, Virgo, Sagittarius and Pisces have two bodies and indicate moderation in changing situations and affairs.

8. Aural Arabic texts 1

i   Complete transcription of من أول من وضع حصاد الشهر no. 3, side 1, item 5, كتابا في الحساب؟.

من أول من وضع كتابا في الحساب؟ وهل كان قبل صاحب هذا الكتاب
الشهير علما يُسمى علم الجبر؟ لا شك أن أغلبنا يعرف اسمه ولكن
مساهمته في حضارة الإنسان يجب ألا ينساها أحد. ويسرّنا أن نقدم لكم
في هذا العدد ومن مكتبة التسجيلات في الإذاعة نبذةً عن هذا العلامة
المسلم الذي دخل اسمه المعاجم الأفرنجية، كتبها لنا الدكتور عبد الحليم

منتصر، وأذعناها أصلا ضمن برنامج خمس دقائق وهو البرنامج الذي احتجب عن الإذاعة مؤقتاً.

هو أبو محمد بن موسى الخوارزمي. وُلد في خوارزم وأقام في بغداد في عصر المأمون الذي ولاه منصباً في بيت الحكمة، وقد برز في الرياضيات والفلك وكان أول من ألّف في الجبر، بل أول من استعمل كلمة «جبر» للدلالة على العلم المعروف بهذا الاسم، ولكتابه في الجبر قيمة تاريخية وقيمة علمية تاريخية، عليه اعتمد العلماء العرب في دراساتهم للجبر ومنه عرف الغربيون هذا العلم. ولكتاب الجبر والمقابلة شأن كبير إذ إنّ كل ما ألّف فيما بعد كان مبنياً عليه، فقد بقي عدة القرون مصدراً يعتمد عليه العلماء في بحوثهم الرياضية. وقد ترجمه إلى اللاتينية «روبرت تشستر» وكانت ترجمته أساساً لدراسات كبار العلماء مثل «لينارد بيدزا» الذي اعترف بأنّه مدينٌ للعرب بمعلوماته الرياضية، كذلك «كردن» و«غراي»، وغيرهم. وقد نشر الكتاب «فردريك روزن» في لندن سنة ألف وثمان مائة وست وأربعين، وفي سنة ألف وتسع مائة وخمس عشر نشر «كابنسكي» ترجمة للكتاب المذكور عن ترجمة تشستر، وفي سنة ألف وتسع مائة وسبع وثلاثين حقق الكتاب الدكتور نشرفة والدكتور مرسي عن نسخة محفوظة بأكسفورد في مكتبة بودلين كُتبت في القاهرة سنة ثمان مائة وثلاث وأربعين للهجرة بعد الخوارزمي بنحو خمس مائة سنة. كذلك يرجع إلى الخوارزمي الفضل في نقل الأرقام الهندية وهي المستعملة في بلاد المشرق العربي وكذلك الأرقام الغربرية وهي المستعملة في المغرب العربي وأوربا وتُعرف في أوربا باسم الأرقام العربية.

والخوارزمي أول من وضع كتاباً في الحساب والأول من نوعه من حيث الترتيب والتبويب والمادة، وقد ترجمه إلى اللاتينية أولا «ردبان» وبقي زمنا طويلا مرجع العلماء وبقي عدة قرون معروفا باسم «لوغارذمي» نسبة للخوارزمي. كذلك ألّف الخوارزمي في الفلك وأتى على بحوث مبتكرة فيه وفي حساب المثلثات ووضع زيجاً سماه السند هند الصغير جمع فيه بين مذاهب الهند والفرس ومذهب بطليمس واعتمد العلماء العرب من بعده على زيجه وأخذوا منه واستعانوا به في وضع أزياجهم. ولا تزال المعادلات التي ألفها الخوارزمي مستعملة منذ عصره حتى العصر الحديث، وبعض هذه المعادلات لا تزال ترد في كتب

الجبر إلى يومنا هذا ناطقة بفضل الخوارزمي على علم الجبر. ويقول ابن خلدون إن أول من كتب الجبر هو الخوارزمي.

وللخوارزمي شهرته الفائقة عند الإفرنج. وقد دخل اسمه المعاجم الإفرنجية، فيقولون «غوارزمو» «الغورذم» «الغوريمس» وكذلك نرى أن الخوارزمي قد برز في علوم كثيرة، أشهرها الجبر والحساب والفلك وإليه يرجع الفضل في تعريف الناس بالأرقام بدلا من استعمال حساب الجمل ووضع بحوث الحساب بشكل علمي لم يُسبق إليه كما أنه ألف في التاريخ والجغرافية والفلك والموسيقى.

ii Answers to comprehension questions relating to من أول من وضع كتابا في الحساب؟

1. Khawarizmi lived in Baghdad.
2. According to the speaker he was the first person to write about geometry, and the first person to use the word جبر in the sense of geometry.
3. His book has historical and historical scientific value.
4. Robert [of] Chester translated his book into Latin.
5. The book was published in London in 1846.
6. Indian numbers are used in the Arab East.
7. Arab numbers are used in the Arab West.
8. These numbers are also used in Europe.
9. السند هند الصغير was an astronomical almanac which combined the views of the Indians, the Persians and Ptolemy.
10. The equations composed by al-Khawarizmi continue to be used to the present day.
11. The speaker supports his claim for Khawarizmi's fame among the Europeans by the fact that his name is found in European encyclopaedias as 'algorithm'.
12. The counting system used before the number system relied on sentences.

9. Aural Arabic texts 2
ii Suggested translation of ما رأي العلم بما يُسمى بقراءة الطالع والابراج؟.

Let us now turn to the future which is the subject of our next topic. It is well-known that many people are concerned about the future, especially those who want to know what their future will be. Perhaps the oddest enduring feature of most current newspapers and magazines is that which is known as reading of the stars or the horoscope. Today there are many people [fans] who are not satisfied until they have read every word the astronomers have written about their future. Such people pay no attention to the saying, 'Astronomers lie even when they tell the truth.' They believe that the movement of the stars and the zodiac and the celestrial orbit has a significant effect on our psychological make-up, mood and personal constitution. They say that the position of every star and solar system in the celestial sphere at the time of a person's birth determines their tendencies and the features of their personality such that their behaviour is dependent on their particular star. History has recorded that a large number of leading figures have believed absolutely in astronomy including Adolf Hitler, leader of Nazi Germany.

But the question which has exercised people and scientists since antiquity is, 'Does astronomy tell the truth?' A French couple, Michel and Françoise Gadila, have conducted a serious scientific-type study to answer this question as discussed in our programme, 'In the footsteps of science'. At that time the couple carried out detailed studies involving a large number of people. They analysed the results, compared them and confirmed the moment of birth of each of the subjects in the study, the position of the stars and zodiac in the celestial sphere, and the effects which their position was predicted to have on the subject's personality. The couple's study which was published two-and-a-half years ago in the respectable scientific journal *Nature* reached the conclusion that there was a link between the moment of birth and an individual's success in life. The couple had studied the lives of many famous and eminent people in a variety of fields and found that every one of them had been born at a moment when the stars foretold that anyone born at that time would become eminent and distinguished.

iii Additional exercise: complete transcription of حصاد الشهر, no. 26, side 1, item 4 ‏.ما رأي العلم بما يسمى بقراءة الطالع والابراج؟

والآن إلى المستقبل الذي يدور موضوعنا التالي حوله. فمن المعلوم أن المستقبل يشغل بال معظم الناس وخاصةً أولئك الذين يريدون معرفة مستقبلهم. ولعل أغرب ظاهرة لا تخلو منها معظم الصحف والمجلات العصرية هي ظاهرة ما يسمّى بقراءة الطالع. فصار لها اليوم هواة لا يهدأ لهم بال دون قراءة كل كلمة يكتبها المنجمون عن مستقبلهم غير مبالين بالمثل القائل «كذب المنجمون ولو صدقوا». فهم يعتقدون أن لحركة النجوم والأبراج ودورة الفلك تأثيرًا كبيرًا على تكويننا النفسي وعلى مزاجنا وتركيب شخصيتنا. ويقولون إن موقع كل نجم ومجموعة شمسية في الفلك لحظة ميلاد الفرد منا يحدد ميوله وملامح شخصيته بحيث أن تصرفاته في ما بعد تظل رهنًا بما يشاء له برجه. وقد سجل

التاريخ إيمان كثير من الشخصيات بالتنجيم إيمانًا مطلقًا ومنهم «أدولف هيتلر» زعيم ألمانيا النازية.

ولكن السؤال الذي حير الناس وأهل العلم منذ القدم هو «هل يصدق التنجيم؟» لقد انبرى للإجابة على هذا السؤال زوجان فرنسيان هما ميشال وفرنسوا غديلا بعد دراسة جادة شبه علمية التفت له برنامجنا «في ركاب العلم». أجرى الزوجان حينذاك دراسات مستفيضة تناولت عددًا كبيرًا من الناس. وقاما بتحليل النتائج ومقارنتها والتثبت في لحظة ميلاد كل من الأشخاص الذين شملهم البحث وموقع النجوم والأبراج في الفلك وما تُوحيها مواقعها من تأثيرات على شخصيته. وتوصلت دراسة الزوجين التي نُشرت قبل عامين ونصف في مجلة Nature العلمية الرصينة إلى الاقتناع بوجود علاقة بين لحظة الميلاد وحظ الفرد في النجاح في الحياة. وكان الزوجان قد درسا حياة كثيرين من المشاهير والأناس البارزين في شتى الميادين والحقول ووجدا أن كلا منهم كان قد وُلد في لحظة كتبت النجوم لمن وُلد فيها أن يكون لامعًا بارزًا.

10. Written English texts
Suggested translation of 'During the period of greatness of the Arab and Islamic empires'.

لقد نشأت خلال العصر الذهبي للإمبراطوريات العربية والإسلامية في الشرقين الأدنى والأوسط حضارة رائعة في ازدهارها والتي تُعرَف بالحضارة العربية. وعندما جاء العرب الفاتحون من الصحراء لم تكن هذه الحضارة في ذروتها كما أصبحت فيما بعد بل إنها لم تكتمل إلا بعد الفتوحات الإسلامية وبمساهمة شعوب أخرى غير عربية مثل الفرس والأقباط وغيرهما. و كذلك لم تكن هذه الحضارة إسلامية بحتة فكان من بين صانعيها العديد من المسيحيين واليهود والزردشتيين، إلا أن الطريقة الرئيسية للتعبير في هذه الدول كانت اللغة العربية والدين الذي سادها وسيطر على نظرتها

إلى الوجــود هـو الإســلام. ويُعــتــبــر هذان الأمــران، أي الدين الإسلامي واللغة العربية، من أهمّ الإنجازات التي قدّمها العرب الفاتحون لهذه الحضارة الجديدة المبتكرة التي تطورت في ظل هيمنتهم.

11. Précis

(a) Suggested guidance questions for the précis in Arabic of عبقرية الحضارة العربية.

١ – ما هي حدود الدولة الاسلامية بعد وفاة الرسول (ص) بقرن واحد؟

٢ – كيف انتقلت عاصمة الدولة الاسلامية؟

٣ – كيف اختلف المجتمع الاسلامي الجديد عن المجتمعات السابقة له؟

٤ – ماذا أخذت الثقافة الاسلامية عن الثقافات السابقة لها في البلدان التي فتحها العرب؟

٥ – ما هو دور العرب في نقل الثقافة اليونانية الى اوروبا؟

٦ – لماذا لا تطبّق التقسيمات الحديثة للعلوم على العلماء العرب في القرون الوسطى؟

(b) Suggested guidance questions for the précis in Arabic of العرب في غرب افريقيا.

١ – كيف يصف الكاتب العلاقة العربية بغرب افريقيا؟

٢ – لماذا يقول ان الصحراء في افريقيا كالبحر؟

٣ – ما هي الاماكن المذكورة في النص، ولماذا يذكرها الكاتب؟

٤ – ما هي السلعة التي كانت القوافل تحملها؟

٥ – ما هي التواريخ المذكورة في هذا النص، وما هي اهميتها؟

٦ – ما هي عنصرية الشعوب التي تعيش شمال غرب افريقيا جنوب الصحارى؟

٧ – في اي منطقة يغلب الدم الزنجي؟